PRAISE FOR OTHER BOOKS BY JUDY ALLEN

EVENT PLANNING
The Ultimate Guide to Successful Meetings, Corporate Events, Fundraising Galas, Conferences, Conventions, Incentives and Other Special Events
(ISBN: 978-0-471-64412-5)

"Allen is a good teacher. Wise planners will add *Event Planning* to their personal reference library as a useful working guide."
—Meeting Professional Magazine

"A blueprint for executing events for 50 or 2,000, with budgets of a few thousand dollars to hundreds of thousands."
—Success Magazine

"*Event Planning* will save beginning event planners from plenty of heartbreak and headaches."
—*Lisa Hurley, Editor,* Special Events Magazine

"*Event Planning* gives readers a blueprint for planning and executing special events with flair. Consider the book as preventative maintenance."
—Sales Promotion Magazine

"A guide to well planned events. *Event Planning* is a must for any PR maven."
—Marketing Magazine

"This book will be a help to all event planners, from rank beginners to seasoned professionals. It provides excellent guidelines as well as helpful details."
—*Katherine Kossuth, Director of Operations and Special Events, Canadian Film Center*

THE BUSINESS OF EVENT PLANNING
Behind-the-Scenes Secrets of Successful Special Events
(ISBN: 978-0-470-83188-5)

"*The Business of Event Planning* is a must-read for those in the event planning business. Strategic in thought and design and user-friendly in presentation, it literally tells you the paths to follow and the pitfalls to avoid. Well told, with examples to follow and stories to relate to, it's the 'how-to' that's a 'must-do' for the meetings, incentive, and event planning industry."

> —*Peggy Whitman, President, Society of Incentive & Travel Executives; and Western Regional Sales Director, Marriott Incentive Awards*

"Written for anyone who has to prepare dynamite meetings and special events, *The Business of Event Planning* is your bible and a must-have desktop reference. Thanks, Judy Allen! You saved the day!"

> —*Susan Fenner Ph.D., Manager, Education and Professional Development, International Association of Administrative Professionals (IAAP)*

"Guidance for new planners, reminders for experienced ones, and useful tips for everyone. This book has it all! It's the key that unlocks the mystery behind event planning, and should be mandatory reading for planners everywhere."

> —*Leslie McNabb, Senior Manager Event Planning, Scotia Capital*

EVENT PLANNING ETHICS AND ETIQUETTE
A Principled Approach to the Business of Special Event Management
(ISBN: 978-0-470-83260-8)

"This is a must-read not only for event professionals, but also for small-business people conceiving product introductions and conference appearances."

> —*Harvard Business School, Working Knowledge*

"Judy Allen strikes again. The veteran event planner…writes with the voice of experience and offers readers guidelines for establishing ethical policies in the office and on-site at events…a good refresher, and excellent reading for novices who need to know how to keep personal and professional boundaries from being crossed."
    —Corporate Meetings & Incentives Magazine

"This book contains invaluable information for anyone who handles events for their organization. A host of real-world stories from the field—the good, the bad, and the ugly—serve as examples of codes of conduct (or lack thereof) as well as cautionary tales of what can happen when ethics and etiquette fall to the wayside. Allen thoroughly examines many scenarios and provides practical advice that any planner would be foolish not to heed."
    —*Charity Village*

MARKETING YOUR EVENT PLANNING BUSINESS
A Creative Approach to Gaining the Competitive Edge
(ISBN: 978-0-470-83387-2)

"For event planners who are tired of being a well-kept secret, *Marketing Your Event Planning Business* offers invaluable advice on targeting talents and targeting clients. It's a wonderful boost for event planners looking to expand their client base."
    —*Lisa Hurley, Editor,* Special Events Magazine

"Judy Allen has crafted another meaningful book in her series on event practices. Every business owner must immediately add this treasure chest of useful ideas to their bookshelf."
    —*Richard Aaron, CMP, CSEP, President of BiZBash Media, NYC*

"Judy Allen has given us the ultimate resource guide to event planning. It's everything you need to know to launch a successful company."
    —*Ramey Warren Black, Partner, Media-Savvy*

TIME MANAGEMENT FOR EVENT PLANNERS
Expert Techniques and Time-Saving Tips for Organizing Your Workload, Prioritizing Your Day, and Taking Control of Your Schedule
(ISBN: 978-0-470-83626-2)

"She has done it again! Judy Allen has written an excellent, educational and user-friendly book, which is a priceless resource for planners worldwide. *Time Management* is an essential book for all planners, new or seasoned. Judy has provided the tools for managing your time which is one of the *most* important skills for event planners and all professionals."
> —*Ysabelle Allard, Meetings & Incentives Planner, Bilingual Meetings & Incentives*

"At last, a time management book written by someone who knows what it is to juggle three programs, six clients, eighteen suppliers and a family in a pear tree! Using Judy Allen's tips have really made a difference!"
> —*Brigitte Mondor, CMP, Event Leader, Microsoft — Maritz Canada Inc.*

"Time is money, and organizing your time is the key to planning a successful event. Judy Allen's new book gives event planners all the tools they need to manage their time most efficiently."
> —*Luis R. Rodriguez, Executive President (CEO), International Standardization, for the Meeting Industry Institute (ISMI), Isla Margarita, Venezuela*

"As all experienced and inexperienced event managers will know, time is one of the main resources that has to be managed effectively for successful events. In this practical skills-based text, Judy Allen explores time management and provides techniques for event professionals to learn and apply to your work. From exploring your current use of time, through prioritising and action planning, to multi tasking, project management and balancing your personal and professional life, Judy provides hints and tips for making better, and the best, use of time, based on her years of experience in the events industry."
> —*Glenn A. J. Bowdin, Principal Lecturer, UK Centre for Events Management, Leeds Metropolitan University*

THE EXECUTIVE'S GUIDE TO
CORPORATE EVENTS & BUSINESS ENTERTAINING

How to Choose and Use Corporate Functions to Increase Brand Awareness, Develop New Business, Nurture Customer Loyalty and Drive Growth

Judy Allen

John Wiley & Sons Canada, Ltd.

National Library of Canada Cataloguing in Publication Data

Allen, Judy, 1952-
    The executive's guide to corporate events and business entertaining : how to choose and use corporate functions to increase brand awareness, develop new business, nurture customer loyalty and drive growth / Judy Allen.

Includes index.
ISBN: 978-0-470-83848-8

    1. Business entertaining—Planning. 2. Public relations. I. Title.

HD59.A456 2006   659.2   C2006-902211-9

Production Credits
Cover design: Mike Chan
Interior text design: Natalia Burobina
Wiley Bicentennial Logo: Richard J. Pacifico
Printer: Friesens

John Wiley & Sons Canada, Ltd.
6045 Freemont Blvd.
Mississauga, Ontario
L5R 4J3

Printed in Canada

1 2 3 4 5 FP 11 10 09 08 07

This book is dedicated to the memory of Daniel (DJMatt) and Bobbie Jo (Beejay), who lived their lives with passion and purpose. Each, in their own way, managed to deeply touch the lives of those who knew and loved them, as well as others who were simply woven into the everyday fabric of their lives. Knowing Daniel and Bobbie Jo, even slightly, enriched my life in ways that have been life changing and continue to have the most wonderful ripple effects. I will always be truly grateful that our lives crossed.

I feel blessed to have had the opportunity to know them. Their so sudden passings brought into my life a heightened awareness of the joy that comes from doing what matters most to you each day, following your passions and taking time to play, and the importance of never leaving anything unsaid. It is important as we go about our days to remember that those who come into our lives—as we come together at work or casually in our day-to-day activities—have the ability to touch our lives and hearts in unexpected ways. Daniel and Bobbie Jo, you touched the lives of all who knew you and more than you probably ever imagined. You are remembered with love and affection.

CONTENTS

ACKNOWLEDGMENTS

WRITING, PUBLISHING AND PROMOTING eight books in six years in both the professional business market and the mass consumer reader market has presented me with the incredible opportunity to learn all aspects of a new-to-me industry and to learn from those who are experts in their fields. I have enjoyed the experiences I have had while working closely on the making of this book with the wonderful teams of professionals at John Wiley & Sons. I would like to thank Robert Harris, General Manager, Professional and Trade; Karen Milner, Executive Editor; Elizabeth McCurdy, Project Manager; Pam Vokey, Project Coordinator; Kimberly Rossetti, Editorial Assistant; Erin Kelly, Publicist; Lucas Wilk, Marketing Manager; Joan Trinidad, Intermediate Accountant; Natalia Burobina, Designer, Interior Text Design; Mike Chan, Designer, Cover Design; Rosa Gonzalez, Contracts Manager, International Rights Department; and Fang Yuan, Translation Publishing Executive, John Wiley & Sons (Asia) for the very special part they have each played in creating a series of books that are in demand around the world and are now being translated in Chinese, Korean, Russian and Polish. I also greatly appreciated their kindness around my mother's illness and a very difficult year.

I would like to thank Daphne Hart, my literary agent, of Helen Heller Agency Inc., who worked with me closely on this book from conception to contracting, and for her contribution in making this book a reality. Once again, I would also like to thank Helen Heller for her assistance.

Working with Michelle Bullard on the structure and copy edit of my books is a joy. I value working with Michelle and have great respect for the insight and direction she brings to each book I have had the pleasure of working with her on.

And as always, I would like to thank my family—my parents, Walter and Ruth; my sister, Marilyn, and her fiancé, Hans; and my nieces, Natasha and Jasmine—and my friends for their continued love and support.

I would like to especially thank Joe Shane—whose business acumen I have the greatest respect for—for sharing his expert professional advice with me, and those who took time out from their busy workdays to read the first run of this book and provide endorsements. I greatly appreciate the valued opinions you've given to readers of *The Executive's Guide to Corporate Events & Business Entertaining*.

PREFACE

SO, YOU'VE BEEN CHARGED with organizing the big event to launch a new product, you have to plan a party to wow new clients or you've been told to pull off a certain strategy and you think a great event would accomplish that. Now what do you do? Executing an event flawlessly is hard enough, but how do you make sure it accomplishes corporate objectives and strategy and, just as importantly, how do you make sure you don't screw up?

Most of my books have been aimed at professional event planners, but this book is for you, the business executive who has to plan a (successful) event for the first time, and has been written expressly to address these key issues.

The meeting and special event industry is a $96.4 billion a year industry and it continues to grow in leaps and bounds as more and more businesses, both large and small, tap into the proven success of utilizing events as a sales and marketing tool to produce extraordinary corporate results. Successful execution of corporate events requires mastery of event design, event development and event marketing strategy, all of which will be covered in this book in great detail (don't forget to review the useful material in the Appendix!).

Understanding the part each of these critical elements plays and most importantly when they come into play—the hows, the whens, the whats, the wheres and the whys to choose and use an event as part of a corporate marketing strategy—is vital to know before you begin to plan your event in order to maximize the personal, professional and business returns to you and your company, as well as your guests' personal, professional and business returns. And this applies whether or not you are handling your company's event in-house or working with a professional event and meeting planning company or incentive house. Inside knowledge and understanding and being able to follow another industry's language is always a powerful asset as you begin to work with venues and suppliers.

Event marketing strategy is very different from conventional marketing. Event marketing strategy embraces psychology and requires the ability to strategically develop events that deliberately create and/or target specific responses and motivate attendees by tapping into people's personal and professional dreams. There is a world of difference between "party planning" (weddings, birthday parties and other personal celebrations) and professional corporate and social results-driven "event planning," which can still include seemingly personal celebrations—such as an award ceremony or personal anniversary—but they come wrapped with a business agenda.

This book will enable you to master the intricacies of using an event as part of your business's marketing strategy, as well as teach you what you need to know about choosing and using an event to its full potential. Corporate events, both business and social, can be used to increase company profits, maximize sales productivity performance, grow brand awareness and recognition, advance employee learning or stimulate sales through motivation. And those are just some of the ways events can be used to promote business growth and meet company objectives.

The range of available events and purposes is vast and it is important to know which style of event to do and when; what event elements are essential to include in order to produce "x" result; and how to stage them in a way that will bring a positive outcome, meet multiple company objectives and become a solid launch platform to build future events upon. All of these very important areas will be covered in great detail in this book.

The Executive's Guide to Corporate Events & Business Entertaining also includes practical advice on the planning and orchestration of an event, and shares expert tips and techniques on how to produce polished and professional business affairs. Red flag areas on what to watch out for on all levels—personally, professionally and company-wise—are covered as well.

The primary focus of *The Executive's Guide to Corporate Events & Business Entertaining* is the strategic event marketing thinking, and how to choose and use events to achieve business objectives and to receive a return on your company's investment of time and money. Should you require in-depth step-by-step event planning "how to" knowledge, for example, if your company is choosing to handle the event from beginning to end in-house or you want a full understanding of what you will be undertaking when overseeing a corporate event, then I recommend you read the Event Planning series of books, which was written for the professional event planning and hospitality industry. They will serve you well as companion books to *The Executive's Guide to Corporate Events & Business Entertaining*. I will be referencing them throughout this book to guide you to which book to read should you require additional event planning logistical support information, need to see sample forms and layouts, require help to understand contract terms and conditions and concession options, identify red flag areas to watch out for, and so on—all of which would be of value for you to know regardless of if you are working directly on your own with venues and suppliers or with professional corporate planners. And if your company is using the services of professional event and meeting planners, these references will also be of benefit to you in helping you to evaluate the proposals you are receiving from planning companies in a bid situation, and provide you with insightful information on how to determine their skill sets and choose the supplier that knows how to bring all the essential elements together.

Acquiring the expertise in knowing how to choose the right event and use the right event elements to bring about desired results is a sought-after business marketing skill in today's competitive marketplace. *The Executive's Guide to Corporate Events & Business Entertaining* will provide you with the understanding, tips and techniques that you need to make informed decisions, and will become an invaluable resource guide that you will want to keep close at hand as you grow your company and improve the style and level of sophistication of events that you plan.

For quick event planning logistical support reference, below is a brief overview of each of the companion books in the Event Planning series:

- *Event Planning: The Ultimate Guide to Successful Meetings, Corporate Events, Fundraising Galas, Conferences, Conventions, Incentives and Other Special Events* (Wiley, 2000)

Event Planning: The Ultimate Guide introduces the fundamental principles of event planning and gives planners a solid foundation in event planning. This book is a detailed blueprint for planning and executing special events without unexpected surprises and expenses. *Event Planning: The Ultimate Guide* contains practical advice on every aspect of organizing and managing special events, such as how to choose the best venue; preparing and managing the budget; identifying hidden costs; scheduling; coordinating food and beverages; selecting decor, themes and entertainment; media; and staffing. It includes many forms, checklists and tips for planning and managing events. This book also features examples of events where things went right—and wrong—and provides techniques to maximize savings and avoid being caught unaware.

- *The Business of Event Planning: Behind-the-Scenes Secrets of Successful Special Events* (Wiley, 2002)

The Business of Event Planning takes event planning to the next level. Its comprehensive coverage includes strategic event design; how to prepare winning proposals and how to understand them if you're the client; how to determine management fees and negotiate contracts; guest safety and security issues that need to be taken into consideration; how to design events in multicultural settings; new technology that makes event operations more efficient; practical tools such as sample letters of agreement, sample layouts for client proposals, forms, tips and checklists; and a detailed case study that runs throughout the book—one company that is organizing two very different events.

- *Event Planning Ethics and Etiquette: A Principled Approach to the Business of Special Event Management* (Wiley, 2003). Harvard deemed *Ethics & Etiquette* a "must-read" for event planning and business professionals.

Event Planning Ethics and Etiquette covers the business side of event planning, including ethics, etiquette, entertaining, acceptable codes of conduct and industry standards. The book provides event planners with the information they need to stay out of trouble, keep professional relationships healthy and profitable, avoid the riskier temptations of the lifestyle and win business in a highly competitive market using ethical business practices. Harvard Business School said this book "is a must-read not only for event professionals, but also for small-business people conceiving product introductions and conference appearances."

- *Marketing Your Event Planning Business: A Creative Approach to Gaining the Competitive Edge* (Wiley, 2004)

Marketing Your Event Planning Business takes readers through marketability, market development and marketing endeavors (business and personal). Topics covered include diversifying the client base, developing niche markets and areas of expertise, establishing a backup plan for use during downturns and innovative ways to solicit new sales.

- *Time Management for Event Planners: Expert Techniques and Time-Saving Tips for Organizing Your Workload, Prioritizing Your Day, and Taking Control of Your Schedule* (Wiley, 2005)

Time Management for Event Planners offers expert insight on time management as it relates specifically to the event planning and hospitality industry. Event planning is a high-pressure, around-the-clock job where planners juggle multiple tasks, multiple time zones and work down to the wire against crushing deadlines and a mountain of obstacles. For smooth event implementation, and for business success, it is essential that planners manage their own time as expertly as they manage an event. This book will show you how to do just that.

• • •

Executing events flawlessly does not mean that corporate goals are being met. *The Executive's Guide to Corporate Events & Business Entertaining* shows not only how to plan and execute the perfect event, but also how to closely tie it in to company strategy and objectives for best results. Covered in detail are how to identify and set clear objectives for each event; which type of function is best suited to meeting your objectives; what you need to establish before forging ahead with organizing committees and reviewing or developing proposals; how to develop a realistic budget, and when to question expenses proposed by staff or professional event planners; the importance of sign-offs; how to identify controversial spending and other red flag areas that could seriously damage the company's reputation, or even put it at financial or legal risk; how to establish spending guidelines and policies on employee conduct at company functions; and how to evaluate the success and results of your business functions.

CHAPTER ONE

THE EVOLUTION OF BUSINESS FUNCTIONS AND THE WAYS THEY CAN BE USED TO SUCCESSFULLY DRIVE BUSINESS GROWTH

CORPORATE EVENTS AND BUSINESS entertaining are used by corporate North America to foster business development and growth and are a major part of a company's communication, sales, marketing and public relations strategy. Staged effectively, they can contribute to a company's success, standing, profitability and expansion and are equally successful with large and small companies that operate locally, nationally and internationally.

Corporate events can be used by businesses of all sizes to solicit new business, create a corporate or brand image, and retain and build loyalty with existing suppliers and customers. They can also be used effectively to elicit peak performance from employees and produce camaraderie and teamwork among coworkers. The corporate event bar has been raised dramatically and the competition to craft something original that will help a business create public awareness as well as industry and media buzz is fierce.

But corporate events and business entertaining not designed with care—without an eye on business ethics and etiquette—can seriously damage a company's image and put the company and its management in potentially high-risk situations if not handled carefully, professionally and appropriately. Corporate boards and chief executives are now seeing how company scandals played out in the headlines can estrange customers, sink stock prices and end careers in a matter of minutes. And many of the transgressions that have been made public have been linked to corporate events and business entertaining.

One company's team-building exercise turned into a case of sexual harassment and sexual battery that ended in a $1.7 million settlement. Their losing sales teams had been asked to eat baby food, wear diapers and be spanked with their competitor's signs.

In another case, a company CEO was removed from his post and sent home to take a position as an in-house auditor when his company was hit with a $190 million sexual harassment suit. The company CEO was accused of improper behavior with one of his staff members both in the office and on business trips when he invited her into his hotel room and made improper advances.

Off-color jokes, permitted at another company's conference, made national headlines and left readers—who were both existing and potential customers—with an impression of the corporation having poor business judgment. As did a teaser mailing for a golf event that closed down an office tower in the middle of a business day, when one of the cans of bear spray, which was tied into the promotional campaign, was released and set off a security alert. Traffic ground to a halt in the middle of the financial district, work was disrupted, and people were inconvenienced for more than two hours while the area was sealed off and surrounded by dozens of fire trucks and police cars. Many of the employees headed for home as a safety precaution.

Another company's promotion ended up with an arson squad blowing up a newspaper box, thinking it held a possible bomb. The box was rigged with a device set to play music, tied into the product launch, when the door was opened, but some of the devices were not securely fastened into place. They dropped on top of the stacks of newspapers and displayed wires sticking out from the recording device, causing great alarm.

As a company grows, so will its business function requirements. The range and style of business functions it puts on and takes part in, and the type of business entertaining that is essential to it as a company will change and grow as the company itself will. Business functions and business entertaining become a part of a company's signature style and convey as much about it as a company—to its workforce, clients, suppliers, potential customers and prospective top-level employees—as does its carefully chosen letterhead and promotional material and how they conduct, present and position themselves in business. But many companies focus more time and effort on these details than they do on planning a corporate event.

Corporate events, done right, become an integral part of a company's image and corporate culture. It is important that a company not allow itself to become stagnant and repetitive if it wants to retain both the competitive edge that using business functions has brought it and its reputation of being a cutting-edge leader in its industry. Business functions become more sophisticated and complex as a company develops and expands their reach in order to meet their changing needs and those of their evolving clientele. There may be "usual" business activities you don't see as "events," such as board meetings, but if you treat them as special functions, with business objectives and follow-up, they can go to the next level and produce outstanding results.

Executives striving to make a name for themselves within their company and industry want a seat on their company's strategic planning committee and are actively vying with one another to be an integral part of their company's decision-making team. It is important for them, personally and professionally, to be viewed as an essential voice within a company's strategic growth plan, and one way to do this is by demonstrating an understanding of how business functions can be used to corporate advantage. They know that meetings and events, successfully implemented, can be a driving force toward ensuring business success, and if they can bring valuable knowledge and insight into the which, when, where and why of corporate events, they will secure themselves a place at the decision-making table.

Possessing the skills required to select the right business function to meet targeted company objectives will set executives apart from their peers and enable them to get the resources (budget, staffing, etc.) and empowerment they need to plan the most effective meetings and events for their division and for their company. Knowing how to justify the bottom line puts them in a position for senior management support. In order to move ahead with confidence in planning their next company function, it is important that they learn what questions to get answers to before contracting and avoid putting themselves and their company at financial and legal risk.

Executives are now being held personally accountable to high-level management for every dollar they spend. Part of that accountability includes proving the relevancy of the dollars being spent on educating, enlightening and entertaining staff, suppliers, customers and the general public through corporate events and business entertaining. Company boards and chief executives are requiring that personnel involved in business function management provide them with evidence that corporate objectives are being more than met by the investment in events and that these expenditures are earning the expected return on investment. If committee and department heads fail to observe company mandates, their divisions can suffer budget cuts and the elimination of jobs, while they themselves may face the prospect of being fired as an example to other company executives and up-and-coming employees.

At one leading automotive company, it was a well-known fact that the corporate executive placed in charge of the company's yearly product launch faced the very real possibility of not being with the company to head up the next one (just like his or her predecessors). In seven years, the company's president had fired seven rising executives who "did not know what they did not know" when they were asked to take on this critical company event. Thrust into a position they were ill prepared to handle, they were unable to achieve the results that head office required.

What they had failed to realize was that flawless event execution does not mean company objectives are being met. They put their focus and energies into a day of orchestrated perfection instead of ensuring that each event element they selected would bring about the desired objective, which was not necessarily financial.

For example, a perfectly produced car launch in XYZ location—which can run in the millions of dollars—means nothing if the dealers whose business the company is soliciting choose not to attend. Many car dealerships carry more than one line of cars and are wooed by each competing company to attend their car launch. The dealers, many independently wealthy, can afford to be choosy with how they spend their time and their money, and if a specific car launch—as it is positioned—does not entice them, they will not step foot on the plane.

Knowing how to qualify and select the right event and entertaining elements that will draw the dealers and get them clamoring to be part of an exclusive event is essential to a successful product launch. But hand in hand with getting the dealers to attend goes the challenge of giving the dealers a reason to pre-order the new line, and all of that was being overlooked in the product launch planning stages. The main focus year after year was on the dollars and cents of budget management, and not on the dollars being spent making both cents (profit) and good business sense after the event had taken place. The executives found out the hard way that coming in on budget without meeting company objectives means that you have run your event at a loss and all the money, time and labor spent planning and producing the event has been wasted.

The Evolution of Business Functions

In the past, business functions were used mainly as a medium for communicating internal corporate developments, such as a company's future plans, prospects, policies and procedures. Businesses used corporate events to foster goodwill between employees and management, encourage company loyalty, raise morale, demonstrate leadership, provide training and show employee and customer appreciation. These traditional business function needs were generally handled in-house. Events were held in the office or at a local hotel and were produced with the help of an audiovisual company and basic equipment.

Traditional business functions include:

- board meetings
- business meetings
- client appreciation events
- conferences
- conventions
- corporate shows
- employee appreciation events
- trade shows

As technology evolved, corporate events developed a more sophisticated style. Companies began holding meetings and events further afield and in a variety of venues. Logistically these functions became much more complex. Corporations seeking new ways to stand out from their competition, take the lead in market share, entice top performers to work with them and retain key personnel started turning to business functions, both corporate and social, to help them achieve their objectives.

Today, business functions are dynamic sales, marketing and public relations tools used by businesses of all sizes. Business entertaining budgets have moved from hundreds to thousands, to hundreds of thousands of dollars, and, in growing numbers, to multi-million-dollar allocations for a single business function.

Advanced business functions include:

- custom training seminars involving emotional and physical challenges
- executive retreats
- gala fundraising events
- incentive travel and premium programs
- award presentation shows
- naming rights
- product launches
- product placement
- special events

The Value in Clearly Defining Your Event

For several reasons, it is important to be able to properly distinguish the type of business function that you are considering holding. First, it will help you establish company objectives and assess whether or not they can be met holding the type and style of business function that is being proposed. Second, it delivers a clear message to your attendees and suppliers, such as hotels, professional event planners, audiovisual companies and so forth, which will in turn help them work in partnership with you to best meet your objectives.

The name you give your function sets the tone and the company's intention. For example, a business meeting paints a very different image or event "energy" than a client or employee appreciation function, even though both can conceivably be very similar in delivery. A business meeting and a client or employee appreciation event can be formal or fun and can take place in a hotel or in a unique venue or location inside or outside. But with a business meeting, the focus is generally on the content that will be imparted to attendees and what they will take away with them and retain, while a client appreciation event can feel more intense and an employee appreciation function conveys celebrating individual and company achievement in a more relaxed atmosphere.

The Types of Returns Business Functions Can Bring

Companies of all sizes and types attend and host business and social functions as a means to:

- increase their company profile
- maximize performance
- grow brand awareness and recognition
- develop new business
- nurture employee, supplier and customer loyalty
- advance employee learning
- stimulate sales through motivation
- drive business growth

Too often, companies put events on and throw parties without even considering such objectives. As such, they waste valuable opportunities, time and money. A strategically planned business function, whether it be put on by the company or attended, can bring a multitude of rewards. But it's key to know which one to do or attend as a company representative; when and why it is better to be the host, sponsor or guest or play a different role; and how to take what you are doing and meet all objectives. It is important that company employees attending business meetings, industry events and so on as company representatives on company time and money be given a clear set of company objectives that need to be met from the outset. It is essential that employees acting as company representatives are not wasting their company's investment of time, money and energy and are not adversely damaging the company's reputation or theirs personally and professionally, which could reflect back on the company. No one wants to be perceived as the person who would "go to the opening of an envelope" and yet many people and companies seem that way. Doing so creates industry buzz that they must not have a home or social life or much to do at work, and that is not the business or personal message you want to convey. It is important to be selective and to be function savvy. Play—social and business functions that are more relaxed—can be work, but it is important to go into such functions with an investment strategy in mind, knowing exactly what return they will bring for all involved.

It is always important when staging or attending a business function that will meet company objectives to keep in mind the target audience and to remember that the audience can be far-reaching and that multiple objectives can be realized from one event.

TRADITIONAL BUSINESS FUNCTIONS: WHAT THEY ARE AND THE RETURNS THEY CAN BRING

Board Meetings

Depending on the company, board meetings can take place daily, weekly, monthly, quarterly or annually. They can be held inside or outside of the company boardroom and are generally attended only by senior executives and the board of directors. Board meetings can run from a couple of hours to all-day affairs, and their focus is on business matters.

Sample Board Meeting Returns

To company heads, a board meeting is a time to come together to discuss company direction and make decisions. The only objective that they may have is to move through the agenda as quickly as possible and get back to business. Whether they hold the meeting at the office or at an outside location does not usually matter and can be thought to be inconsequential, as though the decision of where to hold their meeting will not factor into meeting company objectives, which is not always the case.

Holding a board meeting at the office serves many purposes. It is cost-effective. There is no additional cost incurred for room rental and material, and staff are on hand if they need to be referenced or they can sit in for a portion of the meeting. It is easy to request copies of any pertinent information. The only added expense is for catered breaks and lunches and any special audiovisual equipment that may need to be brought in.

If one of the company's objectives is personal growth and development of their staff, a hidden benefit to holding the board meeting at the office where all the higher-ups are gathered in a show of company strength is motivating staff to aspire to someday be where they are. Seeing life at an executive level can create desire to be part of the inner circle and decision-making process. It will be noted who attended, how they interacted with each other and with office employees and even how they dressed. It is a display of office standards at their very best and a show of what it takes to be part of the executive team. It provides employees with direction if succeeding within the company is part of their goals.

It also creates new energy in the office. Desks and offices are usually tidied and ready for an office walk-through. Employee dress is usually elevated on days when it is known that key executives will be in the office. There will be speculation by office employees as to what will be on the day's agenda and how it could affect the company and them personally. Even what is served for coffee breaks and lunch will not go unnoticed, and it will be discussed should leftovers be put out for the staff to enjoy. They will note any differences between what is offered to company executives and what is offered to them on employee appreciation days.

What can be thought of as a small detail can actually be positioned to work toward or against meeting company objectives. For example, if the message from company executives is the employees are part of the team but the team is served pizza, pop and cake at their get-together while the executives are feted with gourmet fare in front of them—especially if leftovers are put out for them—then their actions are not in sync with what they have been saying. Going out to lunch as a group in a private room so that business can still be discussed may be a better choice for a board meeting in that case. No one would be privy to what the executives ate or how much the meal cost, except those whose job it is to be discreet. On the other hand, if one of the company objectives is to have employees striving to become company executives, serving a "working lunch" of high caliber may fall into giving them a return on their investment for handling it in that manner. Little things like whether or not china cups or foam cups were used will be noted not just by employees but also by senior executives, both of whom companies have invested interest in and are hoping to keep. Many senior executives have been wooed away by a better office, a title, working conditions, perks or concessions.

Business Meetings

Business meetings can take place daily. They take place inside and outside the office. They can be both business and social. For example, a business meeting can take place over lunch in a restaurant or over a game of golf. Attendance is much wider and can include a mix of staff, suppliers and customers.

Sample Business Meeting Returns

Business meetings are a part of everyday corporate executive life. Many a time, executives and those they have met with are heard back in their respective offices remarking, "Well, that was a waste of time." This reaction is too often the case. No meeting, if planned right, should ever be a waste of time, and any that are perceived as such should have their validity questioned and evaluated to see how they could have produced better results for all involved.

Company executives meet with staff, suppliers, existing and potential clients and even the media on a daily basis, but seldom does strategic planning—looking to see how many company objectives can be met by a meeting—come into play when deciding who, when, where and how to meet. Meetings can be arranged by a flurry of e-mails, telephone calls or text messages or by trying to find a clear block of time in invitees' calendars without time and consideration as to the meeting's possible returns on the time, energy and money (whether it is hourly wages eaten up in meeting time or taking a client out to lunch) that will be spent.

Business meetings are filled with opportunity to meet company objectives as well as individuals' personal and professional ones, and receive numerous returns on investment. But each meeting needs to be staged with careful consideration of for whom and why the meeting is being called.

If, for example, one of your company objectives is to always convey to your workforce that they are a valued part of your company's success and that the company greatly appreciates their contribution and dedication, then when a staff meeting is called, timing is one factor that should be carefully considered. Calling a meeting at a time of day that shows a lack of respect for either employee workloads, deadlines or personal life will not help to foster this belief. For some executives, holding an early morning meeting may be easiest for them because coming in early may be a part of their regular routine, but that may pose potential problems for staff workers with school-age children and leave them feeling put upon instead. They may arrive at the meeting filled with resentment instead of feeling like a valued member of the team. Employees of one retail chain that regularly holds its staff meetings at 11:00 p.m. after store closing were understandably put off. The timing of their meetings forces those who have worked the day shift to return late at night to attend the mandatory meeting, which often runs into the wee hours of the morning, and still be prepared to be back to reopen the store early the next day.

It is important to always think about what is being asked of others and how what you are asking serves to meet your objectives. One financial company made a major meeting faux pas when they arranged for buses to take their staff off-site for a meeting so that they could bring all departments together to hear a very important celebratory company announcement and to thank them for their contribution to the company's success. Employees were looking forward to taking part in the day's outing and hearing what had to be said.

The transportation was scheduled to depart for the meeting before the company's cafeteria was open for lunch and return after it and most nearby restaurants were closed for lunch service. Due to the nature of the meeting—a thank you—and the timing of the function—over their lunch hours—employees assumed that refreshments would be served. They had all witnessed the food that had been brought in and served at executive meetings and had even sampled leftovers laid out for them after the company executives' meetings had ended.

Not even coffee and tea had been arranged, let alone a light repast to compensate them for missing lunch and fueling them so they would return back to the office feeling valued, motivated, upbeat and ready to get to work. The company heads had not thought of making that one of their company meeting objectives. Instead, hungry, disgruntled employees were sent back to work and since the company had not even thought to make arrangements to have the company cafeteria remain open later to be available to returning employees, the employees set out to find neighborhood restaurants that were still open or ordered food in at their own expense.

One astute manager did recognize what had just transpired and did make amends with his department by ordering food in for them, but it still did not undo the damage that had been done. For the most part, work came to a halt for the afternoon as employees gathered to discuss what had just taken place. The cost of coffee, tea and light luncheon food was minimal compared to the cost of not meeting the company's objectives and the hours of productivity lost upon the staff's return. The company's investment of time, money and energy had been totally misspent.

The time, money and inconvenience spent transporting everyone to an off-site location also needed to be looked at. If one of the company objectives or desired returns was to have everyone together to show employees or the media, if they had been invited, how large the company had grown and how diverse they were, and/or if they were looking to have the room come alive with congratulatory energy and applause, they needed to consider if there were other ways to achieve the same effect and if the dollars being spent made sense.

Business meetings can be carefully engineered to work toward producing long-term results that will meet future company goals that may have no actual bearing on the meeting that is taking place. They are building blocks and should be used as such.

Executives of one automotive company weighed their options when looking at scheduling a press conference to talk about their upcoming product to see how they could maximize their return. They wanted to tie it into their business meeting and invite the press to sit in on their afternoon session, turning their business meeting into a building block for a pre-event to release the company's future plans and start to build professional press relationships for an impending product launch. They could do something fairly standard—hold their meeting at their facility and give reporters a tour of their plant with refreshments to follow—or hold a private luncheon at a hotel or restaurant and in both cases hope that they had media turnout, which was never a guarantee, especially when the scheduled event had no real hook to draw them in.[1]

Company executives looked at their long-term objective, which was for increased press coverage for an upcoming new product launch that would take place at a time when all their competing car manufacturers would be clamoring for the same, and tried to find a way to promote media loyalty by holding this preemptive business function to woo and win the media's support for when they would need it most. They knew what they did today could work toward, at best, limiting the amount of coverage their competition received and at the very least ensure that the media did come out to cover their own unveiling. They decided they would have to do something more innovative that would allow them to spend maximum time with the reporters and get to know them on a more personal level.

They decided to do a press road rally using their higher end product, which was very alluring to car lovers, to give the media a chance to experience firsthand how their existing top-of-the-line product handled on the open road and get them primed for next year's model. Initially the cost was higher than holding the meeting at their facility or a nearby hotel, but the company's gain for when they would need it the most was potentially much greater. And, if no one from the press was enticed to come to a fairly standard meeting at their plant or luncheon at a hotel, that would be money, time and energy ill spent, with no return today or in the conceivable future.

---

1   *Marketing Your Event Planning Business: A Creative Approach to Gaining the Competitive Edge* (Wiley, 2004) covers event marketing hooks in detail.

The business function was extended from a lunch to an overnight getaway north of the city, timed to when the changing of the leaves would be at its peak. Each member of the media was partnered with a company executive for the ride up. A relaxing "check-in" dinner was arranged and more key members of the company's staff were at each table in order to spend quality time with their guests and have the opportunity to tell them about the new product and build excitement. Following a relaxing morning at the resort, where new designs were unveiled, a luxury motor coach was arranged to transfer everyone back to the city but also to give all the company executives one last opportunity to mingle and mix with the media on a more intimate level.

Bonds were formed and not only did the company receive great press coverage when their new product came out, but when the road rally received a full-page write-up from many of the attendees, the company also received wonderful reviews for their existing line, which helped to spur sales.

Taking the time to weigh their options against how they would best meet their company's present and future objectives brought rich rewards, and not just to the automotive company. The media was also appreciative of having a new story angle—heralding not only the cars but the joys spent enjoying nature, exploring the ins and outs of small towns and the value of getaway jaunts—to present to their paper and their public.

Client Appreciation Events

Client appreciation events can be quite diverse and go from simple and inexpensive to elaborate and more costly. They can vary in tone from elegant to playful, and range in size from a handful of chosen guests to several thousand attendees. For a bank, a client appreciation event could take the form of coffee and cake as a thank-you to all of their customers, a VIP reception and tickets to the theater for a select group or the exclusive use of an outdoor family entertainment complex that has been reserved for the day just for the enjoyment of special guests. Client appreciation events are typically social in nature but packed with clever marketing.

Sample Client Appreciation Event Returns

Client appreciation events provide the opportunity to increase brand awareness, nurture company loyalty, receive press coverage, promote sales and introduce new clients to your products and services. Client appreciation events can be fun, festive or formal and they can be held on-site, at your place of business or at a venue that has been blocked exclusively for your company. They can range in price from inexpensive to over the top and include premium special offers or product giveaways with your company logo (tastefully applied) that will help clients to remember the event.

They can also become part of your signature style, as is what happened for one company when its executives positioned themselves as being the best of the best. They decided that dinner theater evenings would be their signature customer appreciation event. They wanted their clients to feel like VIPs, so dinners were booked in private rooms at only the best restaurants and only the very best theater seats to opening night shows would do. Transfers between dinner and the theater were by limousines so their guests would not be inconvenienced by having to drive between elements. Guests were whisked into the theater. Gift bags with all the show's amenities, including programs and personalized, signed CDs by the cast, were waiting in the guests' chairs. Private VIP intermission receptions gave their customers a chance to mix and mingle and gave their staff an opportunity to meet with them. A decadent post-theater coffee and dessert buffet awaited them when they arrived back at the restaurant after the show and parking passes were given out so that the guests had not one expense to look after.

Their customers came away feeling valued, pampered and spoiled, and anxious to remain on the invitee list. The company also knew that its customers would go home and talk to family, friends and colleagues about their special evening and their wonderful host. The company executives knew that they would get their guests talking about their client appreciation event if they selected shows that gave their guests a certain status among their peers, by making them among the first to see it.

Using this type of business function, which was tailored to meet their customers' desires, was so successful they expanded this to top entertainment and sought-after sporting events and took over private boxes at top facilities in which to fete their customers. They controlled their budget by the number of guests they had attending. Some of their client appreciation events were very small and intimate and they invited only their top customers, while others were considerably larger.

Serving coffee and cake or doing an on-site client appreciation barbecue would not have produced the same returns on investments for them; they may have reached a larger audience but the gains would not have been the same, and the customers they wanted to thank most would never have come out to attend that type of function. They carefully analyzed who their best customers were and looked at their demographics to see what event would hold the most appeal to their clients and how they could stage it to meet company objectives.

They still did the other types of functions to say thank you to their mass-market customers, but remembered to say a special thank you to those who were driving their company's growth. And by doing an event that allowed their guests to bring someone, they also opened the door to meeting potential new customers that shared common interests with their top producers. These individuals would in turn spread the news about their evening and in the process help to spread brand awareness to their circle of family, friends and peers.

Conferences

Conferences are built around educational content and discussion that serves to enlighten and inform participants. They are often viewed as a good place to network and share ideas. There can also be an entertainment element brought into conferences by either the host company or suppliers.

Companies can both attend or hold conferences. Objectives for company representatives attending industry conferences or for a company sponsoring a conference are very different than the objectives a company would have for their own in-house conference where only their own employees were attending.

Conferences can be limited to employees brought in from around the country (or world) to attend the company conference or be industry related, centered around a main topic of discussion and open to colleagues, suppliers and clients. They generally take place annually and can run anywhere from a couple of days to a longer getaway stay. They are not necessarily held locally.

Sample Conference Returns

Company conference objectives need to be reviewed each year so that the conference content and theme can be carefully designed to strategically meet all of them,[2] and so that your participants do not become bored with the format, tune out or worse, decide to sign in and skip out, which is easy to do if care isn't given to selecting the right location to hold your conference in.

The representatives of one company failed to meet some of their conference objectives, such as creating a strong bond between employees, providing a setting for their staff to share ideas and come up with creative solutions for handling common problems more effectively, and so on. They selected as the site for their meeting a Caribbean resort located directly on a busy beach that had great duty-free shopping in town and a multitude of hot nightspots to frequent. Instead of being used as a tool to bring their workers together, the location had the opposite effect. Participants headed out in all directions at night on their own and worse, through the day. Company heads ended up posting key company members on beach patrol and in town to make sure that no one slipped out of the daily meetings.

The destination, type of venue, the layout of the room, seating (tables, no tables), room temperature, the style of meeting, break

---

2   *The Business of Event Planning* (Wiley, 2002) covers strategic planning in detail.

formats and even what is served during the day and how it is served can all help to meet conference objectives. Had this company selected a golf or spa resort located away from town with little or no enticements, it would have been better served. The very nature of that kind of location would give the company the setting it needed to have its participants interacting with one another during the conference and after hours. An afternoon golf tournament with the teams specially selected would have also let the company ensure that the people they wanted to spend quality time together did. Its return on investment would have been considerably greater had the event's planners considered the costs and benefits of their choice of resort.

For another company, this one involved in the manufacture of chocolate, the choice of a Caribbean resort was perfect. The company's event planners wanted to have their employees spend time at a cocoa plantation to see cocoa in its natural form and understand what is involved in the process of growing, harvesting and converting the cocoa into the chocolates their company produced.

The company gained additional benefits from holding a meeting in a location that was tied directly to its manufacturing business. The employees got to know some of their counterparts that were working hard to help them produce a quality product— an added bonus objective that was met. The location also helped to strengthen working relationships. The hands-on learning provided employees not only with greater understanding but gave them valuable knowledge to add to their reputation in the industry as "chocolate connoisseurs," which they could use to help sell their product back home.

The company owners still took care to select exactly the right hotel property to help them meet their other objectives. They chose a smaller resort property where they were able to take over the majority of the rooms and have a greater presence in the hotel. Their employees could not help but keep running into one another. The resort was also very self-contained and off-property draws were minimal, and the destination, location, conference style and content helped them meet and exceed their conference meeting expectations.

One financial conference had suppliers vying for attendees' presence at their private events, which were scheduled to take place after conference hours. Each supplier was anxious to woo and wow participants and have exclusive attendance at their festivities. Their after-hours events were carefully crafted to hold a captive audience and limit the number of other functions attendees could take part in.

One company took over a state-of-the-art entertainment complex that had just opened and created the venue's first virtual Olympics, with participants divided into teams. The event was staged to start with hot and cold canapés with an open bar and then moved into the competition. A celebration dinner and fun awards were scheduled to take place just after check-in, and guests were then given unlimited-play cards for the interactive arcade games and stimulators and, after the virtual Olympic games ended, they could have fun on their own or with teammates or conference friends. The bar was kept open, a lavish dessert display and coffee bar were set up and shuttle transportation back to their hotel was provided.

The guests came, they stayed and they played, and other competing events going on that night sat empty. And the competitive games appealed to the competitive sales force, as did a chance to do something few people had had the opportunity to take part in. A company sending a representative to this event could end up finding out important industry news, learn what the competition has been up to, create a new networking opportunity, find out who to target and solicit to come work for them, and so forth.

Conventions

A convention is not limited to just employees. It has an educational focus as well as a social aspect. They are typically attended by those with shared interests or business concerns and can attract guests from around the world. They are generally held annually and in many cases put on by the industry, for example, trade publications or industry associations.

Sample Convention Returns

Before signing off on employees attending conventions, company executives need to look at the reasons that they are considering sending company representatives to attend. Along with the cost to attend the convention, which can run in the thousands of dollars, there is often also:

- the expense of transportation, hotel rooms, meals, and hosting potential clients or even prospective employees
- the dollars spent on time out of the office
- business not being done while they are out of office
- catch up time once they return

When all is added up the dollars can be considerable. Companies need to make sure that the convention meets their objective standards, which could mean considering the level of educational content and the caliber of who is attending. They also need to make sure that the person being sent to attend is the right person to help them to maximize their return. Several company representatives attending a convention as a group actually cost their company future business from existing and possible new clients, who were also attending, as a direct result of their unprofessional behavior from their dress to their demeanor. Their company had sent junior employees to the event, which had otherwise attracted high-level company decision-makers. No one looked at the list of those who had already registered to first see if the other attendees would be a match for them and could help the company by creating networking opportunities with key players, nor had they taken the time to discuss what would be expected from their representatives in terms of proper displays of company codes of conduct at both meeting and social events held during the convention. Unaccustomed to open bar functions during lunch and in the evening, they too freely enjoyed themselves and forgot that they were in a professional setting. The cost to the corporation was high and had the industry buzzing about the quality of people they hired.

TIP
Remember that the most exciting, memorable, well-planned event means nothing if the wrong people are attending. Pay attention to your attendees.

In addition to gaining new industry knowledge, attending conventions can also be a vehicle to showcase both your company and your talent, which in turn can help develop more business and attract new customers, suppliers and high achievers to look at your company as one that they want to do business with and work with. You can attend as a delegate or take a higher profile approach and become a part of the committee, which could gain you access to top personnel that you might not normally get to spend time with, or become one of the convention's "expert" speakers and use the convention as a platform for both yourself and your company. There are times when it is more beneficial to be a delegate and have total freedom to mix and mingle and meet with potential clients privately, for example, take them for coffee or lunch, and then there are times when it is more advantageous to take center stage and be able to benefit from the different opportunities that are presented to help you meet your personal and professional business objectives. There can be an additional pull to anniversary-year conventions.

Corporate Shows

Corporate shows are a means to showcase a company's product or a message they want to convey, and come under the corporate banner—the company's name is visibly attached to the event. They target audiences that can include both existing and potential customers, and can be private events or open to the public. They can range in size from small, very upscale events to multi-million-dollar staged extravaganzas designed specifically to dazzle and delight guests and attract media attention. Education content is often carefully packaged around entertainment and social elements.

Sample Corporate Show Returns

A corporate show is where companies need to shine, as they are out to impress staff, suppliers, existing and new customers, and the press. When setting company objectives and looking at the return on investment that holding a corporate show can bring, it is important—as it is with every business function—to consider not just the immediate return but what long-lasting ones the company can create as well.

For one company, one of its event objectives was to stage a show and give its audience a compelling reason to buy on-site and to make placing an order for their product as fast and convenient as possible for their customers. The company's event planners then looked at their other company objectives, and while they wanted to use the function to drive immediate sales, they also wanted to devise a means to increase future sales. By simply adding an auto-ship component to their order forms and giving buyers an incentive to sign on for it, each sale went from thousands of dollars to several hundreds of thousands, and their show was an outstanding success. They hired a professional event planning company to handle their event from beginning to end and made sure that their in-house employees were free to do what they most needed them to do, which was sell the company and sell their product.

TIP

Make it easy to do business with you at your business functions.

Employee Appreciation Events

Employee appreciation events can take place both inside and outside the office. They can be as simple as providing a catered on-site lunch as a means to say thank you for getting through a tough week or to celebrate a company milestone, or a full-blown, out-of-the-office celebration. It is a time for employees to relax and recharge their energies. Educational elements can be subtle and worked in, but employee appreciation functions are primarily social and motivational in structure.

Sample Employee Appreciation Event Returns

Employee appreciation events now include exciting new business entertaining twists to help companies meet their goals around showing staff their appreciation. Traditional and themed offerings from the past are being replaced by events that are engaging, enlightening and educational as well as entertaining, and that will elevate the company to the next level.

Stylish and sophisticated are starting to replace casual employee appreciation functions for the entire workforce. Companies are finding that, sometimes, smaller and more intimate get-togethers with each department—or several departments that work closely with one another—holding its own "community" celebration as opposed to companies holding one large function for all to attend are producing better results. All are comparable in terms of dollars spent and what employees experience, but each is designed to meet specific needs within each division and a number of them are taking place out of the office to limit distractions.

One company's owners held their employee appreciation event in a cooking studio with a renowned celebrity chef brought in for the occasion. While they wanted to say thank you for a great quarter, they also wanted to bring together two departments that had been experiencing a little friction to see if spending time outside an office setting would work toward building good energy between them. They wanted their employees to experience a new dimension of working together and designed the event so that their guests would become actively engaged in preparing their own meal and interacting with one another. Their staff was given a hands-on cooking demonstration by the celebrity chef, and employees from both divisions were divided into different groups and were involved in preparing everything from appetizers to desserts. Everyone came together to enjoy what had been prepared and company employees moved from station to station to ensure constant interaction among one another from beginning to end.

The employees came away having been educated as well as entertained. Recipes and shopping lists for the items they prepared, along with custom cooking aprons, became a part of their take-home gift, and gave staff a chance to show off their new cooking talents at home. The long-lasting group dynamics this style of event created within the workplace would not have come about had the company simply held a catered lunch at work. The cost may have been more but the rewards received were far greater and boosted company morale, enhanced working relationships and increased productivity.

Trade Shows

Trade shows contain both educational and social elements. Many times, educational seminars with a top industry speaker are part of the draw. Companies can be exhibitors, attendees, sponsors and guest speakers at trade shows, and there is a time and place for companies to step into each role in order to meet different company and individual objectives.

Sample Trade Show Returns

It can be challenging to create a trade show that is designed to encourage maximum attendance by quality exhibitors and attendees. Organizers—as well as companies spending time, money and energy on attending trade shows, whether as an exhibitor or attendee— face the major hurdles of ensuring that the right elements are in place to entice attendees to register early, have them show up and stay for the duration, leave exhibitors and participants feeling that their time and money was well spent and create industry buzz and anticipation. If you're attending, will this trade show deliver what you need? Would you be better served being an exhibitor locked to your booth, an attendee with the freedom to roam, a host of a private after-show event for select guests or a lead sponsor of one of the top speakers or meal functions?

Companies need to ask whether or not the show is relevant to the audience and decide whether or not that audience *is* their target audience. It is also important to ascertain whether or not the show— and who it is being put on by—is capable of delivering the product, the inspiration, the education and the networking opportunities that are part of the returns on the investment of attending.

If you are attending as an exhibitor, as part of your objectives you would be looking to see if this trade show will attract your prime target audience, if the content and style will drive attendance to this show in record numbers and if it will set the stage for your company to join future trade show endeavors with them. Getting the right people out to the trade show means delivering top industry exhibitors and stimulating educational content with sought-after speakers, and ensuring the organizers have selected the right date, location and time. If any of those vital components are missing or questionable and it is an industry event that it is important to be at and be seen at, it may be better to send out a team of delegates to work the trade floor or look at other viable options that will give you a presence but deliver better results on your company's investment.

In order to get commitment from exhibitors, organizers must be in a position to define the opportunity that the exhibitor will be able to experience. This includes number of attendees, demographic profiles, and networking and branding opportunities. You need the facts before you can decide how and where to spend your money.

Layout can also play a part in meeting tradeshow objectives. If a trade show and conference are both being held, the trade show should not be set apart from the conference program. It should be held where the attendees need to pass through it in order to get to the plenary sessions, receptions and so on.

If your company is taking part as an exhibitor in a trade show, one of the objectives that needs to be addressed in order to get a good return on your investment is how to design your booth so that attendees are drawn to it. For example, do you have a new product that will capture attendees' attention, which is one of the primary reasons delegates attend trade shows, and how will you lay it out so that potential clients don't feel intimidated engaging your sales staff in conversation? Fail to do that and you position yourself for missed sales opportunities.

Ensuring that your company has the means to allocate the appropriate time, energy and resources for pre- and post-show marketing and follow-up also has to be factored into exhibitor trade show objectives in order to achieve maximum results. For example, for pre-show marketing, whenever possible try and set up appointments to meet with customers and prospects at the show.

If you decide to attend as a delegate and not an exhibitor but still want to get your product in front of attendees to increase brand awareness, it is advisable to inquire if it would be beneficial to explain your product/service to the show manager and offer it free of charge. One computer company set up their newest models in an Internet lounge and attendees were able to stop, relax and pick up their e-mail messages as well as sample the new computers. The lounge was set up in a way that the company providing the computers was able to learn about their potential clients.

ADVANCED BUSINESS FUNCTIONS: WHAT THEY ARE AND THE RETURNS THEY CAN BRING

Custom Training Seminars Involving Emotional and Physical Challenges

Team building and motivational elements can be stand-alone events or be built into business meetings, conferences and employee appreciation celebrations as a morning, afternoon or evening activity or even a break. They are carefully designed to evoke a specific reaction from participants. The ultimate goal is to bring the company closer together, open minds to innovative new ways of doing business, motivate and challenge workers to become and do their best, and produce an energy high that will be carried forward in the workplace. Participants can find themselves being challenged mentally or physically or a combination of both. These activities can be built around fun and pleasure or be more serious in nature. It is important when planning this type of business function to ensure that employees look forward to what is being planned with anticipation, not apprehension of failing before their peers, otherwise the purpose of holding this type of business function easily can be undone.

Sample Returns from Custom Training Seminars Involving Emotional and Physical Challenges

Corporations seeking new ways to produce out-of-the-ordinary sales results and become number one in their industry are embracing the new meeting trend of holding their next company function at a venue that offers their employees much more than a ballroom setting.

Savvy business executives know that if they want their workforce to return from company meetings enlightened, energized and enthusiastic, they must move away from old-fashioned meeting setups using conventional function space. Staging a meeting where attendees sit for hours, row after row, sometimes for days on end, in nondescript rooms with little air, has a proven history of being mind-numbing, unproductive and often leaving employees feeling unconnected to the activities taking place. This traditional style of business meeting is the perfect setup for your attendees' minds to wander, their energy to dissipate—especially if a late night of intense socializing has preceded the meeting—leaving them unresponsive to the information being conveyed at great expense.

Companies that are looking to bring cutting-edge performance back to their workplace are moving away from packaged productions and investing their meeting dollars in unique meeting venues that offer their employees the opportunity to take part in personalized interactive experiences, such as spas that specialize in well-being (learning about stress reduction, yoga, etc.), horse ranches, fishing lodges, racecar academies and so forth. These educational experiences are customized and targeted to company objectives and teach participants to look differently at the opportunities available to them at work and in their personal lives.

Companies employing these new training techniques are finding that the skills their employees take back to the office are allowing them to lead their business affairs with more insight, energy and creativity. Glitzy and glamorous audiovisual presentations are making way for specialized instruction that is designed to teach employees how to become proficient in decision-making, efficiently manage their workday challenges, improve communications, build strong teams and identify ways they can effectively move the company and themselves forward. Companies find that their return on investment from this new meeting style extends past their actual event and well into the future.

The key to having your employees responsive to this new meeting format—one that will take them out of a ballroom and out of their comfort zone—is to make sure that all participants have been fully informed as to what to expect without giving away the actual meeting content. To lessen anxiety and heighten anticipation, they need to know up front that they will not be attending a "corporate boot camp." Such events can strike fear in an employee's heart, as they are known for their high-pressure, little-sleep atmosphere, where colleagues are pitted against their peers, judged harshly for failing at their "mission" and told they will be broken down to be built back up.

Participants need to know, so that they arrive relaxed and in a receptive state of mind, that while they will be working hard and playing hard at their meeting, it will be done in a structured and well-supervised format that will be educational, entertaining and engaging. They need to be reassured that they will not be asked to take part in any activities that will put them at physical risk, be embarrassing (such as the example of the having to eat baby food, wear diapers and be spanked) or be against their moral principles.

TIP

Lessen anxiety by letting your participants know what to wear, bring and expect.

Attendees should also be made aware that the tools they will be acquiring will be of great value to them at home as well as at work. What participants will learn from taking part in interactive experiential learning leads to camaraderie, better communication, personal growth and self-mastery. These skills cannot be taught successfully by simply sitting theater-style in a meeting room, eyes straight ahead, with no interaction with the speaker in front of you; they must be experienced firsthand.

One company achieved this by taking its employees to a working ranch set in the great outdoors, where they were asked to play cowboy for a day. And while attendees were enjoying being out of an office setting, roundin' up and movin' out cattle, lessons in teamwork, quick decision-making and organization skills were being imparted—all part of the company's objective. And for those who were wary of horseback riding, there were plenty of tie-in activities that non-riders were able to take part in that taught them the same set of skills.

If companies want to achieve different results back in the office, different means must be used to bring them about. They can create long-lasting change in their corporate culture by moving from mediocre training meetings to meetings that will stir the senses. Unique meeting venues and teaching techniques will deliver extended results and help companies grow in new ways so that they can get roundin' up new clients and focus on movin' out the competition.

Executive Retreats

An executive retreat is a board meeting taken out of the office to a small getaway resort or hotel out of town that offers minimal distractions and an intimate setting. Often the company holding the executive retreat can be the only guests at the facility. The purpose of holding this type of business function is to have quality time one on one without the interruptions that can occur if the senior management, divisional management or some other select group is scheduled to attend or if the meeting is held in the office or locally. A formal agenda is set, but interaction and discussion is not limited to inside a hotel or resort's boardroom or conference space and can take place over golf or dinner. An executive retreat can cover the span of a couple of days or be extended for up to a week. Sometimes an executive retreat can be held before or after a conference.

Sample Executive Retreat Returns

One of the returns from an executive retreat is the opportunity for focused time together to plan future company strategies without other demands getting in the way. It can also be a time for a company's executive force to relax, recharge and rejuvenate; come away with a new perspective on where the company is headed; and get to know one another better.

Many times, golfing is one of the recreational ways this is achieved. One company head looking to do something a bit different and bring his executives back to experiencing what their sales force faced daily opted to have his key decision-makers flown from their retreat resort by sea plane to an uncharted lake. A guide was provided to teach them fishing techniques—patience; how to work together to land that big catch (sales); taking in and processing what is being said; looking for new ways to do something easier, more efficiently and effectively; and working together (cooking their catch using survival tactics)—that are also company objectives that they wanted to recognize in their workforce. Doing something different that took the executives out of their element delivered the messages the company was hoping to convey and gave the executives transferable skills to use back in the office. The company executives also found out firsthand that incorporating innovative new ways to help your company reach its business objectives can pay back many unexpected dividends.

Gala Fundraising Events

Supporting a charity or being perceived as champions of a specific cause can be beneficial to a company in terms of good will, media exposure and generating new business. There are many ways that a company can participate in gala fundraising events, and each will meet different company objectives. Companies can be actively involved as lead sponsors, attendees, silent auction contributors and committee members. There is a time and a place to do each, so it is important for companies to carefully weigh their options and decide how they wish to be involved or be perceived before they tie their name publicly to an event.

It is important for a company to have a clear policy in place regarding involvement types, goals and requirements for involvement, so that no ethical corporate boundaries are crossed. For example, accepting an invitation to attend a fundraising event as a guest of a supplier could be considered as crossing a boundary, while having the company purchase a ticket on its own would avoid the appearance of being "bought" and accepting social outings in exchange for business.

As a company, you need to determine your objectives for becoming involved with a charitable organization, for example, public image, access to a new client base, community good will, increased brand awareness, company beliefs and so on, and which style of gala fundraising event will help you meet them. You also must determine your positioning—committee chair, sponsor, patron or other, as each will help you meet a different set of objectives—and decide how you will be handling your event if you decide to take on the role of hosting the fundraising endeavor, and your *level* of involvement.

First, you must decide what philanthropic cause will be the best fit for you as a company and your corporate image. Do you want to be known for supporting the environment, education, sports or the arts, be a champion of something tied to children in need, or support research or a specific cause? Once you choose the type of philanthropic cause you wish to underwrite, it will help you to design a business function event that is the perfect fit for your company and the cause you are supporting, and one that will help you meet all your event objectives as well as help the nonprofit sector.

It is important to identify everything—being very honest—that you hope to achieve from this venture (e.g., are you looking simply to tie a company event into something that gives back, or are you also looking at the event as a means to link your company name to a specific cause, promote your brand to potential new customers in addition to helping others, etc.). What you and your colleagues will be undertaking, both personally and professionally, is an investment of time, money and energy, and you will need to be able to enlist everyone's full support.

You also have to decide if you will be handling the event on your own or doing it in partnership with a nonprofit organization. If you are working in partnership with a nonprofit organization, they may need to play a major part in the event decision-making process as well. Both you and the nonprofit have company images, rules and regulations, legal issues, and terms and conditions to meet and uphold. For example, it may or may not be a requirement that their board of directors is actively involved with your committee members and that all promotional material featuring their organization's name or logo is approved by them before you can produce it.

Sample Gala Fundraising Event Returns

There are many types of corporate fundraising activities that you can undertake, from supporting and sponsoring a local community event to helping a family in need or raising funds for someone's medical emergency, to sponsoring national or worldwide fundraising efforts. Some can be gala productions, while others can cross over and be tied to other company objectives, such as team building.

One company that wanted to do something for children in need held a team-building event where they turned the backyard of a safe house for children into a wonderful playground haven. The looks on the children's faces when their new backyard was unveiled brought tears to everyone involved in the project.

Teams were not competitive; instead, they all had to work together on timing and logistics. One team was in charge of providing food all day long; another team installed protective fencing; one poured concrete and put in a basketball court; others worked on setting up the swing sets and so forth. Corporate sponsors were solicited to help contribute money for supplies and food for the volunteers.

The following year, this same company decided to make a summer camp for underprivileged children handicapped-accessible. It meant widening pathways so that wheelchairs could be accommodated, redesigning washrooms, putting in ramps and more. They also enlisted the support of local suppliers to help them with expert guidance and direction and provide corporate sponsorship. One of the added benefits to the company was that employees had to move outside of their comfort zones—cold calling, learning to negotiate and so on. In each case, they first checked with the nonprofit organization to see what type of team-building activity would most benefit them. Some organizations, such as Habitat for Humanity, may already have corporate team-building options in place.

Another company wanted to undertake a community project that everyone in their offices across the country could partake in, representing their area. Each region pulled together to put on their own fundraising golf tournament on the same day to support the local branch of the nonprofit organization they had selected to support. It was an overwhelming success, and the bonus was that the employees got to spend quality time with potential new customers while also raising money for a good cause and working together as a team.

One company that had an abundance of outstanding musical talent decided that, as a team-building event to raise money, they would work together and stage a live concert. Their effort was so successful it has become an annual event and each year they choose a different charity to support.

But you have to be careful—business event theme faux pas tied to fundraising events are starting to make national headlines and are costing companies their good images. A company's marketing efforts and reputation can be undone in a matter of minutes by theme events that have not been well designed and thought out as to all possible ramifications. For example, a major beauty manufacturer sparked an international protest among Hindus who felt that a Bollywood gala fundraiser the company had sponsored had appropriated their culture and was disrespectful to their religion. "Fashion Careless," as opposed to "Fashion Cares," was the headline flashed around the world, with details of the dishonorable use of religious imagery at the event.

TIP

Fundraising events draw media coverage, so your success or failure can circle the globe before you realize it. Plan carefully to avoid any unnecessary risk.

Incentive Travel and Premium Programs

Incentive trips (travel) and premium (gifts/merchandise) programs are implemented to increase sales and motivate staff. "Winners" of incentive rewards can be taken for a day of pampering at a local spa or even be whisked away with their partner and fellow winners to an exotic locale for up to two weeks to celebrate sales success. For tax purposes, meeting components are often a part of incentive programs. Incentive trips and premium programs, when staged right, have the ability to meet a number of company objectives.

Sample Incentive Travel and Premium Program Returns

Premium programs have been successfully used by both large and small companies. For smaller companies, premium programs are a good way to introduce motivational programs to employees and to customers. They can be as simple as a summer sales blitz, with the premium prize being a top-of-the-line barbecue combined with boxes of quality beef to enjoy. Or, they can be a promotional program involving your own company product, for example, customers coming in to sample new ice cream flavors, and having the opportunity to win enough ice cream and all the supplies to host a neighborhood ice cream social, which in turn introduces the product to even more potential customers—meeting an additional company objective. To enter the contest, customers may have to drop by the store and deposit an entry form in a drum; for customers not having seen the newspaper ad, entry forms would be on hand at the store. Finding a way to draw customers into a new store location may be another company objective met.

Incentive travel programs can be held locally, for example, a full day of pampering at one of the best spas in town, with VIP touches such as being picked up in a limousine, having a private lunch for two, having a luxury robe to wear, or even two-week getaways at some of the world's top resorts and taking part in one-of-a-kind life experiences, such as a custom African safari. Incentive travel programs can be for couples on their own, or a group of in-house company employees or outside sales staff. Incentive programs can be designed around the employee and a guest or even be expanded to include children. Some incentive programs are designed for the family, such as trips to Disney World.

For years, companies have been using premiums and incentive gifts as a marketing tool to meet their company objectives.

While trends and hot gift items may change, their value has not diminished and is stronger than ever. Premiums can be used as a theme incentive teaser to launch a program; as a marketing mailing piece to customers to stimulate sales and increase brand awareness; as a handout at a trade show booth where one of the objectives may be to attract new clientele and build a mailing list; as a room gift (welcome, nightly or farewell) for a conference; as an appreciation gift to staff or customers and more.

One company's dynamic teaser campaign using premiums combined with a great incentive destination had their employees lining up sales in record numbers, so much so that they outgrew the hotel they were booked at and had to move the program to another equally sought-after—but much larger—hotel in the same location. They ended up putting a two-tier incentive in place, with the top winners flying out in advance and staying at the original property. This successful business function set the tone for the next year, with everyone clamoring to achieve sales, resulting in back-to-back incentives being run. The incentive destination, which hit all of their company and sales staff's objectives, plus the carefully chosen premiums in the company's strategically planned teaser campaign and the targeted incentive gifts on site, helped to create this demand and enabled the company to receive outstanding returns back from its investment.

Award Presentation Shows

Award presentation shows take employee, supplier and industry appreciation events to the next level. While they are created to honor the best and give recognition, they are also a very successful marketing tool. Companies hold in-house award presentation shows and can also get involved in industry award presentation shows as sponsors, attendees and nominees. All serve specific purposes and help to grow business.

Sample Award Presentation Show Returns

Award ceremonies crafted with creative ingenuity and delivered with timely precision have the ability to boost company and supplier images, promote brand loyalty, create public awareness, increase sales, provide award-winning recipients a platform on which to shine as they bask in their 15 minutes of fame and give the audience something to aspire to as they picture themselves walking across the stage next year. But if care is not given to how these events are presented and structured, they can easily create the opposite effect and leave winners feeling as though the efforts they were being rewarded for were minimized.

It is important to remember when designing an award presentation that the presentation needs to meet the expectations of not only the award winner but the company's suppliers, customers, employees and their family members, and the award recipient's family members, which could all conceivably make up the audience. Each of them will be coming to the event with their own set of expectations and personal agendas, so building in ways to help each of them meet theirs over the course of the event will also help corporations meet their own. For example, although the guests are there to congratulate the winners, most people are there to network with the judges, entrants, winners and invited guests. It is important to structure your function to make sure there is networking time before and after the official award presentation.

Naming Rights

The arts, strapped for cash, opened the door to naming rights. Theaters, opera houses and the like are now found bearing corporate names for a specific period of time, such as 10 years, in exchange for potentially millions of dollars. In addition to having the building, room or facility named after their company, corporations are usually able to use the venue as a means to showcase their product. For example, if an automotive company bought the naming rights for a specific property, one of the concessions that they may have included is the right to have their product on display. Another concession could include exclusivity in that no other automotive company would be able to hold private events at their venue or display their company name, logo or product in any way.

Sample Naming Right Returns

One computer company rocketed to national public attention by purchasing the naming rights to a very established government-owned facility that staged some of the country's top entertainment shows. To the general consumer they seemingly came out of nowhere since their name was not a household one. With all the press they generated, though, they soon became well known, as the public became engaged in discussing the merits of naming rights and the human interest reasons why the company president decided to take this route as opposed to spending the same dollars advertising in more traditional ways that could soon be forgotten.

As one of the concessions, they also received exclusivity of all seats to sought-after shows for private pre-opening shows for their select customers, with post-show parties staged at the venue attended by their guests and performers for 10 years. They felt that they had more than met their company objectives to increase brand awareness and gained a high-image profile for their company by making this very public move. And in some cases, purchasing naming rights can also provide tax benefits to companies, which is an added bonus.

Product Launches

When bringing out a new product, a company may look at doing a number of different product launches, each designed to meet the needs of different target audiences and each with their own set of objectives. Separate product launches may be held for employees, those selling their product, consumers buying their product and the media. Some can be orchestrated to hit all at once.

Sample Product Launch Returns

One department store looking at launching a new product line staged an industry first by doing their fashion show down the side of a building. They received advance buzz and great press coverage on the day of their launch. Because of all the news being generated, both employees and consumers were very aware of the new line that would now be available in their stores. And doing something that had never been done before—and doing it well—gave the department store extra cachet.

A global electronics company that distributes consumer and broadcast products worldwide found that choosing an unexpected venue, such as a warehouse, club or gallery, in an easy access, convenient location open over the lunch hour, worked well to pull in their attendees and helped them receive a return on their investment. They found that the new art gallery they took over for their product launch was an interesting backdrop for their high-end television launch. In the evening they opened it up to their dealers to invite their VIP customers (end users). It was a unique touch that proved to be very successful. Their customers found it refreshing to get out of a hotel and be among the first to see the art gallery—and the product—on an exclusive basis. The location and their event delivery appealed to the company's high-end market target audience, helped them meet their sales objectives and worked to enhance their brand image.

Product Placement

Traditional ways of marketing a product or service to consumers are no longer working as well as they did in the past. Consumers have limited time and they are not spending it reading or listening to advertising. They are, for instance, taping shows and fast-forwarding through commercials.

Sample Product Placement Returns

One fast-food company looking for new ways to tempt consumers to watch their commercials and meet their marketing objectives created an ad that allows television audiences to view a hidden message—how to get a free sandwich—in their commercial that they can only see if they play the commercial back in slow motion on a VCR or digital video recorder. Viewed normally, the commercial looks just like any other television ad.

To circumvent this trend, other companies are now looking for fresh ways to place their products in front of or in the hands of their consumers. They don't want to take the chance that viewers will suddenly want to become interactive with their television set, or spend precious time—time more valuable than the cost of a sandwich to most—and create more work for their consumer by having them tape and play back their commercials to find their hidden messages, which may or may not ever be seen. Instead, these companies are arranging to have blatant product placement appear on television and even whole shows built around a specific product or service. They are planning themed business events, such as big screen viewing parties for selected guests. Celebrating their company's product placement gives them a reason to get together and talk about product but as a "seemingly" very soft sell. Companies are paying millions of dollars to be able to do so. They want their product imbedded into the show and into the minds of their consumers.

Virtual product placement ads are now becoming common as well. Products that were not in an original scene are being added digitally and targeting a specific network audience. For example, the backlit ad on top of a New York taxi was digitally changed to advertise a specific casino to a viewing television audience that was located in that state. The cost to do virtual product placement in this manner was in the area of $10,000 and considerably less than a traditional 30-second spot on the same show that could be fast-forwarded or played on mute.

Companies are taking innovative product placement concepts a step further and are now actively looking for ways to incorporate product placement into the business functions they do and partnering with others, such as one music company that had CD lids made to fit beverages that were being given out free to guests attending another company sponsor's theme party. The CD featured one song from a new singer whose new album they were about to launch.

For smaller companies, product placement could be sponsoring a local children's sports team, having their name on team shirts and hosting the celebration party for the parents (potential clients) and team members, which may or may not include samples of their product.

And sometimes product placement can bring together interesting corporate partnerships. One television network is promoting their upcoming season by introducing their shows on more than 35 million eggs being sold in grocery stores. Eggs will bear messages such as "Crack the Case" for a detective show or "A Grade 'A' Comedy" applied by the newest technology, enabling them to reach viewers in their homes. If they wanted, they could host egg-themed parties, such as brunches, or host tie-in events in local grocery stores.

Product placement is not limited to taking place on television, in the movies, on stage and in magazines and books. The objective is placing your product in front of your targeted audience, and in order to meet your objectives it must be done well.

One beverage manufacturer created a business buzz, but not the kind they were looking for, with a combination public product placement and product launch themed event that went terribly wrong. Working with their ad agency, a 20-ton, 2½-story flavored ice pop was unveiled at Union Square in New York at the start of summer to advertise the company's new frozen treats. The huge blocks of ice melted and the street was flooded with a gooey mess that sent pedestrians and cyclists slipping and sliding—and to the hospital. Not only did the company have a failed promotional event on their hands but they also could have been liable for city cleanup costs and lawsuits from those who were injured. They did receive major media coverage—just not the kind they were looking for to bring a return on their investment.

Product placements must enhance and help build—not tarnish—a company image through well-thought-out event designs, and corporate executives must be able to spot red flag areas in events proposed by their company's advertising agencies and public relations firms. Companies can never forget that along with their product, their company image is being placed in front of their customers. One of their objectives should be to deliver successful execution as well as produce great consumer goods and services.

Special Events

A special event can be a company milestone celebration. Or, it can be an event that has been created especially to meet a specific company objective and will be hosted by the corporation, such as one honoring someone who has made a great contribution to their industry. A special event can be a small, intimate affair, a private event for thousands or televised to millions around the world. They are often one-time events.

Sample Special Event Returns

A special event is a stand-alone event created around a specific occasion such as a company's 50th anniversary, not a company's yearly holiday party. It is designed to take place for a reason, be it a person or purpose, and can be used as a creative way to meet many company objectives. For example, a number of companies are now hosting private celebrity or sporting special events that only their customers whose purchase contained a specialty item can take part in. The special event is being used to meet company objectives of brand awareness, being thought of as cutting edge, nurturing customer loyalty, developing new business, increasing sales of a particular product and receiving media attention, and was created for the sole purpose of doing all of the above.

Conclusion

In conclusion, business functions and business entertaining provide the means to meet many company objectives and bring about a return on investment but it is important to know why you are holding them, which one will give you the best results—since many styles may meet the same needs but not to the same extent—and where, when and how to use them effectively for maximum results. It is important to know how to clearly define and set company objectives so that you are in a position to choose the best style of event to deliver them. Understanding each style of event and its potential returns is the first step in being able to successfully choose and use the right business functions in order to bring about a return on your company's investment.

CHAPTER TWO

HOW TO QUALIFY YOUR COMPANY OBJECTIVES FOR A PROPOSED BUSINESS FUNCTION

TO SUCCESSFULLY DESIGN the right business function to deliver the results you are looking for, it is important to examine and set all possible company objectives at the outset and prioritize them. Knowing your key objectives will help you choose the right vehicles to meet them. Avoid the desire to designate the type of event that you want to hold before you begin to consider your business objectives.

Several types of business functions may meet some of the same objectives. For example, a product launch and sponsoring a gala fundraising that will showcase your new product could both conceivably bring about media exposure and brand awareness, but would provide different levels of return in each area. It is important to decide which business function will meet more of your primary requirements so that you can then move forward to determining the role that will best serve the company. If you decide to hold or take part in this particular event, at this specific time, how will you meet this precise set of intentions? For example, what capacity—host, attendee, sponsor and so on—will help you achieve more of your goals (the results, once you lay out costs and benefits—not pros and cons—can be very surprising) so that you can then look at how best to strategically plan and stage all of the essential elements for maximum results?

Defining Your Basic Objectives

Ask yourselves these questions to determine your needs:

- What is the purpose of our proposed event, for example, do we want to introduce a new product? Motivate sales for a specific product and reward top performers? Attract new clients? Thank existing clients and show appreciation for their business support? Build company loyalty? Bring the company together to celebrate our past year and announce our company's future plans?

- What are our future plans for company growth? Are there other areas that need attention now or in the upcoming year or years that it would be of benefit to start addressing now? It does not matter at this stage whether or not they initially seem to be related. As you plan one event, you have to have one eye looking forward so that you don't duplicate ideas, and you may be able to design and use this proposed event as a solid launch platform for your next event.

- Can any of these objectives be combined so that we can achieve layers of multiple returns from one event, such as launching our new product at the end of our business meeting and opening it up to customers, suppliers and key employees, and giving them a reason to place a pre-order at the event to stimulate sales?

- Why do we think holding an event will give us the best possible results? For example, why hold a media event to release news of a new product as opposed to taking out national ads in newspapers and magazines at this particular point in time? Print ads might be more effective when the product is actually in the stores. Holding a media conference—having media authorities test-drive new cars and write about their experience on a corporate sponsored weekend away planned to showcase the product (e.g., car rally)—could enable us to reach different target audience markets and have actual user credibility as opposed to just the advertiser saying the product is great.

- Who is the main target audience we are creating this event for? And who are our secondary, third, and so on, audiences? For example, creating pride in the company for employees of all levels could be an added company objective to holding an event that is tied to helping a specific cause, such as providing relief to an area that has been hit by a natural disaster. An additional company objective could be picking up media coverage that will give your company community and national exposure.
- What does our company need right now to grow financially and in industry position, become stronger and attract and keep new clients and the best caliber of employees?
- How will our proposed objectives—if met—help us as a company meet our present and future needs?
- Have we missed an important growth component that could be added to our event's objectives?
- If all of our objectives are met by holding this event, what will have been this event's value to us as a company?
- How will the company benefit by doing this event and how will it affect us as a company if we do not hold this event? What is the cost to us as a company if we don't hold this event?

It is important to know and make a list of all of your company's objectives, once again present and future, and not limit them to a specific department. If you can address and build in layers of critical company objectives, and strategically design your event to target and meet all of them—both company and department—it can be of tremendous benefit to the company as a whole, and will be money well spent because you have maximized the event's potential delivery and return on investment. You could conceivably find yourself working with a larger event budget because of this.

While a department may decide its main objective is to run an incentive program to move a certain product, crafting it so that it becomes the buzz of the industry will profit the company if the cream of the industry decides that your company is the place to work at. Attracting the best employees is always a company's objective.

What goes on in one company is always the water cooler topic of conversation in another, so use this to your advantage when creating events and put out the image you want to project and protect. After all, employees will talk, suppliers will talk, industry media will talk and so will customers and the general public. That is always a given. For example, does your company want to be thought of as traditional, tired or cutting edge? If keeping your image as number one and cutting edge is one of your company's objectives, then one of your event's objectives must be that the event itself will generate that kind of PR for your company.

Before you start shaping and structuring your event, begin by creating five lists of objectives. The first one will be a list of all department objectives—present and future. Do not limit them to this event at this time. The second list to compile will be a list of company objectives—present and future—and make sure that it encompasses all of the company's hopes and dreams, regardless of whether or not they are in place as yet. The third list will be a list of department and company objectives that can both possibly be met by holding this event. The fourth list will be a list of attendee objectives that the event will be required to meet, which is very important. The fifth list, after careful review of lists three and four, will merge parts of the two together and become the primary event objective list that you will design your proposed event around. And these can include objectives that are both small and large, short term and long term, and so forth.

Whether or not you handle your event in-house or hire a professional corporate event planner (contract or company), you and your committee members and/or those designated to help you with this project, and the person and suppliers actually putting together the proposal for your event, will need to know your objectives so that they can address each issue and build in exactly what you will need to meet each and every event objective.

The clearer and more detailed you can be with your list of objectives, the better your end results will be. It is also imperative that you rank your objectives in order of importance so that you and your suppliers know exactly where to put the main event focus.

Sample objectives:

- increase sales by "x" percent
- inspire sales for specific products, which are "a," "b" and "c," by "x" amount
- motivate sales staff to meet personal and company. sales targets for the coming year
- reduce workplace accidents from current figures of "x" to "y"
- increase productivity by "x" and meet company-guaranteed delivery deadlines
- attract "x" number of new customers by "y"
- move from number three in industry rankings to number one

A business function, carefully designed, should meet numerous company-targeted goals as well as those of individual departments. Goals should not be limited to strictly monetary matters—coming in, on or under budget. For example, there can be many returns on the investment of hosting an award ceremony in addition to whether or not the event came in on budget. Each player in the event—the client, sponsors, suppliers, customers, employees, award winners and family members—can each take away something different, and in many cases there can be multiple rewards. The company may decide to host an award presentation to create employee recognition and loyalty, and having spouses present validates the efforts the family supported during the year. These non-monetary types of returns should be included when looking at your company objectives because they can generate powerful returns that will have long-lasting effects on your company's business growth.

When preparing a list of all possible company objectives that can be met, you need to look at them from every angle and from the perspective of everyone that could be attending. It is essential that companies know who will be in the room for each event so that they can create the perfect showcase that more than meets their attendees' level of anticipation. Everything from the entertainment to the food to the decor to even delivery must be planned to the demographics of the group. For example, a younger crowd will not appreciate a Broadway song and dance after a company dinner as much as they will a high-tech multimedia show with special effects. The age, sex, geographical location, level of sophistication—everything—must play into the mix as you begin to lay out your objectives.

> **TIP**
>
> Know your audience and you'll be better able to get their attention and keep it.

A good way to begin this exercise is to start by looking at all possible objectives in four different categories to help you produce the end result, which is a successful event that surpasses your company goals:

- expectations from all involved
- emotion
- exposure—internal and external
- expenses—hard costs

Expectations from All Involved

Companies must never lose sight of the fact that for their objectives to be met when using business functions and business entertaining, they first must meet the expectations and objectives of everyone involved. Your audience—employees, their partners, suppliers, customers, media, general public and so on—will all be attending, hoping that they will come away fulfilled and that they will receive return on their own investment of time, money and energy. They are looking to come away educated, enlightened and/or entertained. Fail to keep that in mind and stepping into individual expectation shoes could leave you failing to meet even your basic objectives.

> **TIP**
>
> Combine enlightenment and educational elements with entertainment to make guests feel totally engaged in the moment.

We live in an era where time is a very precious commodity and people are taking steps to make sure that they spend both their personal and professional time wisely. In the past, for example, when suppliers opened their doors at holiday time to invite their customers to partake in the season's cheer, they often could be guaranteed a reasonable turnout of their top supporters with little or no thought going into their event. That is not the case today. Creating celebrations that allow guests to come away with a sense of joy is an important trend. It is a busy time of the year and guests are choosing not to go to parties when they don't feel they will come away with their spirits elevated. They are weighing their costs, for example, time out of their life to get there and back and any backlogs that could result, cost of dressing the part (new outfit, hairdo, etc.), and the potential drain on their energy. In many cases, if the holiday get-together is just going to be an open bar and refreshments, they are opting not to go, and hosts hoping to have quality time to schmooze their customers are not meeting their objectives.

More and more companies are turning to entertainment specialists to help them meet this challenge, as the age base of their staff grows and there is more diversity and sophistication in their workforce. Companies today are looking to have their guests engaged from the moment they walk into their holiday event and they are hiring professional MCs and hosts to keep their event's energy level up and consistent. They are open to new ideas and they don't have to be extravagant. In many cases, clients are looking for a toned-down event—in appearance only—with the budget remaining the same as an over-the-top affair but totally tailored to attract their guests' attendance.

One company held a wine tasting conducted by a very respected wine expert for their upscale customer holiday event, featuring the types of wines that were sought after and held great appeal to their clientele. They also made sure that the guests knew that they would be going home with a thank-you bottle of their favorite selection. Both the host's and the guests' expectations were met and the evening was an outstanding success.

On the flip side, a company that built their event around one speaker covering one specific topic found themselves facing an empty room on the day of their event. The speaker and topic that they had chosen had zero appeal to their targeted audience. All that had been planned was the speaker and light refreshments, and neither served as a draw to bring people in.

Knowing your target audience's likes and dislikes is extremely important, as is knowing what else is taking place around the date of your event industry-wise, world-wise and personally (e.g., a long weekend). Without attendees there is no event. Another company failed to realize that they had scheduled their event over World Cup, which was of major interest to their guests, and had to cancel their event due to lack of response. Had they turned their event around to being a showcase for watching the World Cup and celebrated the playing teams in a way that held great appeal, such as in the same manner that Oscar parties are done, with theatrical flair and big screen staging, they could have ended up with a waiting list.

Remember to ask:

- Who will be in the room?
- What is the main age group?
- What are their likes and dislikes?
- What will we be doing that will make our event stand out as a "must-attend" event?
- What "WOW factors" can we build in that will tap into our audience's personal and professional desires, for example, getting someone with the name and reputation of Warren Buffett to speak would be a "must-attend" event for those in the financial industry.
- What other things are taking place that could limit attendance at our event?

Emotion

It is important to look at the emotional connection your event could potentially bring to your company or product. Will what you are proposing to do and how you are looking at doing it leave people feeling good, bad or indifferent after attending or hearing about your event? The emotional component needs to be examined closely as to what can be done to ensure that emotions are evoked in a way that will help you to meet your objectives.

For example, one organization that required sponsors to host their final evening dinner extravaganza at their convention knew that if their event could be staged to win over their audience's emotions, they would win over their existing sponsors for next year as well as attract new sponsors and media play. They had tied their event to a nonprofit charity and in their finale they included before and after images of the children being helped by the funds that their sponsored event would help raise, and those images captured the hearts of both sponsors and attendees and left them feeling good about their association with the company.

A company that produces toothpaste, toothbrushes or anything that is related to oral hygiene could consider supporting a wonderful nonprofit association like Operation Smile, which calls on volunteers to help children with facial deformities smile for the first time. And so could manufacturers of lines of lipsticks. Clothing manufacturers could tie into charities that help women in shelters learn how to dress to go back out into the workforce again. One company that each year sends terminally ill children and a family member on a plane ride to the North Pole to see Santa (the flight is actually a flight to nowhere and Santa emerges halfway through the trip from the cockpit) and receive presents tugs on the heartstrings of the nation as they watch the children's faces light up with joy. When given the choice between buying the same product from two similar companies, many people reach for the product of the company that does good for families that need joy in their lives.

Emotion is very much a tool that many companies use to help them meet their objectives, which are not limited to increased sales and may include boosting their company image both inside and outside their company. The partnering opportunities to do something wonderful are out there, and both the charity and the company come out winners. Emotion can be used to garner public good will, drive sales and promote customer loyalty to your product.

In the case of an organization involving sponsors as part of the farewell event for their conference, after their first event they found that in addition to the original event sponsors being back on board, two additional sponsors were lining up to be a part of the next one. Each year they continued to build on their emotional hooks and found that new sponsors were no longer waiting to be approached by them post-event, but had begun coming up during the course of the evening asking about sponsorship opportunities for the next year. In addition to receiving sponsorship dollars that allowed them to take their conference to new levels, the company and their sponsors also began receiving extensive television, newspaper and magazine coverage due to their success and how warmly their conference was regarded. One of their objectives that served them well was always making sure to invite potential new sponsors and the media to their farewell event so that they could witness firsthand their audience's response.

Questions to ask as you design your event include:

- When our guests walk out the door, what emotions do we want them to be carrying home about the event and our company? (They can be very different depending on your event objectives.)
- What holds emotional appeal to our targeted audience and how and where can we tap into it during our event?

Exposure—Internal and External

Internal exposure is exposure within your company, your industry and your circle of existing suppliers and customers. External exposure is related to brand awareness and attracting the attention of the world at large in a favorable way to build name recognition and create a center of attention to draw new clients and business opportunities to your company.

It is important, when setting objectives, to look at the exposure your business function can receive both internally from your staff and externally from others pre-event, during and post-event in the form of media attention—newspapers (local and national), magazines (industry and non-industry), television (local and national) and the Internet (worldwide). You can get additional external exposure through press releases, holding a press conference, inviting the media to your event as guests, producing your own marketing pieces and submitting stories and photographs to the media. Take note of what other companies are doing and not just those in your related field. Pay attention to the stories that fly around the world about companies via the Internet or are picked up by newspapers, magazines and television. Many times they are company generated and are not the result of the media seeking them out. There is usually little or no cost involved, and could simply mean hiring a professional journalistic-style photographer so that the pictures meet media criteria, or inviting the media to cover your event.

In order to first capture media interest, you must have a hook that will appeal to the media's specific readers. Your hook can change to address different audiences. And for internal media exposure, look for ways you can piggyback on what already exists to hit your targeted audience. For example, one real estate company capitalizes on their award presentation post-event by honoring their winners in a congratulatory advertising insert in one of their industry's leading publications. Doing this brings tremendous exposure to their company as to how positive their sales results are, raises the profile of both their company and their top achievers, showcases their event, is a means to entice top talent from other companies to consider working for them and introduces them to prospective new customers.

Questions to ask include:

- What type of internal exposure would be applicable to this event and benefit our company?
- What type of external exposure would be applicable to this event and benefit our company?
- Where are our competition receiving media exposure from (simple ways to check this out include going online to Google News and putting competitors' names in the keyword search to see what comes up under news)?

TIP

You can set up Google News to alert you to news covering topics and specific company names once a day, and display stories that are relevant to your business. Pay attention to what and how the subject is being discussed and how many newspapers are carrying the same story. It is important to also begin to create a media contact list.

Expenses—Hard Costs

Never assume that your proposed budget will resemble anything close to your final reconciliation. As you begin to design and contract your event, you will begin to firm up "estimated" costs. It is important that your event cost summary (which is your proposed budget) needs to be done "menu style," broken down item by item to make sure that the dollars being spent make sense and that every dollar counts toward helping you meet your event objective[1] and continually updated so that there are no unexpected surprises at the end. Periodic reconciliation is a must and imperative before final payment—not final reconciliation—goes out to suppliers.

Note attrition dates; these are your deadlines for bringing down guarantee numbers and so forth by a certain percentage and avoiding cancellation charges. Not only these dates should be noted on your critical path but also those with a time buffer built in so you

---

1   In-depth details on how to do this are covered in *The Business of Event Planning* (Wiley, 2002).

are not leaving critical decisions to the last minute—at which time it might be very costly to make changes.

While proper budget management is always of paramount importance, the money spent will have been wasted if you stay within the allotted dollars but fail to deliver the results the event was conceived to produce. The dollars being spent must make good business sense. Events must be designed and strategically planned to produce maximum effect while being cost-efficient. Executives must become masters at finding creative cost-saving measures, designing events that meet and exceed client and guest expectations, and showing budget restraint without jeopardizing meeting company objectives.

When deciding whether or not to proceed with a product or service, it is important to look at how an item will meet the event's objectives. If a quote is higher than the budgeted amount, it is important to discuss how these additional costs will be recovered. For example, purchasing advertising in an industry magazine will incur costs, but the anticipated return on investment is that more paying delegates will attend, thus meeting a conference objective of increased attendance as well as providing the extra revenue to offset the advertising cost.

Look at the type of group that is getting together. A group that is in training sessions all day may not need to be in a five-star resort. Using properties in smaller cities for meetings can often mean lower room rates, food and audiovisual costs, and room rental rates. As long as the transportation costs don't outweigh the cost savings of having the meeting in a smaller city, this is often a good option, especially if participants are traveling from across the country. As well, properties will often offer clients incentives to travel off-season.

Savings can be realized in all areas. For instance, under transportation, instead of doing individual transfers, use scheduled pickup times. Although it means a longer wait for attendees, costs are much less. Or, allow for longer wait times between flights in order to completely fill up the coaches. Pay attention to food and beverage costs that can quickly escalate. Hotels and convention centers often charge huge markups on bottled water and participants often take bottles for consumption after the meetings. Jugs of water, while not as convenient, are much less costly, but be careful about refresh costs as hotels and convention centers are now beginning to charge to refill the jugs.

It is also important to take into consideration the financial and cultural climate of the company when you are defining your company's expense objectives. Employees who have experienced cutbacks will have a poor response to a flashy event. Some companies would rather compromise quantity rather than quality, while others would rather cover all of the bases on a much more scaled down level. All of the various costing factors that can impact a program's cost and effectiveness must be reviewed based on the primary objective that will drive the greatest return. For example, if a company's key objective is to improve customer satisfaction, the budget may be focused more heavily on meeting content versus group leisure activities.

Questions to ask include:

- As I evaluate my list of event objectives, which cost items will help us to meet them?
- As event elements are laid out, will they be effective or do we need to reassign dollars in order to create a more effective delivery? For example, does the money being spent on a themed coffee break help us to meet our objectives in any way or would we be better served having a standard coffee break and allocating those extra dollars elsewhere?
- Are we spending major dollars meeting objectives that are on the bottom of our list or are the dollars being spent in ways that will ensure that we meet our primary objectives?

Providing Added Value

Using the previous example of an award presentation, a sampling of a company's added value and non-monetary objectives could include:

- saluting their employees' outstanding efforts and acknowledging their achievements (expectation)
- ensuring that the nominees, not just the honoree, are also considered winners (emotion)
- ensuring that all goes as planned and time doesn't run out before everyone has been acknowledged (expectation)
- recognizing any significant others that are in attendance, such as having them stand, be applauded and receive a special gift to thank them for their support and dedication so that next year's potential winners will be inspired at home as well as in the office (emotion)
- sending winners away having enjoyed a priceless life experience that is worth striving for (expectation and emotion)
- entertaining your guests and keeping them there until the last award (in order to meet that objective there needs to be a three- to five-minute WOW factor at the event: great AV, great awards, suspense to see who the big winner is, an entertainment component that builds to the top award, an engaging MC, celebration of all winners and the evening ending with an emotional motivational bang) (expectation, emotion, expense and exposure)
- creating an event that is cutting edge and positions the company as a leader in its industry and in its customers' eyes (exposure—external)
- leveraging post-event returns, for example, by posting a happy snapshot of the events, including the awards presentation, on the company's website for all the staff to see and be inspired by (exposure—internal)

- showing company strength and delivery through planning and proper preparations so that those on stage appear confident and poised (expectation, emotion and exposure)

Prioritizing Your Objectives

As discussed earlier, once you have laid out all of your objectives and categorized them as to what return they will be bringing you, the next step is prioritizing them so that you will be able to make informed decisions regarding strategy, inclusions and proposed expenditures. It is essential that you can clearly identify your "must haves" and what is most indispensable to you. Your "must haves" are what will bring you returns on your investment and help you meet your top event objectives. As you look through your event design and related costs with meeting your primary objectives top of mind, you will be able to quickly and efficiently decide what to keep in and where you need to make adjustments to both your event design and your budget.

TIP

Realize that not every objective is a "must have."

By doing this, you have basically laid out your wish list. While it may be possible to meet all of your company expectations from your upcoming business function or business entertaining venture, it's not always the case. Circumstances and cost control can play a factor in what you can do, and you want to make sure that what needs to be addressed most is at the top of the list. For example, if it was determined that having a WOW factor would give you the most returns for your investment, then that would need to be stressed in your request for a proposal or quote from your suppliers.

When you set out to determine your priorities, it is important that you do not look at your proposed business enterprise in isolation. Each undertaking is a business-building block and should be viewed as such. Your company's past history, present direction and future goals all need to be factored into the equation. You need to assess which items on your list of objectives have served you well in the past, if they are benefiting you now or could be if they were in place in the present, and if they are in keeping with your company's future plans.

What you do today will affect what you do tomorrow and how your company is perceived by your employees and by others. For example, one company decided that launching a company travel incentive would help them meet many of their company objectives. It would:

- work toward creating an inner circle of top employees that others would strive to become a part of
- potentially increase sales for selected products
- give their best sales staff a chance to relax
- enable staff to get to know one another and share their proven sales techniques
- give senior management time to spend with key members of their team and learn from them what else they could do to take sales to even greater heights, see how they conduct themselves outside of the office and assess their leadership skills with an eye toward future promotions

While this company had not previously held sales incentives, many of their senior staff members had participated in them in the past when they worked for the competition, so they knew how they worked logistically. They and their staff were tremendously excited about their upcoming program. The destination and program inclusions far outshone what their competition had been doing, and they were looking at positioning themselves as the company who rewarded outstanding sales results with extraordinary rewards, such as their two-week, first-class, all-expenses-paid getaway to an exotic locale. Unfortunately, they failed to look at whether or not their sales staff could meet the extremely high target figures required to qualify, how many would find the targets achievable and how the results from this year's incentive program would influence next year's. The company prioritized sales goals as a primary objective but did not create an event that could deliver at the target levels set.

It is important as you prioritize your event objectives that they are first reachable. If they are not, not only will it affect the return on investment of this year's event but on future ones as well, because they will fail to motivate staff who were striving to meet impossible company targets, fell short and came away feeling defeated.

In this instance, the company contracted airline seats, hotel guestrooms, and meeting and venue space based on their projected numbers, which were not based on reality. When the numbers did not materialize—as could have been expected had they taken the time to really work the numbers before launching their program— they were left with having to pay considerable cancellation charges, even with the attrition worked in, and higher costs per person because they no longer had the numbers to command better rates and concessions. The higher costs per person were no longer covered by the sales targets that had already been established.

The actual program was wonderful and those that did partake had an amazing time and were pumped up when they returned, looking forward to the next incentive program and wondering what could possibly top this one. And that is another thing the company had neglected to look at when selecting this year's program: What could they do for next year to top this one going out? What could they do now to redeem themselves and their program since they had designed the event such that the cost far outweighed the benefits? They knew they would have to scale back in a big way in order to achieve the results they were looking for.

They now had a greater appreciation for their main competitor's programs and how they were positioning themselves. Their competition had their priorities straight, and they were using their incentive programs as present and future business-building blocks.

Their competition's "president's club" had started out small and very exclusive. It was first class from beginning to end, but started off with a three-night program held in North America. The second year's program, due to attainable goals and the success of the first year, was a three-night stay in London. That was followed with another three-night stay, but this time it was fun in the sun. Their next program was held back in Europe.

Their numbers were growing and what was working for them was the back and forth between fun and sun and sightseeing and shopping. The stays started to get longer but quality was never downgraded—it was still first class all the way. Instead of holding one incentive program a year, they were now running incentive programs every three and four months and sales targets were being met and exceeded.

All of their objectives were being met many times over but they were still not prepared to do what the other inexperienced company had done—put the reach too far and made it unobtainable in order to present something splashy. Someday they would set lofty sales goals, but only when it was doable for their sales staff.

What they did do, however, was reexamine their incentive program strategy to see where and how they could grow it and still produce the results that they were looking for. One of their new objectives was to further challenge and stimulate sales by their top performers. Their solution was to devise a two-tier program. All their president's club winners would travel together to the incentive destination for a three- or four-night stay. At the end of the program, their new incentive program would kick off and their "president's circle" winners would be whisked away first class from the destination to an exotic location for stays of up to a week, while the rest of the president's club, who were returning home instead of jetting away, were left planning their sales line of attack so that next time they would be on the plane with their partners heading off to a wonderful week of enticing delights. Another encouraging tactic that the company brought in to spur more of their sales staff to greater heights was to assign suites to all president's circle winners on the higher level incentive program.

Prioritizing their objectives and then looking at how business functions and business entertaining could be brought in to help them achieve objectives not just today but tomorrow helped that company grow in leaps and bounds. Had they not sat down to take the time to map out their master plan, they would not have had the success that they did. They never had to backtrack or downsize their program or substitute quantity for quality; they devised a means to get both. Each program built on the next and created desire to be a part of this prestigious club, as the president's club and president's circle members were respected not only in their offices but in their industry as well. Their outstanding performances were also creating impressive résumés and they stood out in the eyes of company executives. Meeting company objectives had in turn set wheels in motion for their participants to create their own personal and professional objectives, too.

In the end, the company and their employees met far more objectives than they had originally planned on. As their programs grew, so did their company objectives. They allowed neither to become stale. As they worked on today, they took the lessons learned from their past programs, revamped their present events to incorporate them and always kept one eye on how what they were doing now would or could affect their company's future objectives.

Another company, just starting out with incentives, did their homework. To reach one of their company objectives—improving motivation—they looked for ways to ensure as many people as possible reached their sales goals and took part in their incentive program. Their core objective was to increase quarterly sales, although an incentive program, which they believed to be the perfect vehicle for them to achieve this, was never originally budgeted for. They wanted to have a high-end incentive with limited resources.

They started out with a tiered incentive structure to allow more winners to be included, but structured it so that their top level could still be richly rewarded. The program was a weekend theater extravaganza.

Destinations were the highly desirable top-tier city, London, and the second-tier city of New York. The third tier was a location that was many of the participants' home city. The program was over a long weekend and this made it even more desirable, as participants appreciated not having to take too much time away from their families.

Each site's event included a number of low-cost, high-impact elements, such as personalized cell phones with paid-for local calling, makeup artists, personal shoppers, limousine transfers, luxury robes, private chef kitchen dinners in the best restaurants in town and a gift certificate for a shopping spree.

Attendees loved every element. For those close to home, they felt like celebrities in their own city and did not for one moment miss getting away to another destination. Sales revenue well exceeded the company's original target and top-tier losers were still made to feel like winners. There are many ways to meet company objectives; the key is finding the right one for yours that will deliver as many results as possible.

Will the Event You Are Proposing Help You Meet Your Company's Criteria?

In addition to looking at the past, present and future company objectives that you are looking to meet through specific business functions and business entertaining, it is important to look at what will be going on within your company as a whole. Are there any competing or comparable events that will be targeting your same objectives, and if so, when are they taking place and could they help or hinder your efforts?

It is possible to leverage off of other departments' events. One company receives huge savings from contracting to use the same hotel and supplier for events two years in a row but not necessarily for the same departments or style of event. The savings are substantial and by looking at what other departments were doing and pooling their negotiation clout, they both came out winners.

Too many departments are focused on their own internal efforts and do not take the time to become informed as to what will be taking place in the company as a whole or in their industry. Not knowing can be a costly mistake and, despite your best efforts, produce less than desirable results. Two separate divisions in your company may be going after the same suppliers for sponsorship dollars for their individual functions, or hoping to get the same customer base out to attend their event. Your event may be scheduled to take place at a time when your target market is out of the country attending an industry convention, or two similar-style events are running back to back. It is important to know what is going on in your company as a whole so that each business function can play its own part in making the company a success, and so that there are no missteps.

It is vital that you take the time to research what will be taking place in your industry, when it is scheduled to take place and who is likely to be attending. It is possible to do companion-style events where your event complements what will be taking place elsewhere or what has taken place in another department or even within the industry.

For example, one growing trade show trend is collocating more shows together in order to create greater critical mass to draw people from farther distances and to take advantage of synergies between complementary events, that is, getting people to enter the second show rather than leave the building after they have finished walking through the first show. This gives attendees more choice and one-stop shopping opportunities and gives exhibitors the chance to meet more prospects. It is similar to the power centers that are popping up all over the place. Collocating also lends itself to being able to brand a trade show as being the biggest and a must-see if customers want to find new products, which in itself could help a company trade show exhibitor or attendees to meet objectives.

Conclusion

In order to qualify your company objectives for a proposed business function, companies must:

- lay out all of their proposed event objectives
- define and categorize them to see which specific needs they are targeting:
  - expectations from all involved
  - emotion
  - exposure—internal and external
  - expenses—hard costs
- prioritize them, keeping in mind past, present and future objectives
- critique them as to how they will help you meet specific objectives
- check to make sure that there are no other competing or comparable business functions taking place at the same time

CHAPTER THREE

SELECTING EVENTS TO SUCCESSFULLY MEET SPECIFIC COMPANY OBJECTIVES

IT IS KEY THAT YOU UNDERSTAND what each type of event will deliver and how it will play into meeting your specified objectives. There is a time and a place for each of them, but it is essential to know what event to do or attend, when it is most advantageous, in what capacity your company should be involved and what your presence—or lack of presence—will say to your employees, customers and suppliers. For example, within the context of holding a trade show, a company can hold a trade show, attend a trade show, sponsor a trade show, be represented at a trade show by having a senior member of the company act as a keynote guest speaker, or have a company representative on the chairing committee of a trade show, and each one of these alternatives has its pluses and minuses.

Each type of event represents an investment of time, money and energy, but they all bring different results. Being able to pinpoint which business function to choose to meet a specific company need at a particular point in time is invaluable to company executives. And to be able to do so successfully, you need to be able to envision the maximum returns on investment from all angles and position accordingly your company and the role your company employees play.

TRADITIONAL BUSINESS FUNCTIONS

Board Meetings

A board meeting is generally called to review company direction, review polices and procedures, and map out future plans.

Board Meeting Options

Remember with board meetings that the location can work toward meeting company objectives as well. Board meeting locations include being held:

- in the office
- out of the office, for example, in-town hotel
- out of the office overnight stays, for example, in-town or out-of-town hotel

Effective Board Meetings

Board meetings can be used successfully to review a company's standing, for example, if they are where they wanted to be, and if not, why; map out a company's future direction; and strategically plan the best means to reach their goals. Board meetings are a time to focus on company matters and to make them the primary objective. It is a time when the top minds of your company are together in one room, and company direction and growth needs to be the number one concern on your agenda.

Look for ways to make the best use of your time together so that your board meeting can be as productive as possible, for example, holding working lunches in the room so that no one loses their train of thought and you can move through your agenda more quickly and more focused than breaking the day and the mood by going to a leisurely lunch. Better to save that until the day has wrapped up, especially if any board members would be likely to enjoy an alcoholic beverage or two over lunch.

TIP

Peoples' attention declines after a heavy lunch, so plan for it. Perhaps adjust your content or change locations. Always allow for a mid-afternoon break where attendees can move around.

Structuring Your Meeting for Maximum Success

If you stop and change the mood and the setting from business to pleasure (social lunch) or start with pleasure (early morning golf tournament) and then try to shift gears into business, it may be difficult to get back to where you were or where you need to be. In the end, you may not have as productive a day as you could have. It is better, for example, to start the day early and work straight through in a business frame of mind and then break for a game of golf and dinner than to schedule an early round of golf first and then move into the meeting. The mind-set in each scenario would be completely different and so would be your returns. You want to make sure that when you have the most expensive minds of your company gathered together, you spend their time and your time wisely in order to get the best return on your investment of taking them away from their day.

Companies can meet more of their business objectives from attendees at a board meeting by making sure that they have their attendees' undivided attention. It is important that everyone involved has cleared their agendas and that their time and their minds are solely on the meeting at hand. All attending need to know, before going in, what will and will not be tolerated in terms of interruptions from their staff, checking in for messages or leaving them, and stopping to take calls or make calls that are not relevant to what is being discussed. It will change the energy of the room and minds will be wandering from matters at hand.

TIP

Ask attendees to turn off their cell phone ringers during the meeting. Let attendees know there will be periodic breaks so they can check for messages. This not only keeps attendees focused and allows the event to flow smoothly, but it also gives the meeting an air of importance.

Attendees need to know in advance what the company objectives are for the meeting with respect to how communication needs should be handled so that they can properly instruct their staff. What are their specific times of the day they will be able to call back to their offices to check in for messages and touch base with their staff, check their Blackberries or have access to a computer? This all needs to be established and conveyed well in advance of the meeting.

Attendees also need to know the schedule of events, which includes start and stop times, so they can make any necessary adjustments in their personal and professional lives with respect to any time commitments and time constraints they may encounter. Making sure that your top executives are focusing their attention on your intentions without interruptions will deliver better rewards and results at the end of the day.

Once you have been able to clear everyone's schedule and bring your senior staff members together, you want to be able to maximize having them all together in one room at the same time. There are pluses and minuses to taking a boardroom meeting out of head office and to a hotel, but if your meeting is going to take more than one day, there are two strategic techniques that you can employ to help meet more of your board meeting objectives. The additional costs for both, if done right, can be offset by the added value they bring.

First, regardless of whether you decide to hold your board meeting in the office or at a local hotel, consider including overnight stays so that you can then layer your meeting objectives and add social elements to allow your executives to bond more closely with one another and discuss common issues in a more relaxed atmosphere. That way, you are keeping their focus on work and what has been covered during the day. If you break at the end of the day and your attendees adjourn to go back to their offices or homes, you run the risk of losing their focus and having them not return as planned.

Second, make sure to book a boardroom or conference room—whether in your office or in a hotel—on a 24-hour basis, and ensure that it is one that can be locked so that everything can be set up once and left and no time is lost at the start and end of each day.

Business Meetings

A business meeting should only be called when you can clearly define the purpose of pulling people together. Don't call a business meeting without having a clear agenda of what needs to be accomplished.

Business Meetings Options

Business meetings can be held in a private or public setting. They can be pure business or business mixed with social elements. Business meetings can be held:

- local—in or out of the office
- out of town
- out of country

Effective Business Meetings

A business meeting offers the opportunity to create layers and layers of company objectives that could be met while participants interact with one another both professionally and socially, just as company executives can. If two of the company objectives are making sure that the costs for an out-of-town meeting come in on budget and that specific individuals meet and have time to exchange ideas with one another, then having shared accommodation would help to bring about both objectives. Care would need to be given to the rooming list and ensuring that participants the company wanted to spend quality time together were matched up. The same can be done—meeting company objectives of key people spending time with one another—when selecting golf tournament teams, dinner seating partners and so forth.

For maximum returns on business functions, company executives have to focus attention on not only what is going on at the front of the room but on other areas as well. In-room and out-of-room dynamics should be as carefully orchestrated as the meeting's content and flow. Every element can play a part in paying back major dividends. All too often companies stop short of using each and every means possible to contribute to their functions' successful delivery in providing maximum returns on investment—because some company objectives could at first appear to be unrelated.

Business meetings run the risk of becoming very predictable and stale, and as a result failing to deliver a powerful punch. If a company wants different results they need to strategically stage their meetings to produce them.

Start by setting the tone for your business meeting by providing your attendees with a dress code. Requesting casual attire will meet and deliver different results than will a business suit and tie; one will evoke a spirit of relaxed camaraderie among attendees, while the other will demand a more professional, respectful demeanor from them. Your attendees will go into their meeting with different mind-sets and expectations both of the meeting and of what they will take away.

Most business meetings have social components built into them, such as coffee breaks, lunch, post-meeting cocktails and dinner. Each one of these elements can be turned into a mini event and strategically designed to meet a different objective. If you are including them, look for ways to use them to your advantage.

During its staff meeting, one company staged yoga stretching breaks with healthy, tempting refreshments specifically selected to not cause extreme spikes in blood sugar levels that would cause their employees' attention to fade once they were back in the meeting room; to get the employees moving so that their energy would be up; to see how well their employees reacted to being taken out of their comfort zones by having them try something new, which was a company objective; and to provide them with something different than the expected standard coffee and Danish. The employees returned to their meeting with renewed energy and focused attention, thanks to moving around and refueling.

By positioning their coffee break as an opportunity to lay the groundwork to meeting a company objective, the company received a return on their investment of unproductive time (the time for the coffee break) and money (the cost of the coffee break). The coffee break would have been an expense they would incur regardless of if they did or didn't use it as a means to produce a company benefit. By staging a simple coffee break as a mini event within their main event, they were able to maximize effectively the time and the money being spent, as well as their returns on their investment.

Another company successfully did this by having "tee breaks." Their participants got advice from golf pros and had the chance to perfect their putt before their tournament later in the week.

Don't overlook any aspects that could bring you returns. Some cost nothing but awareness and pre-planning. For example, one company lost its attendees' attention by holding a meeting in a room that overlooked palm trees and the ocean. Employees were more caught up in the swaying trees and agile surfers than in the meeting content. The company could have solved the problem by closing the shutters and positioning them to let in light but not distracting scenery. As an alternative, breaks could have been scheduled on the terrace to let attendees enjoy the spectacular view and allow them to return to the session mentally stimulated by the scenery. Walking back into a pure business setting would help to re-center their minds back to the business at hand.

TIP

The layout of the room, the temperature of the room, what the window looks out onto, the type of food you choose, and whether or not and when alcoholic drinks are served can all impact participant performance, which in turn will have a direct effect on your meeting efforts.

To obtain the most from your business meeting, pay careful attention to what is being required energy-wise from your participants. For example, if you are looking at holding your business meeting out of town:

- look at destinations that can be easy reached with direct flights and relatively short flight times—don't have attendees arrive exhausted and jet-lagged
- select a meeting space that is capable of holding all your meeting needs and breakouts under one roof so you don't lose time transporting attendees from one location to another
- ensure that there are attractive venues for on-site dinners, good restaurants, great weather and some free time for relaxing
- have controlled changes of scenery for energy boosts but move them around in the right way and at the right time; holding your meeting and meals day in and day out in the same meeting rooms can be very mentally draining

Client Appreciation Events

Why we feel it is important to thank our customers, suppliers, staff and so forth at this time is a question that must be able to be answered before moving forward with planning a client appreciation event.

Client Appreciation Event Options

Client appreciation events can cross over to many different event styles. Client appreciation events can be:

- fun—coffee and celebration cake on-site, barbecues, sporting events, top entertainment events
- formal—dinner theater event, gala sit-down dinner and dance
- small, intimate VIP event
- large informal or formal event

Effective Client Appreciation Events

Client appreciation events are a means to thank existing companies, nurture customer loyalty and attract new business from present and potential clients. While they are a thank you, client appreciation events are also a marketing tool and should also be planned with an eye on what can be done to promote ongoing promotional mileage from the event.

Client appreciation events must be classy, not tacky. One financial company looked carefully at who its top-producing customers were and what they shared in common. They found that golf was a passion for a majority of the people.

The company representatives then weighed their options. They could put on their own golf tournament at a very exclusive golf course, which may or may not attract the attendance of their customers, or buy into a very high-profile celebrity golf tournament, which would have major appeal to their clients. The second option had the added bonuses of allowing them as a company to give visual support to a cause they believed in and one that supported their image in return, would please their customers, and would draw their customers to their event within an event.

They decided to maximize their exposure and brand awareness to others who would be attending—potential new customers—and approached the charity for lead sponsorship opportunities that would place their name in front of both existing and possible new business and the press who were covering the event. To give them one-on-one time with their top customers, they created a pre-tournament event that would give them time to mix and mingle.

As they already knew their customers and this event was held to thank them, their prime objective for this golf tournament was to give their clients a life experience that they would long remember fondly. The company received tax benefits for their sponsorship contributions, which was an added incentive, and executives had their pictures taken while handing over an oversized check to the organization, a picture the media picked up and ran. As a result, the company gained additional good will exposure in their community, as well.

Post-event, they sent their customers framed pictures of themselves in their foursomes with the celebrities—one of their negotiated sponsorship terms—as a reminder of their day, along with quality clip-on golf towels with their company name. The picture frames bore a very discreet logo and tied into the message of the day, and more than likely would be displayed on the clients' desks or walls. These items would provide the company with added promotional benefit, as would the golf towels when the clients were out on the golf course with their friends.

Two things that you want to avoid at a client appreciation event are disappointment if your event fails to deliver a message of thanks to your customer and having your customers unable to attach a value to their worth to you. For example, one local drug store at tempting to woo seniors to their stores for "client appreciation" savings and a much hyped "thank-you" party (timed to when seniors had received their monthly pension checks) merely laid out store-bought cookies on a plate and served coffee in foam cups. Seniors looking forward to the thank-you party were sorely disappointed that the value of their business was not even worth their time and effort to be there. The store was guaranteed to have poor attendance at their next such venture. Another small store did it differently. They offered the incentive of savings but their celebration included an over-the-top, oversized sheet cake—which gave their patrons something to talk to each other about—and entertainment provided by a local community group, plus chairs and small tables set out for the seniors so they could relax, enjoy the festivities and think about shopping. This setting also gave the owner and staff a chance to mingle with their guests as they refilled coffee cups. This event experience became an outing for the seniors and the next client appreciation event the store held was eagerly anticipated. That month the store did something different. They had a huge display of customized miniature cupcakes laid out instead of the lavish oversized cake and again gave their customers something to talk about to others who had stopped by.

To get more from your participants at a client appreciation event, make sure that your function clearly shows them that you know who they are. Ultimately, the event is about them. You can design your event to give you the results that you want, but if your event lacks personal appeal to them you will not get the turnout you desire.

One thing to decide when you are designing a client appreciation event is whether it is appropriate to include your clients' partners or invited guests. For example, a dinner theater client appreciation event would be better received and attended if the client was not expected to go on their own and could bring a partner to share in the celebration, but a single invitation to partake in a golf tournament would be acceptable.

Each type of event can be layered and produced in a manner that will bring about the exact result that you are looking for. It is important to weigh which one and which way will bring you maximum rewards. In the above golf tournament example, had the company's main objective been to spend quality time getting to know potential or new customers—as opposed to thanking existing top customers that they had established long-term working relationships with by giving the customers a life experience that they would always link back to the company—the company representatives would have opted to have held their own tournament, which they could have total control over and stage for their best results. They would have been seeking an entirely different set of objectives, which would have required them to change their entire plan.

Conferences

Setting a conference theme helps to establish the framework content to build your conference elements around. You want to present a strong company message that your participants will remember and work with you to further company objectives.

Conference Options

Company conferences can be held:

- local
- out of town
- out of country
- holding and attending

Effective Conferences

A conference is content-driven, and discussion is focused on specific pre-selected topics. Delivery is of paramount importance. Conferences provide the opportunity for employee training, education and enlightenment, and for attendee networking, motivation and inspiration. For maximum effectiveness, ensure that your conference has a strong hook, a solid launch platform and a sharp focus.

Prepare attendees in advance as to what to expect by including a detailed itinerary in their travel or other pre-conference documents. Be sure to include start and stop times, dress codes, what is and is not included, for example, if meals are included or will be at attendees' own expense, and what attendees should bring, along with any other special requirements. The more prepared they are, the better the returns on your investment will be.

Also, you will need to communicate whether or not guests will be allowed and at whose expense. Is the company hosting spouses or will spouses be allowed to accompany your employee only if the employee pays for their partner to come? Will you be offering events for your attendees and their guests combined, or events for the guests while the attendees are busy? And if partners are permitted, be prepared in advance to answer the question that will be sure to come from your employees: can they arrive in advance of the conference or extend their stay and take some personal vacation time?

If one of your executives will be speaking at your conference or someone else's, ensure they're a comfortable public speaker. Most studies show that the number one fear for most people is not death but public speaking. It didn't help calm people's public speaking jitters when during the live finale of Donald Trump's *The Apprentice*, one of his top company executives found his nerves getting the better of him and was rendered speechless, paralyzed and panicked with fear, unable to answer the questions asked of him despite numerous attempts.

> **TIP**
>
> If public speaking isn't your thing, consider setting up a speaking club within your company, or join Toastmasters or another public speaking group.

Company executives are often thrust into the spotlight at conferences, and while they may be comfortable conducting meetings with their staff, the thought of speaking in front of their colleagues, employees, suppliers and clients can leave them uneasy. They may look to their company to provide guidance on how to pull off a polished and professional presentation. Today, executives need to be skilled in not just strategic event design and management but stage management and show flow so that they can help alleviate their speakers' public speaking fears and make company presidents and fellow executives shine on stage.

Those in charge of their own corporate presentation preparation should work closely with those who will be speaking on stage as well as their chosen audiovisual and communications company on the timing of their speech and the show flow. As the designated speakers and presenters begin to prepare their speech to fit with specified timelines, it will help them to know that they need to count on speaking between 120 and 130 words a minute, including pauses. For example, if speakers are looking at being on stage for a one-hour time period and talking the whole time—with no question and answer, back and forth with fellow presenters or the audience, or other speech interruption, such as pausing for a film clip or waiting for someone to come on stage—they would need to prepare a speech with a word count of about 7,000 or 8,000 words.

Hiring a professional speechwriter to work with your presenter is essential for maximum returns. The difference they can make to your presenter's delivery is well worth the money being spent. Using the services of a skilled speechwriter can mean the difference between your presenter delivering a presentation that has your audience falling asleep or listening intently to the message that is being given. Professional speechwriters have the ability to take a presenter's stuffy and dry outline and turn it around so that the end product is warm, clear and possibly humorous, and conveys a powerful message to your audience.

Don't wait until you are on-site to schedule rehearsal meetings. Pre-event rehearsal time should be booked with all company presenters in attendance, as well as the speechwriter. More than one pre-event rehearsal may be necessary. Holding pre-event rehearsals will enable your presenters and their staff members who are speaking to become comfortable with their speech, their timing and delivery, and working with TelePrompTers, microphones and each other. This is an essential presentation preparation step that should not be missed; it will make your on-site rehearsal flow much smoother.

Always be prepared to make changes to speeches on-site right up until the last moment, and have a backup plan in place going in. Many executives have found themselves needing the use of the hotel's business center in the middle of the night before the presentation. Hard copies of the scripts should be printed in large font to act as backup should there be any TelePrompTer glitches.

Having a professional master of ceremonies to introduce each speaker or presenter is another option that should be considered and one that delivers a return on investment. Trained MCs are experts at moving your show along and keeping all on stage to their timelines. MCs can also jump in where necessary and fill any time gaps with experienced ease. You will find that many sought-after MCs are proficient in several languages. It is important that the master of ceremonies attend all pre-conference and on-site rehearsals as well so that they can familiarize themselves with the content and the individuals presenting.

Consider having professional hair and make-up teams on site so that your speakers are presented perfectly groomed. Holding a full dress rehearsal (including hair and make-up) will also allow your lighting technicians to make any necessary adjustments in advance so that they can display your speakers and presenters in their best light for photographs and filming.

Be sure to have mini personal care kits backstage for the speakers, and find out if there are any essential items your presenters must have before going on stage. One company president, flown in from Asia, refused to go on stage until a specific hair product was made available to him. His speech was delayed while staff scrambled to find a store open on a Sunday morning that stocked that particular brand of grooming aid.

TIP

Your personal care kits should be filled with essential items such as extra pairs of panty hose; clear nail polish to stop runs; make-up for touch-ups; scarves to protect clothes from make-up; hair spray; breath mints; a brush; a comb; tissues; handkerchiefs; feminine products; deodorant; contact solution; bandages of different sizes; stain removal sticks; styptic pencils; safety pins; tape; a mini stapler for emergency hem repairs; miniature scissors; a lint brush; energy bars; bottled water; keys to hotel rooms, car, home and so on; and any required medication.

As savvy executives know, these items should be costed and presented as part of an initial budget projection so that the costs to be able to present a polished conference can be allocated in advance, everyone has an understanding of all that will be required and there are no budget surprises at the end.

Conventions

What elements are so compelling that holding or attending a specific convention would be a "must attend" event is a question that needs to be answered before moving forward when planning to stage or take part in a convention.

Convention Options

It is important to weigh the costs and benefits of attending a convention in each of these capacities:

- company representative attendee
- committee member
- speaker
- exhibitor

Effective Conventions

Conventions, like conferences, are content-driven. When deciding which conventions to attend, it is important to consider the topics being covered; how and what they will add to the attendees' business and management skills; the caliber of the speakers, for example, are they top speakers, known experts in their field or unknowns looking to raise their professional profile; the type of participants that will be attracted (local or international); and the level of attendees (junior or senior executives) to determine what company objectives being there would fill. You want to make sure that if you are sending a company representative to a convention, they are not merely there to fill a seat or to obtain a take-away skill that will benefit them professionally but not the company should they ever leave.

Clearly state the intended objectives that the company expects to be met if the company is prepared to invest the money and time in the employee or employees slated to attend. For example, some companies sending participants to hear top speakers at their expense request that upon their return the attendees present a synopsis of what was learned to other staff members who were unable to attend, so that the message and material is shared.

If networking with attendees from around the world—or with select participants—is one of the company goals, then this must be stated up front. Too many times, employees or peers attending the same convention travel in packs, stay within their comfort zone of sitting beside and attending meal functions with those they see everyday at work or at industry functions, and do not take the time to develop potentially helpful relationships for the company. Valuable international networking opportunities can easily be lost if company expectations are not clearly laid out.

Should you choose to use sending a company representative as a means to meeting a corporate objective, such as establishing an industry presence at the event, networking and so forth, remember to brief company employees on expectations for dress and behavior as well. If they are going as company representatives, they have an obligation to conduct themselves in a manner that is in keeping with company standards both during the day while attending the conference and out and about at related business entertaining events. Employees should also know if there will be any repercussions for skipping the convention to shop, sightsee or nurse a hangover from partying too much the night before. One company manager was so incensed by the out-of-line behavior of one of his employees—as stories began to filter back to the office while they were still attending the convention—that they made the employee pay back all convention costs including air, hotel and meals.

Limits should be set for what will and will not be covered on expense reports. This will give staff an idea of what is and is not expected of them. At another convention where customers were also in attendance, one company's representatives were so drunk and poorly behaved that customers took note of who never to do business with again. The company who sent these employees to represent it made a costly mistake and one that will have lasting repercussions on the company's future growth. There are times when company executives will want their representatives to wine and dine specific attendees, but limits do need to be set in advance so that there is no miscommunication after the fact.

If the speakers are top notch and the level of attendees is excellent and has value to the company, sending one or more representatives to work the convention may be advisable. If there is any other possible company business that could be conducted pre- or post-convention in the destination, set up meetings in advance in the hopes of "getting more bang for your buck."

Corporate Shows

The level of attendees, and the calibre of exhibitors that a corporate show attracts, are considerations to keep in mind whether staging, taking part in or attending a corporate show. Ask: Does it fulfill a specific need, or is it just filler? Is the show likely to appeal to its desired target market?

Corporate Show Options

Corporate shows can be:

- small, intimate VIP upscale shows
- large-scale staged productions filled with special theatrical effects

Effective Corporate Shows

A corporate show is a business function designed to showcase a product or personnel, increase brand awareness, develop new business, nurture company loyalty and drive growth.

Corporate shows can include many social components, such as areas to relax in and enjoy a meal and a beverage or interactive exhibits that feature well-known experts—part of the enticement— demonstrating the product and inviting guests to be "hands on" as well.

Many companies focus on creating an event that will get attendees and the media through the door—a main objective—but forget one important element, which is to give them a reason to buy the goods or services. This is one of the major purposes in holding a corporate show! To get the most from your attendees, both new and existing clients, at a company corporate show it is important to offer those in attendance a means and an enticement to buy your product at the event or in the near future.

It is important to always bear in mind that a corporate show is not a client appreciation event. A corporate show should be staged to showcase your product, conduct business and build a mailing list of interested buyers for future follow-up.

TIP

Mailing lists can be obtained in many ways, such as from advance ticket sales, check-in registration or by holding draws for door prizes.

If media coverage to promote consumer brand awareness is another company objective, it is important that you spend time making sure that any reporters covering your event are well taken care of and have everything they require to make their job easy. After all, you want your attention to detail to come across in their coverage. The more polished and professional you make them look, the better your company looks. Remember, you are putting your company image on display for the world to see. Find out in advance if the reporters have any special requirements, for example, easy access parking for camera crew trucks, key executives available to them for live television coverage and so on.

Media require special handling, so make sure that they have all that they will need to report on your event, such as specialty prepared press kits, and ensure that they are warmly welcomed at their own private check-in registration and properly attended to. One of your event's objectives should be building lasting relationships with the media, and respecting what they will need to do their jobs and meet their objectives is important.

Reporters are looking for stories and angles that will interest their viewers, while companies who are looking for media coverage are hoping for free advertising and writer or television reporter endorsement of their product. Both sides have two very different sets of objectives going in, and knowing the media's and displaying professional respect by doing what you can to help them meet their objectives can go along way toward meeting yours.

A company corporate show is a major investment of time, money and energy. Proper planning and preparation must be in place. Time management is of the essence. Critical paths[1] must be laid out and adhered to, as you cannot afford to run down to the wire and have everyone giving less than their best. The days before your show need to be spent giving final direction to all staff members involved, not on fine-tuning show elements, which should have been attended to and in place well before the final week. Your staff needs to be fully versed on the company role they are to play. This is the time to

---

1   Detailed information on how to create a timeline for a special event can be found in *Time Management for Event Planners* (Wiley, 2005).

bring professional staff in to handle what needs to be done on-site so that all key members of your staff are available to mix and mingle with your guests and not be tethered to a registration desk. Make use of your staff's talents.

> **TIP**
>
> When it comes to assigning tasks, make use of talents.

Due to the social nature of this type of event, directives must be given as to expected codes of conduct. Staff need to know exactly where and what the boundaries are. This is a business event for them and for the company, and should be stressed as such. Proper dress and decorum must be in place. Do you want your staff eating and drinking in front of guests? If not, a separate meal room should be set up at the event. Will they be permitted to drink alcoholic beverages? There is too much at stake to have your event undone by a loose tongue or an inappropriate action by a company member, and everyone needs to be at their best to sell the company and the product and produce sales as a direct result of the show. A corporate show is a high-profile event and all must be done in advance to not compromise any part of it. And it must be a quality event from beginning to end.

Employee Appreciation Events

It is important that an employee appreciation event be staged to match the level of "thank you" your company wishes to display. For example, a celebratory dinner may be more in line with a company landing a major multi-million dollar deal than pizza and pop in the office.

Employee Appreciation Options

Employee appreciation events can take place:

- in-office casual affairs
- out-of-office fun, semi-formal (end-of-year celebrations) or formal (awards) events

- employees only or expanded to include partners and family members

Effective Employee Appreciation Events

The number one objective of an employee appreciation event is to have your employees come away feeling that they are a valued member of your company. They will be looking to be entertained, not educated, unless it is something that adds value to their personal lives. One company's employee appreciation event, for example, was a barbeque and activity day. Professionals were brought to the event site to teach employees how to roller blade, fly fish and so forth—this event was meant to be a thank you. Your event, however, can be designed to motivate, inspire company loyalty, leave employees on an emotional high and/or serve to attract quality new employees to your company through industry chatter.

To ensure that your employees truly enjoy themselves at their employee appreciation event, remember to tailor it to them as well as to meet your company objectives. For them to come away truly feeling appreciated, they need to know that you know who they are—their demographics and what they would enjoy. Do not show less effort for them than you would your customers. A company is only as good as its employees, and your customers are looking to do business with companies who do not appear to have a revolving door when it comes to keeping employees, and enjoy working with staff who know and can meet their needs. An employee appreciation event is, after all, a business function that is used to thank employees for what they bring to you and your customers.

Ensure your employee appreciation event lives up to employees' expectations. Be very careful as to how it is presented. If it is a spur-of-the-moment thank you, an informal atmosphere and casual fare is perfectly acceptable, but if this is an "event" in employees' minds and one where anticipation is building, make sure that proper planning and care go into it, especially if it is an event where spouses and family are attending. Employees want their company to shine in the eyes of those they are closest to. A well-thought-out thank-you event validates their hard efforts and long hours, and shows that the company values what they do. Don't cut corners and don't have one standard for company executives and another for employees and expect staff not to notice or for it not to have lasting ramifications that could, in the end, affect productivity, loyalty, service and sales.

Trade Shows

Trade shows—with all the used components—can deliver many returns, but poorly designed they are easily deemed a waste of time by attendees and exhibitors.

Trade Show Options

Assess in which manner attending a specific trade show would best serve you to meet company objectives. Company representatives can attend trade shows in the capacity of:

- company representative attendee
- trade show as company exhibitor
- trade show as company sponsor
- representing your company as a trade show speaker

Effective Trade Shows

Companies are looking to take part in trade shows that deliver. Each is carefully choosing which ones to sponsor and/or attend as a supplier and customer. It is important that the trade show live up to expectations, deliver the numbers hoped for and be viewed by all as informative, interesting and inspiring. It must be perceived as entertaining and engaging. Business audiences like to be wowed, dazzled and delighted as they are educated and enlightened. It is important that trade shows stay on top of cutting-edge trends in order to provide value for all parties involved.

Quality educational content is a deciding factor for many companies considering their trade show attendance options. Great speakers attract quality exhibitors and attendees to a conference. For many today, if there is not a conference or educational portion to the trade show, the decision is not to partake.

> ### TIP
>
> If you're going with the tried and true, it better be worth it. Add new elements to keep your event young.
>
> Look what can be done for little or no cost to generate interest, and media coverage. One bridal trade show did theirs with flair by showcasing the "most expensive wedding cake in the world" at $20 million. The wedding cake was covered in diamonds. Much was made of the security protecting the gems! This was great promotion for the show, the diamond company and the wedding cake designer for very little dollars; this showcase gave them maximum exposure and draw appeal. It was excellent value in comparison to cost.

Take the time in advance to create a pre-show strategy and set return objectives for company employees who will be attending a trade show as a representative of your company (on company time and company expense). It is important to plan ahead, especially if it's a large show. Starting at the entrance and working your way up and down the aisles can cost you time visiting with suppliers that may be known to you but that are not on your business agenda. You also run the risk of wasting time in idle chitchat with sales people whose products are totally unrelated to your needs. You might not make it through the show floor and might miss the opportunity to meet a specific supplier or view a product that would have had potential benefit to you or your company.

For best results on your investment of time, obtain an advance copy of the floor plan, mark your company's "must-see" booths and map out your best route. Do not leave your preparation until the day of the event or you will lose precious time. Pre-schedule on-site appointments with new and existing suppliers that you wish to meet. Remember that it is difficult to talk business at the actual exhibit booth with your competition all around. Either have something prepared in advance to hand out, for example, if you are looking for a specific quote from them, or know your options with regards to where you can go for some privacy, such as an on-site trade show café or nearby restaurant or coffee shop on which you have already checked out their hours of operation and busy times. Once you have made your way through the show and met with everyone that was important to you, you can then set out to discover new suppliers and look for new marketing ideas that might translate over into your business.

If the show is large and the caliber of exhibitors excellent, companies should consider the number of attendees they will need to work the floor to their best advantage. By pre-assigning everyone's show route you can maximize your trade show results and ensure there is no duplication.

It is important to promote your participation and let potential attendees know that you have new information to share with them. Communicate with key customer accounts before arrival, and if possible offer them something of value if they come to your booth. For best results, make sure that your giveaway is pertinent to your current or future business relationship, for example, a high-end home accessories exhibitor may offer her retail customers a free in-store merchandising consultation as part of her incentive to book at a show—something that is beneficial to both parties.

One of the best ways to attract attendees to exhibitors' trade shows or particular show booths is to have "interactive hands-on" demonstrations that can be offered in a booth as small as 10' x 10'. Make sure that your exhibit defines what you're offering and stands out from the many, many others around you. Adding something unexpected will also help draw attendees to your booth. Participants are always on the lookout for something new that they can use in their own work.

It does not matter what product or services you are selling; if you don't create an eye-catching exhibit and a reason to stop, you have wasted your company's time, money and energy. If all you are doing is taking up space, everyone will pass by your booth. If you do not have the funds to do it right and make a splash, you would be better served not exhibiting but taking on the role of an attendee or putting the dollars you have into effective sponsorship opportunities.

At one trade show, an exhibitor had a DJ playing songs, but at the same time, had percussionists who were playing along with the music. The percussionists added an interesting touch of live performance and could be something companies might choose to investigate. There may be the potential to use percussionists at one of the company's future functions where they might need to draw customer attention, for example, at a corporate car show targeting a young audience who would be drawn in by the live performance. Performers can also create custom songs around a product.

Look for ways to encourage attendees to linger in your booth. There are many different ways to do this. For example, exclusive comfort rooms, where select attendees can relax, enjoy a light refreshment (even be pampered with a neck or foot massage) and return calls to the office, can be set up and manned by exhibitor staff. Rest stops on the trade show floor or in exhibitors' booths are also of benefit. Specialty coffee machines, cotton candy or candy apple booths (or decadent apples covered in chocolate and caramel) and other fun—not commonplace—offerings will entice attendees to drop by, sit and chat a while. Post–trade show parties are also a good chance to meet with attendees in a less formal business atmosphere but the key here is designing a party that guests will want to attend and not leave to go to the next one on the party circuit list.

If, as an exhibitor, you are considering giveaways, ensure that the item is either something brand new that has not been seen on the market or an item that will be used either by the attendee or one of their family members. Attendees are not interested in trinkets that have no lasting value and will trash them.

It's very important that you have on hand sufficient quantities of collateral material for attendees. Keep it simple. Time is valuable for both parties. Exhibitors need to be conscious that attendees want to receive your information in a brief, streamlined and efficient manner. Attendees today want bullet-point information, not fluffy descriptions full of adjectives.

To continually attract attendees to trade shows, many shows have expanded their conference sessions and look to sponsorship as a means to provide quality speakers at a low cost to the attendee. Many trade shows adopt a mandate of helping their attendees to grow and develop professionally and are updated on what's hot and who's hot from a topic and speaker point of view.

More and more trade shows today are successful in securing sponsorships as companies realize that they can drive business growth from their existing customers by strengthening their strategic alliances with them. Retaining and growing business with existing customers is easier than going after new business. Trade show marketers are finding that more companies are willing to listen to sponsorship ideas than ever before—some in conjunction with having exhibit space (which may or may not be a negotiated concession and part of the terms of sponsorship) and some as a stand-alone business event within the trade show, with the company preferring to have flexibility to move around and work the exhibit floor.

Companies find that sponsoring a top guest speaker is very well received by attendees. The returns that sponsorship can deliver include brand awareness to potential new customers, a higher profile for the company at the event and in the industry, a means to give back something of value to existing customers and increased business growth. If the speaker has a book published, a signed copy with a customized book jacket (with the sponsor's name imprinted on it) makes a long-lasting gift for the attendee and a lasting "feel good" reminder of the company that sponsored him or her.

In order to maximize time with attendees, some companies sponsor an exclusive luncheon or dinner around a sought-after speaker and position key members of their staff at each table to "host" and get to know the participants, as opposed to sponsoring a morning or afternoon session, which will leave them little time for interaction with those in the room. The speaker does not necessarily have to speak on industry-related topics. Topics that lend themselves to personal and professional development in business can draw record number of attendees. For example, one company featured a speaker who had climbed Mt. Everest and spoke on what you need to require from yourself to be able to scale the mountains in your life.

One means of establishing a strong company presence at a trade show is having a member of your staff as one of the event's main speakers or sitting in on a panel discussion. This is often an available option to both large and small companies and can even be a means of attending a conference for free if your company does not have the available funds to pay the related costs. It is essential, however, that the person stepping up to take on the task is capable of delivering a memorable performance in a way that will make both him or her and your company look good.

One speaker's comments made the newspapers and received television coverage, but not in a way that reflected well on them. The off-color comments—by a woman, not a man—were deemed "the most inappropriate thing I ever heard" by one attendee. And the newspapers reported that "there was a gasp in the room when she said that." That's not the kind of press coverage you want to receive and have your industry and existing and potential customers chattering about. Ground rules should be set out not only for speakers that you hire at an event but for speakers that are going out and representing your company in an official spokesperson capacity.

Questions you want to ask about your potential speaker include:

- Do they have top-level expertise on the subject they will be talking about?
- What is their experience with public speaking, for example, are they members of Toastmasters?
- What speaker's presence will they radiate, and what company image will they project on stage? Will they come across as confident and knowledgeable? Arrogant? Too laid back?

Being a sought-after speaker at an industry event helps to raise both your professional and company profile. In the eyes of new and existing customers, suppliers and industry peers you are perceived as an expert in your field, and people are drawn to do business with those that they perceive to be the best of the best.

Many times if you are asked to speak within your own industry, there is little or no monetary return for the time and energy that you must put in to plan and prepare the speech. What can be negotiated is access to the mailing list of attendees who have signed up to hear you speak so that you can send a post–speaking event mailing, which can be beneficial. While it is possible to request that the trade show pick up the cost of any handout information during the session, you may want to consider having that as a company expense, as it is important that what is handed out, essentially a marketing tool, reflects your company image and printing and design standards. Should you decide to do a handout piece or premium item that has your company logo on it, ensure that it is relevant to the attendees and something they will use again, and not something that will be left behind when they depart the room. Make sure that whatever you do or hand out has added value to you, your company and to the attendees.

ADVANCED BUSINESS FUNCTIONS

Custom Training Seminars Involving Emotional and Physical Challenges

Custom training seminars can be done in both large and small groups. They can cross over departments as well.

Custom Training Options

Custom training seminars can be successfully used to meet company objectives around:

- personal growth
- professional growth
- business skills development

Effective Custom Training Seminars

Elevated education and enlightenment is one of the main objectives of custom training seminars. If you want extraordinary results from your employees, make investing in their personal and professional growth and developing their business skills to better serve them, your customers and the company a priority.

It is extremely important that all possible be done to alleviate any possible participant anxiety. They must know in advance what will be expected from them going in—physically, mentally and emotionally. That doesn't mean you have to give away the details of what they will be experiencing; only that it will be enjoyable, that no strenuous physical demands will be placed on them and that they will not be made to look bad or be embarrassed in front of their colleagues. After all, it is not necessary for your employees to be put through extreme conditions or master extreme sports in order to realize extreme benefits, and there have been stress-related deaths from custom training seminars that were not properly or professionally run.

TIP

This might not be the time to surprise your employees. Find out if they have physical limitations and prepare them for emotional and mental pressure, but reassure them that what will be asked of them is absolutely doable and in some cases alternative options will be available. For example, if they can't do a high ropes course, other options will be made available for them to take part in that will deliver the same results, such as a low ropes course.

It is important to know your objectives and then look for how they can be best reached without causing undue concern in advance of or during the course of the training. During one company's seminar, the company set up tent camping for some of their corporate employees wanting a total getaway from office routine or staying right in the resort. Cooking was done in Dutch ovens and everyone got involved. The setting provided many opportunities for the participants to interact with one another, work as a team and employ new ways of thinking. They also set up a low ropes course that allowed their attendees an opportunity to move past fears, build trust and grow personally, as the true objective was not about scaling a wall or jumping off a telephone pole but about taking one step more than they felt comfortable with. Hiking (perhaps combined with geocaching), rappelling, skeet shooting and archery are just some of the other activities that can be customized to meet and teach company objectives without causing trauma or drama.

Look for innovative ways to bring about the results you are looking for and that engage both your attendees' minds and their bodies. For example, Miraval Resort & Spa, rated one of the top getaways by Conde Nast, are masters of transformational learning and mindful decision-making. Corporate groups have the opportunity to practice what they hear and experience in their meetings and challenge their creative and intellectual preconceptions. Custom experiential activities at Miraval can be built around overcoming fears and self-doubt via equine experiences; self-awareness through private desert journeys, meditation and creative expression; and how to reduce stress at home and at work through spa and yoga teachings. The same results can come about through pampering and not cause your employees to panic about what demands may be placed on them or experience any inner turmoil going in.

Custom training seminars do not have to be expensive and they can take place in an office setting. One company hired a motivational company to design a mock game show around a company product. Another had its staff take part in a fun board game that was designed to teach negotiating skills.

Executive Retreats

A great deal can be accomplished in a relatively short time when you take company executives away together to a setting that allows them to focus on the business at hand without outside distractions competing for their attention. This is why exclusive takeovers of fishing retreats and private island getaways are popular selections for executive retreats.

Executive Retreat Options

Executive retreats can take place:

- locally
- out of town
- out of country

Executive Retreats

Executive retreat objectives are usually met by combining business and pleasure elements. Social and group activities, as well as the business meetings, are crafted to bring company executives together in new ways and stimulate thinking. They are designed to meet objectives as well as return company heads refreshed and ready to take on company challenges. Golfing, deep-sea fishing, skiing, tennis, polo or learning how to drive a racecar have all been incorporated into executive retreat getaways, as have been fine dining experiences and sampling and learning about premium wines. Regardless of the events, it's key to tie these elements to business skills that can further the executives back on the job.

Choose an intimate setting, not a large resort, with little or few distractions. For an example, planning an executive retreat in Las Vegas, while perfect for a product launch or an incentive program, may not be the best choice for a corporate retreat. A resort that your company can take over exclusively would be preferable. Make sure that it can meet your business requirements as well as your social and group activities.

Set the ground rules going in about calls from the office and clients. The objective of taking the meeting out of the office and extending the stay is to have focused time to work uninterrupted on company issues and direction. You want to ensure that the meeting of minds is not constantly starting and stopping or it will defeat the whole purpose of being away.

Gala Fundraising Events

It is important to always make sure the cause supports the company message and image.

Gala Fundraising Event Options

Companies can play major roles at gala fundraisers as a(n):

- attendee
- sponsor
- host

Effective Gala Fundraising Events

Corporations are looking for custom creativity, not cookie-cutter gala fundraising events to put on, sponsor or attend. If company representatives are looking to position their company as a leader in their industry, it is important that all they do is perceived to be one step ahead of their competition and that includes all of the events they tie their names to. They want to be the talk of their industry and top of mind to customers, suppliers and even potential new employees. People are very selective today with how they spend their time, and if an event is deemed to offer nothing new to draw people to attend, the company will not meet their objectives or receive a return on their investment of time and money.

Nonprofit organizations have to be top of their game when it comes to strategic planning, technology, theatrical staging of events, creativity and so on to produce events that not only are flawlessly executed but also produce desired results. What they do and how they do it reflects back directly on the top sponsors and in some cases the guests supporting them. When a company chooses to support a nonprofit organization, they must do so with care to ensure that the organization's standards, target audience and codes of conduct are the same as theirs. Brand awareness, community and national good will, a new sales market, and an opportunity to launch new products (silent auction donations or other) are all benefits of being involved in gala fundraising events. Cause marketing is a growing phenomenon.

Companies of all sizes are exploring—not exploiting—ways of how they can partner their brand, their products and their sponsorship dollars with nonprofit organizations whose causes and public image are a match for theirs. A well-run and publicized event can be a positive marketing experience that brings awareness to both the charities and the corporation equally, and the cause benefits.

There are opportunities available at all financial levels, so even the smallest companies can participate. One company with minimal dollars volunteered to provide the gift bags—not the contents—for attendees, and the bags sported its company logo along with the nonprofit's event theme logo. The bags became a walking advertisement for their company, as it was designed such that people would use it again and again to show their support of the cause and the pride of having attended the event. They ended up having much more visibility than the products that were donated for inside the gift bags. The company received maximum exposure for their sponsorship dollars—which were minimum because that was all they could truly afford at the time—because they carefully looked at the options available to them and weighed their return on their investment. The nonprofit organization was thrilled to have the sponsorship dollars to create a quality gift bag that would serve an extended cause of marketing and event promotion.

Go to any high-profile gala fundraising event where tables run in the tens of thousands of dollars and you are very likely to find a number of stockbrokers attending and working the event. It is a rich—in every sense of the word—target market for them.

They may choose to attend in one of two ways. They may purchase either 1) a couple of tickets at the most expensive level, one that includes attending a VIP reception or selective seating options, and be free to mingle, mix and exchange business cards with other patrons whom they hope may soon become clients; or 2) a table, and invite prospective clients and their partners to join them for an evening out supporting a worthy cause.

The cost of the tickets is usually a tax benefit for individuals if they purchase them on their own or for their corporation if their company decides to pick up the cost of the tickets as a business-entertaining venture. It brings brand awareness to the company, potential new business and a certain cachet.

It is important before investing money this way to look at the past history of the gala fundraiser and see if the audience meets your company profile. For example, a gala fundraiser that is open to the public and has a minimal cost to attend is going to produce a very different level of guest than an upscale fundraising gala where tickets for two are more than $1,500 a couple.

Visit the organization's website and review past programs to see who the sponsors, patrons and committee chairs were. You will be able to tell from that if the gala is a fit.

When you sponsor or host a gala fundraiser event, keep in mind who will be responsible for actually running the event. If the organization is taking on the project and running it with untrained volunteers, and the event falls short of guest expectations, it will reflect back on the sponsors or host. It is important to establish how the event will unfold and be managed before committing your name to the venture.

One high-profile fundraiser was a total disaster from beginning to end due to the inexperience of the committee head. Not only did the gala run at a substantial loss, but the attendees—a very high-society crowd—were very disgruntled and left early. It was sheer chaos from a design and show flow perspective, and was made worse by the fact that more than half of the volunteers who had committed to be on hand to run the event never showed. The guests blamed the lead sponsor for letting it run so out of control.

If you are contributing your company name and sponsorship money, be hands on from the start and state your terms and conditions up front. Sign off on any proposed changes to the role you intend to play. Your company name and credibility—and the nonprofit organization's—is on the line. Sponsorship or hosting, done right, can be a very rewarding and winning proposition for the company, their employees and the nonprofit organization on many levels

> **TIP**
>
> Gala fundraising requires gala thinking, so go big, go smart or go home.

Incentive Travel and Premium Programs

Hit the right motivational buttons, and incentive travel and premium programs can deliver outstanding returns and become a very important contributing part of a company's financial growth.

Incentive Travel and Premium Program Options

Company reward programs can include:

- incentive travel program
- premium program
- combination teaser premium and incentive travel program

Effective Incentive Travel and Premium Programs

Incentive travel and premium programs can be either combined with premium teasers used on incentive programs or stand alone to increase sales and create talk in the industry. Incentive travel rewards can range from one- to two-week events. Premium teasers tied into the marketing campaign can help to increase awareness and motivate staff. Premium programs on their own usually include some high-ticket items, such as large screen televisions or even cars, given as rewards for top sales during a specific time period. They can be used to promote new product or push existing stock or services.

Smaller companies who are just starting to use incentives and premiums as a motivational tool can also build programs around themes. A pampering theme and gifts can escalate from gift baskets and luxury robes to a weekend stay at a top local spa resort, or anywhere in the world for bigger budgets. A summer fun theme can include family admissions to theme parks, fireworks, dinner cruises, fully catered backyard barbecue parties and so on.

One of the newest trends for employee and customer appreciation premium gifts are items geared to lifestyle. Look at what will excite and motivate your recipients. Electronics are hot— portable CD/DVD players, iPods, flat screen televisions, digital cameras, cell phones—things people can enjoy on their own leisure time and are no longer business-related, like the leather portfolios or briefcases given in the past. Lifestyle gifts come in all prices and range from propane BBQs to beach coolers/warmers, mini fridges, Lego NBA Challenge (for families) and gourmet foods. A boxed set of feng shui candles was a popular lifestyle gift at one corporation.

Another major change is that these items are not bearing a logo. Companies are no longer prominently displaying their corporate name or logo on the premium and incentive gifts they give as rewards. Companies arc instead looking at who the recipient is and what the objective of the gift is. Fresh, new items that are quality made and that can be tailored to the customer have become important commodities in premium and incentive gift items.

When combining an incentive travel program with premiums, having them tied to the destination and having them be symbolic is very effective, especially if this is combined with versatility. One financial company who has successfully used both incentive travel and premium programs looks for premium and incentive goods that will serve the dual purpose of accentuating the event and being useful after the event has ended. For another company, a custom leather passport jacket with special features and designed in a crocodile pattern for an exotic incentive doubled as an evening bag after its program. The logo was very subtle and located on the inside of the item. Another company that used premiums both in their teaser campaigns and as room gifts in the destination during their incentive program found that an African zebra head letter opener given as a premium gift item is still being used today in the office by winners. To keep the momentum going, teaser items usually become bigger as the campaign winds down. Premium room gifts can be divided into different categories/levels, with upgraded gifts going to top performers as an added sales achievement incentive.

Incentive travel programs must involve a destination that will have major appeal to those you are trying to inspire. For one company that was very family oriented, an all-expense-paid trip to Disney World, in which their employees took not only their partners but as many family members as they qualified for from sales results, had it hitting record numbers. The company chose the right destination and did the right thing by opening it up so that family members could also take part. No parent wants to fly off to Disney with his or her partner and leave their children behind. Support on the home front was major. The following year the company took them all to an all-inclusive resort in the Caribbean that catered to families, and parents glowed to see their children having so much fun. When the next family incentive was launched, a cruise, everyone was ready to sell and sail. Another company used this same strategy successfully when it realized that many of its staff were of Italian descent and yet many of them, despite having family in Italy and longing to go, had never visited. The company also worked into its incentive program a means so that employees could extend their stay pre- and post-event so that they would have leisure time to visit with family members. The company tapped into who its employees were and marketed what would cause them to produce uncommon results.

Premium Item Considerations

When choosing a premium gift, keep in mind corporate image, for example, if you are known for being trend-setting, you will want the item to project that image; who the recipient is; and how sophisticated they are—what type of item would capture their attention. For example, a well-traveled, high-profile participant could easily discount an item that to them is a commonplace, been there/seen that giveaway, whereas to someone starting out, the same item could be enticing.

You don't want your gifts left behind in a hotel room for the maid or thrown in the garbage; you want them packed, in hand and being used either at the office as a subtle reminder to others of what they too can take part in next year or at home to remind the participants of the wonderful time they had. Your gifts should give them well-deserved bragging rights and create the desire within them to qualify again next year. It is, therefore, necessary that you choose your items carefully. It is important to keep top of mind that you want the item to be treasured not trashed, otherwise you limit the financial investment return. The cost should always provide a benefit or add a meaningful or memorable layer to a life experience.

Ask yourself:

- Is the item meant to be a throwaway fun item or to serve a dual purpose?
- Is it of the quality, look or design that the recipient would actually use?
- Will it spark conversation?
- Does it have appeal?
- Is it innovative?
- Is it something that we wish to have associated with our company name, for example, not risqué, of inferior workmanship and so on?
- Is the likely benefit worth the cost?

You also have to look at how the item will work to meet your objectives. Is it a service item such as a teaser, or one that is expected to last long term to help brand the event? Either way, it is important to tie it to the theme, corporate message and/or destination. One company who had a great on-time delivery record and was holding their product launch at Disney decided to give customized his and her Mickey Mouse watches as their welcome gift. The watches captured the corporate message, the theme and the destination, and were useful.

TIP

Knowing what can and cannot be shipped into or out of a country or be brought back into your country in packed luggage or carry on is key, as you don't want the gift to be confiscated or guests questioned or delayed going through security and customs. One corporate client whose farewell destination gift was a brass flower vase whose bottom was filled with sand and sealed to give it balance caused their participants stress upon return when their gifts were drilled and checked for drugs.

Always keep quality top of mind when looking for teasers, promotional giveaways and premium program gift items. A pen that leaks, a gift that easily breaks, or clothing that is not colorfast in the wash or has lettering that will crack will not leave behind a positive company message for the recipient. And look for premiums and incentives today that can serve a dual purpose, provide lifestyle value, have longevity and be treasured, not trashed.

Award Presentation Shows

Award presentation shows can deliver multiple returns and must be designed with great care for maximum benefit.

Award Presentation Show Options

The popular award presentation show styles are:
- dinner, with awards presented afterwards
- theatre-style awards presentation, followed by dinner and a celebration in a separate room

Effective Award Presentation Shows

An award presentation show is a business function that is designed to acknowledge outstanding performance. It can be used to showcase company employees and the company as well. Press releases and photographs can be sent out to industry publications and local newspapers and television stations for added exposure. A marketing piece can be prepared and sent out to customers, giving companies an opportunity to put their name in front of their clients and, if combined with a "celebration" promotional offer, can promote sales as well. Maximizing internal and external exposure should be a part of company objectives around holding an award presentation event.

Having an award presentation executed theater style as a separate event prior to the dinner works well if there are several awards to be presented. This format allows the audience's focus to be on the main stage and the award recipients and enables a smooth flow with no interruptions (such as dinner service). Following the awards portion, guests are invited for cocktails and dinner and the award recipients can then mingle with their peers, receive congratulations and celebrate by enjoying a nice meal. This allows your winners to have the opportunity to bask and extend their 15 minutes of fame, and set the stage for inspiring next year's winners. The theater format commands attention and quiet from the attendees and brings the award ceremony itself to a whole new, respected platform.

It is recommended that you use an actual theater, not a room set in theater style. The theater has a more upscale appearance and raises the bar on the ceremony. This format also cuts your ceremony time down and allows for a separate, celebratory bash extravaganza in a separate room or venue following the ceremony. Using this format alone raises the importance of this type of event. Start the ceremony earlier and have your guests into the celebration party by 8:00 or 8:30 p.m.

It is possible through creative means to stage your event to meet other company objectives. For example, marrying an awards presentation with a "cirque" number is visually pleasing and can be symbolic of teamwork, strength, flexibility and unity—qualities that successful people in the workplace share. An event such as this is popular because it is short in duration and requires relatively little space, but can be effective in conveying a subtle company message that will support company objectives.

Keep the show simple and to the point. Too many different speakers at the podium may be distracting and too many speeches can make the show long and drawn out. Avoid using the platform to make special announcements, and stick to the agenda of honoring the award recipients and their achievements. Prepare a detailed script of the presentation and hold a rehearsal prior to the event in order to work through the details. It is important for all of the participants to know what is expected of them and to get a feel for the stage in order to achieve a polished look.

Naming Rights

When weighing the return on naming rights opportunities, always keep your target market in mind to help you determine if it is the right fit.

Naming Rights Options

Naming rights options include:

- buildings that house the arts
- theaters
- entertainment centers
- parks
- sporting complexes
- festivals or other special events, for example, fireworks competitions, sports events, concerts tours by top name entertainment, golf tournaments, skating shows and so on.

Effective Naming Rights

Naming rights have gained importance as companies seek new ways to get their names in front of their current and potential clients.

They generally extend past one year. It is important to map out your company direction to make sure that the target audience you will reach today is the same target audience you will want to market to three, five or ten years down the road. Along with purchasing naming rights for a building or a performance and so forth, you also want to negotiate naming rights that will be exclusive to your company for the length of time that your company holds the rights.

When having a building, complex or special event named after your company, it is essential that your negotiated concessions are a match for meeting your company objectives and that the building or event is a match for your company image and standards today and into the future. Will this venture complement what you are setting out to do as a company? Tax benefits should also be investigated as well.

Remember that if you want to acquire naming rights, you also want to be able to obtain the rights to tie in ongoing exclusive events for your employees and customers, both existing and those you are targeting, and you want to be able to do this for as long as you own the naming rights. For example, if your company is purchasing the naming rights to a yearly theatrical performance that is staged during the holiday season, one of the terms of the agreement could be that on opening night each year all seats are reserved exclusively for your guests, followed by a post-performance party at the venue attended by the principal performers.

Product Launches

Product launches can be tiered to meet multiple objectives.

Product Launch Options

Product launches can be strategically planned to address one or more of the following areas:

- customer focus
- dealer focus
- media focus
- public focus

Effective Product Launches

Product launches always have the key objective of giving attendees a reason to place an immediate order. While you are focused on launching and moving a new product or service, do not forget to look at add-on sales opportunities for existing goods.

You must give attendees a reason to come other than just to see your product. They know they can purchase your product or service through normal channels without giving up an investment of personal time. One drug manufacturer held a very successful product launch event at a major theme park, which it had taken over exclusively for its guests. Doctors and their families were invited to enjoy the day without the usual lineups and crowds. Partners and their children enjoyed breakfast and entertainment in a separate area while the doctors attended the formal product launch and sit-down breakfast. All came together post-launch to relax and enjoy the day as a family, and company employees were on hand to make sure that the doctors were well looked after and to continue interacting with them.

One real estate company launching their product—multi-million-dollar condos—and hoping to attract and convince potential customers to attend their sales event, staged private performance parties by invitation only. These were small, intimate affairs that featured top named artists performing exclusively for the targeted guests. The guests' desire to be part of such an exclusive event and to see a close up, private concert by a well-known name in a very relaxed setting drew them in. They attended knowing that they would be sold to, but the seductive soft-sell technique (taking part in something few could) was more effective in getting them to attend than had the company simply held an opening event in which potential attendees would be held captive listening to a sales pitch over canapés and cocktails. That would have been easy to say no to, while being part of an elite event that held ego appeal wasn't quite as easy to turn down. The real estate company representatives also received media play about their building and their exclusive event and had their guests talking about their evening to their circle of friends—potential customers—the next day as well.

Remember when setting company objectives to always keep in mind both internal and external exposure. If you are launching a new product, you want to make sure that word gets out and that you maximize promotional opportunities. Make sure that the media, both local and industry, are a part of your event and that they are as top of mind as your guests are.

Product Placement

Product placement must be done skillfully and creatively so that it does not come across as a hard-sell infomercial to your target audience and leave them mentally tuning out.

Product Placement Options

Product placement can be used in a:

- stand-alone event
- product imbedded in another company's event, production or product

Effective Product Placement

Brand awareness and sales are two of the major objectives tied to product placement. Product placement can also be used to launch a new product or service to a targeted audience and an event can be built around the exposure. For example, on one business reality show that attracted millions of viewers, companies were vying—and paying top dollar—to have their products used in a challenge or to have the teams design a new product that they could then launch in their stores to draw viewers in. The one-hour show served to become a one-hour infomercial about a company and its products. It also provided the perfect opportunity for companies to have their own company "viewing party" for their top customers. Having their product featured on the show also provided the means for companies to have an excuse to contact their customers to tell them about the show, invite them to their event and to do follow-up marketing after the show ran. The next day the company received media mention in the many columns that were written up about the show and how the challenges and competitors did.

It is important if you as a company tie your product to another company's product, production or event that the other company's elements reflect what your company stands for, that you do not lose control of how your product or service is positioned or used and that you request final sign-off authority.

Special Events

Special events can encompass many things, including one-time events and annual celebrations.

Special Event Options

Special event options include, but are not limited to:

- milestone celebration
- honorary event
- small, intimate affair
- private company event
- televised event

Effective Special Events

Evoking emotion is one of the top objectives tied to special events. As a company you are looking for your attendees and the media to come away embracing the company and what it stands for and ultimately your product as well.

A milestone event can be wrapped in layers of memories and take your guests from the past to the present and into the future, and your event can be wrapped in layers of warmth and emotion geared to continued company support that translates into sales. For example, a company's 50-year anniversary celebration could be designed to showcase the company, how it has grown, how it has continued to meet the needs of their customers—and now their customers' children—and how the company has served the community and the world at large. Media exposure—local, national, world and industry—should be another company objective tied to special company events.

It is very important to make sure that if you are billing a company event as a "special event," it is exactly that. Your guests will be walking through your venue's doors anticipating an extraordinary event with unexpected surprises that have been designed to delight them.

Deliver an ordinary event without the "extra" and you will have lost your guests' attention and most likely their attendance at future company events. In order to deliver the extraordinary you need to know your guests' profile inside out. If you want the best from your attendees at a special event, you have to give them yours. You want to woo them and wow them but you first have to know who they are.

This is the time to creatively design an event that will touch all of their senses and will have people talking about how amazing it was, not just for days but years after the event. It is important to align your company with event planning industry professionals that are masters at creating strategically planned events that have emotional and theatrical creative impact to help you pull off exactly what your event requires. If you do not have the dollars or the right creative elements in place to stage an effective special event that will meet the needs of your guests and deliver it in the manner it needs to be done, whether it is large or small, then wait until you can. Do something else in the interim, otherwise the dollars you spend will be wasted and will not deliver the level of return that you would expect from a special event.

The success of a special event is not so much tied to the amount of dollars being spent but to *how* they are being spent, as evidenced by one company that held a special event tied to a worldwide theatrical gala premiere. Guests included top government officials, celebrities, including many notable Oscar winners, high society and media. The company representatives knew that their attendees had been there, done that, and that the only way to excite them was to give them something totally unexpected, which they did with the help of an event planning professional.

Instead of holding their event in a hotel ballroom, a venue that had never before closed to the public was transformed into an enchanted forest. Guests were transported from a magical evening at the theater into a breathtaking setting that was inspired by the play. Their special event was billed a "beauty of a bash" and a "fantasy whirl" in the papers and on television the next day, and guests were so enthralled that no one wanted to leave. They stayed until the sun was beginning to rise.

Knowing what their attendees needed and staging the event to produce exactly that allowed the company to meet and exceed both company and guest expectations and fulfilled even more of the objectives than anticipated. Had the representatives simply held a post-event reception in a hotel room, their guests would have made a brief appearance and left. They knew that they had to offer something that would captivate the attendees in order for the company to in turn have a captive audience. An army of their staff was on hand to mix and mingle with guests, and the event's planners took the time to prepare the employees to act in the role of gracious hosts. With the eyes of the world watching their theatrical debut they wanted to make sure that the post-party reviews were as warm as they hoped the play's would be, which they were. In this example, the special event run as it was actually cost thousands and thousands of dollars less—almost half of the cost—than it would have had it taken place in a more traditional venue such as a hotel ballroom, but expert help was required to design it and successfully execute all the moving parts.

A special event must be exactly that—special. It can educate, enlighten and entertain but it must do it well. It is designed to be an event to get people talking and it is not the time or place to give less than your best or else objectives will not be met. Special events do not necessarily translate into extravagant expenditures but do mean giving attendees a life experience that they will long remember. Special events should always be designed and strategically planned to be meaningful, memorable and magical.

Conclusion

Once you've set your objectives, you'll have to decide what event you want to hold to meet those objectives. Not all events lend themselves to meeting every possible objective, so it's important to understand what your involvement in each type of event will deliver.

The successful selection of the most appropriate type of event will mean a more effective use of time, money and energy. This is a skill that executives tasked to plan their company's events will find invaluable.

CHAPTER FOUR

TAKING STOCK AND PLANNING AHEAD

PROFESSIONAL EVENT PLANNING companies are continually sending their sales representatives back to their corporate clients to have them qualify the requests for proposals they receive from them, because based on what has been submitted, it is immediately apparent to the planners that proper research and development into the proposed event has not been undertaken—there is no rhyme or reason to the requests being made. If they were to continue based on the limited amount of information received, the event would fail to yield a return on investment and likely not meet a single company objective.

Companies that are handling their events in-house—working directly with a hotel or other venue and suppliers—run a great risk of designing an event that will not deliver a return or meet a targeted objective if they have no one on board that has experience in identifying a proposed event's red-flag areas. Taking stock of your past events and their results will help you to avoid repeating past mistakes and to build on previous successes.

Having a good understanding of where you've been gives you a better foundation on which to develop the framework of future events and develop a three-year or more event master plan. Longer plans are often beneficial, because while most companies only do a three-year strategic plan for their entire business now, due to advance bookings, sought-after hotels and venues can be booked far in advance of three years. Initial deposits on hotels and venues to hold space are not necessarily a major investment. Some companies would rather forfeit the deposit dollars, or negotiate terms in their contacts that would allow them to use their deposit in other ways or at a sister property should their event not proceed as planned, than run the risk of space not being available at a specific property when they are ready to move forward. This generally happens with hot venues and hotels that you know your company has a successful history of holding events at, especially if you need to block a majority of the location's function space and there are only a limited number of hotels that can handle your ballroom, breakout rooms and food and beverage function needs. If you do look at booking past the three-year planning mark, negotiate your cancellation clauses and dates very carefully to minimize your financial risk. For an incentive program you may wish to remain within the three-year time frame due to "hot" designations changing and new luxury hotels opening.

TIP

Professional event planners try never to book a hotel or resort for an event within its first six months of opening. The first six months of operation gives the property time to work out any kinks and for their staff to come together and perform as an experienced team. This also provides a time buffer for event planners in case the opening date is delayed so they do not end up scrambling for leftover space at another location.

Hotels and resorts may offer "soft opening" specials to entice businesses to use their property immediately after opening but should you choose to go that route be prepared for growing pains, make sure that you have more staff on hand than you may normally require, negotiate your terms and conditions carefully and include financial considerations or reimbursements should there be any opening delays or services that are not fully functioning.

Regardless of whether or not you are handling your event through professional event planning staff or in-house, qualifying a business function should take place within a company before a request for proposal or quote is sent out to prospective event planners, hotels and other related industry suppliers. To use business functions and business entertaining as a successful marketing, sales and communication tool, always map out a three-year master plan. This plan will be amended and adjusted as your company grows and evolves but will serve as a blueprint that will help you qualify your event—properly frame and set the stage for your event—which will aid you in preparing and submitting a solid request for a quote that will deliver exactly the results that you are looking for.

Tracking Your Present Business Function and Business Entertaining Activities

You must first understand where and on what your company has and is spending their total event dollars—not just department dollars—and most importantly how much is being spent, who it is being spent on and if you have been able to see any measurable results from the event expenditures. Only then can you can begin to successfully map out a three-year business function and business entertaining marketing plan. One category that needs to be researched and included in your findings in addition to business functions is business entertaining.

Business entertaining is usually defined as being when one or more company representatives host one or two—seldom more than a handful—business associates or existing or potential customers for a casual one-on-one get-together and the cost is expensed back to the company. It is a hard business cost and not one that can be recouped by billing it back to the company, although this does take place in a number of industries where the cost of taking a customer to lunch is creatively costed back into future invoices[1] so that the company hosting actually bears no real cost of entertaining the client.

---

1 See *Event Planning Ethics and Etiquette* (Wiley, 2003).

Business entertaining by its very nature is a combination of business and social activities, often viewed as relationship bonding or building. It is in one sense a one-on-one client appreciation event and can range from "doing lunch" to sharing common interests, such as taking an afternoon off to enjoy the first ball game of the season in prime seating. Business entertaining can consist of but is not limited to:

- business lunches
- business dinners
- sporting events (baseball games, hockey games, basketball games, car racing, etc.)
- social events (golf games, deep-sea fishing, tickets to a gala fundraiser or top show, etc.)

Many companies are very surprised when they sit down to do the math to find out the number of dollars that are being spent on the exact same client through more than one department. This may be happening in a number of ways. For example, you may find that perceived top customers may be being wined and dined during business lunches and dinners, invited to client appreciation events, taking part in company incentives, as well as being hosted at a number of other company events by more than one department.

The hard questions that need to be asked include:

- Does their business warrant that number of dollars being spent on them?
- Has the volume of business they have produced grown?
- Are they a good source of referrals?
- How many of your departments are wooing the same business through functions and business entertaining, that is, is there major duplication going on?
- Are these customers really where your company's business function and entertaining dollars should be spent, and if so, which customers are proving to be the most beneficial?
- How much demand are you making on their—and your company employees'—personal and professional time

to plan, prepare and attend your company functions and handle business entertaining one on one?

One company's executives were shocked when they finally sat down to review the business function and business entertaining expense reports and lists of who had been hosted that they had requested from their various departments. They saw just how many dollars in total they were spending on one client whose business remained consistent and whose spending never increased, who never referred business and was always nickling and diming them on their costs. They were aware that this particular client was always dropping by unexpectedly at lunchtime to visit various department heads who, being well aware that this client was deemed one of their "good customers," invited him to lunch at the company's expense.

Cross referencing showed that there were many weeks when this one customer was enjoying not one but two or three expensive lunches on the company, but the various departments involved had no idea that the other was entertaining the customer as well. Once this was uncovered, the company was able to make the decision that the return on business was not there from this particular client.

They reassigned dollars that had been spent on him elsewhere in efforts to develop and grow business with potentially more lucrative clients. Their original client was still invited to very specific company functions and events but the free business lunches, which added up to substantial dollars over the course of a year, came to an end. When the invitations to lunch started to decline, replaced by coffee in the office, so did the client's carefully timed drop-ins. Other departments still made him feel welcome, but the company developed an internal policy of bringing the client back to his assigned sales representative when he showed up in their departments, and thereby left the when and where of hosting the client for lunch up to the sales representative.

Nothing was said directly to the client about his tendency to drop by only at lunchtime to visit various departments that were unrelated to his actual business with the company and to suggest lunch, knowing it would be at the company's expense. There was no need to embarrass him. The company simply took back control of the dollars they were spending that were not producing a return on their investment. The customer's level of business remained the same, as did the company's level of service to their customer, but his drop-ins declined considerably as it was readily apparent that his sales representative was not likely to offer two or more free lunches in a week. The sales representative still saw her client out and about at their favorite restaurants, but now he was dining on another company that he did business with.

Cross referencing what is going on in different departments also allows companies to see where duplication is occurring and look at new options. A company might be better off launching a product with an event that has a WOW factor than each department holding their own individual events. Doing one main event could work toward creating sales synergy and introduce existing and new customers to new areas of your company.

Taking Stock of Past and Present

When a company decides to hold an event and contacts a professional corporate—not social—event planning company or venue such as a hotel or convention center, one of the very first questions the sales representative of the venue will be asking is the history of the event and of the company. This information aids them in many ways. First off, they will be able to tell the caliber of the properties your events have been held at and advise you as to whether or not they would be the right fit, if you may be better served by a different property and how their facility differs from the ones you have used before.

The information you will be compiling when you create your event and company history will be invaluable not only to them but to you as well. Further on in the chapter there will be more on how to collect and create a company history.

If your company has traditionally been holding corporate events at three- and four-star properties and the hotels and resorts that you are now considering are five and six stars, there will be very noticeable differences in costs, facilities at the property, guestroom amenities, food and beverage options and so on. You will need to weigh your options carefully to see if this is the time and place to take your event to the next level. There can be repercussions in the following years if it is then necessary for a variety of reasons to move your events back to three- and four-star properties. Doing so may send out a silent message to employees, participants and the industry that may or may not be valid, such as that the company is going through hard financial times and is cutting back. The reason could be entirely different but what is perceived could be damaging.

One woman loved the five-star luxury resorts that she chose for her personal vacations, and when she became company president, the company's incentive programs took a huge but not well-calculated leap to meet her desires, not those of her sales staff. In the past they had enjoyed incentive getaways to all-inclusive resorts or cruises, which are semi all-inclusive and were a great success. At the all-inclusive resorts everything was paid for—all bar drinks, all meals, accommodation, most sport activities and water sports (additional costs applied for motorized water sports, and golf may or may not be included), some tours, in addition to the private ones that had been arranged exclusively for their group, nightly entertainment and all tipping. The sales staff could go away, totally relax, feel rewarded and not have to spend money on anything but personal items, and that gave them a great sense of personal relief. At the all-inclusive resorts, often the running joke was who was going to pick up the next round of drinks, since in actuality, no one had to worry about it. On cruises, while bar beverages are not traditionally included, special arrangements had been made to have complimentary wine and beer with meals, for a private nightly cocktail reception and special bar beverages through the day. As with an all-inclusive, all meals, entertainment and a number of activities were included and tipping was looked after by their company. The incentive reward was a match for the sales staff and next year's destination—launched at the end of this year's—was eagerly awaited. That changed with the jump to a five-star resort in a faraway destination.

The company, trying to stay close to the original budget, was eating up major dollars on airfare and guest accommodation. In order to try and save dollars, they limited the number of participants who would be able to qualify for the incentive getaway, which was self-defeating. A sales incentive's goals should be to maximize sales and the number of people that can travel, even if it means running back-to-back programs or moving to a larger hotel because the incentive was so successful.

The company also found, in trying to meet the demands of their company president, that they could no longer include three meals a day for their incentive winners; they now were providing only breakfast and dinner most nights. Some dinners were at leisure and at the group's own expense. Drinks were at their participants' own expense, other than a welcome and farewell cocktail reception and wine with dinner. Activities were limited to just one group activity.

The change to the winners—with the added costs they were now expected to pick up—felt dramatic and was a cause of anxiety to many. The resort they were staying at was far removed from inexpensive food alternatives and eating at the hotel, where a soda came in at over $10, was not an option for most. Many of the incentive winners actually started to take extra food from the breakfast buffet to save for their lunches in order to be able to have a noonday meal. Winners came home feeling stressed, not successful, and the next year's incentive campaign to another luxury resort fell flat as there was no inducement for them to want to go and find themselves placed in a similar situation—being in paradise but with no means to enjoy it.

That luxury style of incentive reward, for this particular company, would be better left until the company and their sales targets are in a position to pick up the expenses for their participants in the manner they have become accustomed to. And staged right, each campaign building on the next, many companies are able to do exactly that, including picking up all personal expenses such as mini bars, spa and golf packages and even shopping at times, but keeping them as surprises for their guests when they checked out of their hotel or resort—their winners never knowing when or what additional unexpected bonuses would be taken care of for them.

In this example, reviewing the history of past and present incentive programs that had been successful for the company and comparing it to what was being proposed should have triggered red flags to both the corporation and the resort they were booking their stay at. In the end, to meet both the needs of their employees and their sales objectives, it was necessary for the company to take a step back to review what was working and how it could be enhanced to bring extra value to their participants. Doing so also enabled them to look at how they could structure their incentives so that in the coming years they would be able to whisk their top salespeople away to wonderful resorts where they could enjoy a relaxed reward. Their participants had loved the cachet of being able to say they had stayed at the five-star resort, but they couldn't undertake the additional financial burden of also having to take their family on a vacation.

In the end, the company was able to come up with a solution that pleased both sides. Instead of a seven-night, all-inclusive stay at a four-star resort, they began to enjoy three- and four-night stays at luxury resorts in North America with all of their main expenses looked after. The sales staff had a wonderful experience and no added expenditures except for personal items. As they became more comfortable with the new direction, their motivation returned, sales targets were raised, stays became longer at the resorts, more exotic but not too far flung locales, such as Mexico, Hawaii, Bermuda, the Bahamas and the Caribbean, started to come onboard and staff were meeting and exceeding the sales targets.

It is a building process, and learning curves on both sides have to be factored in. Knowing your history will help you to have a better handle on what to expect from everyone involved.

TIP

If your original plans aren't up to snuff when considering past learning, move on. You can and should do better.

Knowing your history will also help you avoid unpleasant surprises at final reconciliation time. As you start to negotiate with your event suppliers, one of the questions they will ask you is how many people you will be basing the costing and contract on. The rates that are then offered are based on your meeting those guest numbers. Provisions are made, however, for a slight drop in numbers, and you will find release dates and attrition dates—when you can reduce your numbers without penalty or with minimal charges that should be strictly monitored so that you do not incur any unnecessary costs—in your contract.

Looking at your event history, you will be able to tell how many participants your contract was based on, and when you compare that to your final reconciliation, you will be able to see exactly how many guests attended as well as the guestrooms required, meeting space required and so forth. Knowing your past guest numbers is a critical component in accurately predicting your costs.

Within business functions and business entertaining there are two types of pricing: fixed costs and per person costs. Fixed costs are lot costs where you are given one price for a specific item, for example, staging. Your stage, depending on the design, will cost the same to set up whether you have 100, 500 or even more people in the room. The cost for your stage, as well as all related charges, for example, union labor, can be divided to give you a per person cost for budgeting purposes. The per person number will change as your guest count goes up and down but the cost of your stage will be fixed.[2] The cost to charter a private yacht for a dinner cruise could be another example of a fixed cost. The price to rent the boat is the same no matter if you are holding a party for one or a party for a hundred. The same would apply to items such as entertainment, decor, audiovisual and so on.

The more accurate your numbers going into negotiations, the closer your budget projections will match your final budget reconciliation. Should your numbers drop, you will find that your vendors have the right to reassess your costs, and their new pricing

---

2   *The Business of Event Planning* (Wiley, 2002) details how to set up and manage an event budget in detail.

based on your adjusted guest count can make a major difference to your projected expenses. For example, meeting room rates are negotiated with an eye on how much food, beverage and, in some cases, guestroom revenue they will be receiving. Some properties will offer concessions on move in, setup, day of, teardown and move out days' site rental costs. If your numbers drop, fees in the tens of thousands and much more, depending on how large a space and how much time you require between move in and move out, can be implemented as per the terms and conditions in your contract. Room surcharges can also be tacked on and the facility also reserves the right to move your event to another room should your numbers fall below what was contracted. This can impact your staging, lighting, audiovisual, decor and other costs that have all been based on using a specific room and moving in and moving out at contracted times.

Failing to meet your estimated numbers can have a domino effect on your costs and your event. One company executive liked to project large numbers in order to receive preferred rates going in and would estimate 400 guests attending, when in fact past history had proven time and time again that guest count for this particular business function came in at approximately 160 guests. In the end, time and energy were wasted, with both sides having to prepare numerous re-costings as the numbers moved steadily downward. The costs charged ended up being exactly what they would have been had he originally gone in with a guest estimate of 160, although additional expenses were incurred as some cancellation charges applied that would not have had the executive gone in with truer numbers at the start.

A past and present history will also give you a sense of what your company has been paying out in terms of guestroom rates, meeting room charges, food and beverage costs, and so forth, which will help you to assess the quotes received for future business functions. You will quickly be able to see where prices are out of line and where you may be able to negotiate cost concessions and make informed spending decisions. For example, knowing past bar beverage expenditures may help you to decide to go with a flat open bar rate or to base your bar on past actual consumption. If the guests you are inviting are the same as in the past and you have been able to ascertain from your past records that they are heavy drinkers, then choosing a flat open bar rate to control liquor costs would make the best sense.

Compiling and Charting Your Business Function and Business Entertaining History

Most of the information that you will need to create your company's past history can be found on final business function reconciliation and expense reports. To better serve your company with regards to decisions, it is wise to look at total spending as a company, broken down by department, as opposed to just researching one department, in order to discover where duplication is occurring. If spending from one department to another is in line and you are all using the same hotel properties, venues and suppliers, together you may have better buying power. If, for example, you can go to a hotel armed with facts and figures showing total money being spent at their property by your company, a more favorable rate—or preferred rate—may be negotiated along with special concessions.

If possible, a three- to five-year past history, or longer, should be compiled to give you a clear idea of where your company has been. To that information you will be adding what is currently underway and future planned business function and business entertaining endeavors. Once you have your master chart or blueprint in place, it is easy to maintain, and as part of the final reconciliation process an event history summary can be requested so that it can be input and everything can be kept up to date.

The time and energy required to put the initial blueprint together will pay off as you will be able to clearly see how, when, where and why your dollars are being spent, and you will be in a position to clearly address the issue should more funding be required in one area or another in order to maximize your returns. You will also be able to see patterns emerging—successful and not—and this will help you to decide what to eliminate, reassign or propose doing. You will be in a position to ascertain if a solid business function foundation is in place and if the framework of the types of events the company is building will produce the results you are looking for to drive the business and produce sales growth.

Creating a Travel History

From each of your final business function reconciliations, you will want to pull the following business function history summary for each event that you have done, and add your current event spending to your blueprint as well. You are mapping out not only your company's past history but the history of the events that are being contracted now and in the future. You are creating a "big picture" overview of what has taken place and what will be taking place so that you can carefully assess your plans and make any necessary adjustments to present and future events. Having this overview will also benefit your suppliers, who will need to know past, present and future contracted history in order to help you avoid duplication of ideas, which could lessen the effectiveness of the events you have planned for the future.

- date of travel
- actual number of participants
- guest profile/demographics
- gateway cities (if air travel was involved)
- total airfare spent
- total number of participants that required air transportation
- average air cost per person
- guestroom breakdown, for example, how many suites, how many single/king guestrooms, how many double guestrooms (shared two-bed accommodation) and room rates
- total accommodation costs
- meeting room spending and meeting room charges
- audiovisual spending

Continued

- total food spending
- total beverage spending
- total group activities spending
- total entertainment spending
- total spending (including expense reports related to the event)
- total cost per person
- company objectives going in
- company objectives met
- executive history success summary

This list can be broken down even finer and include categories such as room gifts, promotional items, communication costs and so on, depending on your company needs.

Once you have all the facts and figures at your fingertips, the next step is identifying which one of the categories each event fell into. Was it a traditional business function?

- board meeting
- business meeting
- client appreciation event
- conference
- convention
- corporate show
- employee appreciation event
- trade show

Or an advanced business function?

- custom training seminar involving emotional and physical challenges
- executive retreat
- gala fundraising event
- incentive travel and premium program
- award presentation show

- naming rights
- product launch
- product placement
- special event

What some companies have found when they prepared their master blueprint is that some departments were actively involved in planning both traditional and advanced business functions while others had not progressed beyond traditional events. The company as a whole was not in sync with how to choose and use business functions to meet company objectives and in many cases the same individuals—existing and potential customers, participants and employees—were being invited to many of the same events. And many of the events they were staging were simply being recycled with little or no effort made to tap into new audience markets. Nor was an effort made to design and produce effective business functions that help the company to receive a better return on their investments by meeting more company objectives, which would open the doors to potential new company growth and direction.

Once you have prepared your business function and business entertaining history summaries and classified them as to which category they fall into, the next step is to identify the nature of the event. Was one of the main objectives to:

- educate
- enlighten
- entertain

It will be interesting to note where your company has been placing its focus. You will be able to tell this from assessing each of the business functions you held. Then you'll be able to look at the results that they have produced and determine how successful they have been to date. If you find that all of your company business functions are falling into the category of entertaining your customers with no regards to educating or enlightening, these may be new avenues that you might wish to explore. Likewise, if you have been heavy on education and enlightenment, there may be a place for an entertaining event that will help you meet new company objectives or that can be combined with education and enlightenment to produce new results.

It may be hard to determine at this time how successful past events have been in meeting company objectives if they were not well detailed going in and the results noted. The only real reference you may have is whether or not they came in on budget. To avoid this, ongoing and future business functions should clearly outline company objectives in requests for proposals or quotes. This will serve a dual purpose. Your suppliers will gain added insight as to what you are trying to achieve and will be able to offer creative suggestions to help you achieve your goals—remember they do this on a daily basis, not once a year—and their input and experience can be extremely valuable. And you will have a clear record of your company objectives going in so that when it comes time to review them post-event and prepare an executive history summary, you will have everything that you need available to you. With the time lapse that can take place between planning and holding an event—some events are years in the making—people and committees change through retirement and moving to new positions or jobs. Memories get clouded as new projects with their own set of objectives come along that could be taking place well in advance of others on the books, and it may not be possible to get clarification on certain issues.

Oncc you have taken stock of the bigger picture taking place in your company and prepared your master blueprint of what has taken place, what is taking place and future business functions as a company and individual departments, you can then begin to formulate a three-year plan that will allow you to maximize your returns on business functions that are built on a solid platform of company history knowledge. And remember that the information that you have compiled will also be of great significance to your suppliers in addition to helping with your negotiations by enabling you to be very specific with your proposal requests. You'll gain added insight to serve you and your company in many ways.

Building Your Three-Year Master Business Function Plan

As you map out your present and future business functions, begin to look for duplication of events and participants/guests from different departments. Carefully review the categories where each of the scheduled events fall as well as where they stand with regards to education, enlightenment and entertainment in delivery style to see if they are one sided or equally balanced. Assess how that has been working to meet company objectives.

Take careful note of the time of the year for which the business functions are being scheduled. Timing is everything and this applies to when you hold your event as well.

One automotive company in the past had been holding their dealer product launch program, which was designed to educate, enlighten and entertain, well before the product was available in its showroom. They took the dealers away at great cost, put on a multi-million-dollar show, got them excited and sent them home to wait months before the new product was ready to roll into their dealerships. In the meantime, their competition successfully held their events closer to the date when product would become available. These same dealers returned home from the competitors' events pumped up with enthusiasm for the competing products, the first company's product was long forgotten.

When the first automobile manufacturer's executives reassessed their present and future three-year plan, they noted that the same top dealers that traveled on their incentive programs, which were held later in the year, also attended their product launch. Both these programs were being run by different departments. Once this was brought to the attention of both divisions' event planning decision-making executives, a better option, one that would allow them to maximize their return on both business functions, presented itself.

Their first step was to move the date of their product launch to be more in line with the release date of their product so that the message and motivation their product launch delivered was no longer being lost. Keeping the incentive program running after the launch of their new product was perfect because it was being used to reward sales on new product. That did not need to be changed. The only thing that needed to be done was to slightly adjust the time period the reward incentive ran to give the attendees more time between the product launch and the incentive to meet sales targets. Further review of their three-year plan allowed the company to delete some duplication of other proposed events and reassign the funds to create a brand new client appreciation event—a three-day getaway—for their top dealers, to run in the earlier time period that was now vacated by shifting the dates of their product launch to a better time.

The objectives they tied to their new client appreciation event were to thank dealers for past business, provide them with a reason to help them move existing stock to make room for the new product, show them a teaser in the form of a prototype reveal for what would be upcoming, and give them special pricing for pre-orders. Their new mission was to increase sales on older stock and lock in sales for pre-orders before their competition had their product launches. Along with wining, dining and wooing their clients by saying thank you for past business, they successfully increased their present and future sales and gained quality one-on-one time with their best customers. It was only by mapping out and stepping back to see what had been done, evaluating each function's level of success, looking at company direction and seeking ways to expand the reach of each individual event that they were able to come up with a new business function plan that helped them to meet and exceed their sales expectations both for the present and future.

Identifying When (and If) a Business Function Should Take Place

Once you have a clear idea of your past, present and future history, it is important, before committing to holding a new business function, to know exactly why this proposed event is taking place, when it would best serve you, how it can be designed to help you meet as many company objectives as possible and how it fits into what is presently on the books and under deposit. Once these issues have been addressed, you can then begin to prepare a results-specific proposal for a request for proposal from suppliers and venues that will clearly spell out to them exactly what you are looking for. Questions to ask yourself to reach this stage include:

- What type of business function is being proposed, for example, meeting, conference, incentive?
- Why is this type of business function being suggested? What are our primary company objectives?
- Is there another type of event that could meet or exceed the company's goals, perhaps using fewer internal resources/ less money?
- What other company objectives could this type of event be designed to meet?
- Will this business function educate, enlighten and/or entertain our guests, or be a combination of two or three style categories?
- Will this business function bring the company short-term results?
- Will this business function lend itself to long-term company growth?
- Who will be our attendees?
- Why are they being invited to take part?
- What is the lifetime value of this participant to the company (i.e., will we realize a return on our investment in them today or over the years)?
- When is this business function scheduled to take place?
- Is this the best time for an event of this nature? What does our business function history tell us?
- Are there any timing issues to consider, for example, religious holidays, school breaks when parents may book time off? Will we get maximum attendance?

- Are there other events going on in the same location that we must consider, either to our benefit or detriment? For example, are we looking to go to Miami Beach during March Break?
- How much planning time will this allow us? Is it sufficient given our other business commitments?
- What else is going on in the company at this time? Are there any conflicting or competing events taking place over the same time period?
- What else is taking place in the industry at this time?
- Does the budget that we have allocated allow us to do this function in the way it needs to be done to produce the greatest results?
- If we wait to hold this event, could it be more advantageous to us?
- What event inclusions have worked successfully for us in the past with this particular target audience?
- How do we need to structure this event to maximize its full business return potential?
- What do we want this business function to say about our company to our employees, attendees, suppliers, existing clients, potential customers and the general public?
- Will this event work toward enhancing or diminishing our company image?
- Will this function be able to be done in a manner that reflects who we are as a company, such as when a high-tech company's event is cutting edge and holds appeal?
- Can we fully commit the time, energy and money that this project will require to make it an outstanding success?

Conclusion

By mapping out a long-term master plan, your events can meet their marketing, sales and communications objectives more effectively. And having a good understanding of where you've been gives you a better foundation on which to develop the framework for this plan.

You will adjust this plan as your company grows and evolves, and doing so will ensure it will always provide you with the details you need to prepare and submit a solid request for proposal that will deliver exactly the results that you desire.

CHAPTER FIVE

SPENDING YOUR COMPANY'S DOLLARS WHERE THEY MATTER MOST

NOT ALL EXPENDITURES ARE CREATED equal and produce the same results. It is important to be able to assess how to structure your business function and business entertaining events and choose the inclusions that will ensure that you receive the maximum return on your investment and meet all of your objectives. In addition, you must be able to determine the total amount that should be spent on a business function, how to allocate the available dollars to achieve the best possible outcome and when to say no to a function.

It is equally important to be able to know how and when to question expenditures proposed by peers and by event planning companies. For example, Tyco CEO Dennis Kozlowski was accused of charging to Tyco a portion of the $2 million birthday bash—on a Greek island with company executives wearing togas—held for Kozlowski's wife in 2001. Was this social affair, attended by corporate executives and paid for in part by the company, a corporate event run amok or one that should never have taken place under the guise of being a corporate gathering? Hard questions need to be asked and answered.

Obtaining sign-off on allocated budgets by company heads such as the CFO and company lawyers is important especially in cases of what could be perceived as controversial spending. One well-known event planner was recently quoted as saying, "One of my favorite ways to burn money is with fireworks because it burns very quickly. And when it comes to fireworks, you can never have enough." While fireworks can be effective and they have their time and place in meeting objectives, you do need to know when to say when and how much is enough.

Executives need to take care that they and their company's money are not being burned as a way to add to someone else's income and that what is being suggested will produce the results they are looking for. For example, at an event held in Hawaii, an event planner had an entire Chinese setting shipped in. Stone slabs were shipped from California on a barge, and the whole garden at an upscale golf estate was replanted for the event and would need to be returned to its natural state—at the host company's expense—at the end of the function. In some cases this expense would be warranted and in others a waste of time, money and energy. The key is knowing the difference.

If you are the one approving what could be perceived as an extravagant expenditure and are being held personally responsible for spending your company's dollars wisely, you need to be clear about what you are signing off on, how it will help you strategically to meet your company objectives and why this inclusion will bring about the best results. This applies whether or not you are handling your event in-house and working directly with venues and suppliers, or working with a professional event planning company.

Business entertaining and business function excesses, if not carefully monitored, can cross ethical boundaries. One company decided that throwing a bachelor party for a supplier with whose company they did substantial business was a reasonable business event expense. The bachelor party details, which included charting private aircraft, renting a yacht, and hiring women and a dwarf, became known to the press, was posted on the front page of a major financial newspaper and damaged the business credibility of both the company and their supplier.

It is important not only to set company standards around entertaining and event expenses but to know the company policy of your attendees as well. Will they be permitted to attend sporting events, theater evenings, hosted dinners or other types of events? Would they be in violation of their company regulations if they accept an invitation to more high-ticket events, such as taking part in a sales incentive program that is not an in-house initiative? These considerations have to be factored into the types of events that you are choosing to use to meet your company objectives.

Each company will have their own internal policy of what is and what is not excessive spending in terms of gifts and how business is being wooed, wined and dined. For some companies and businesses, a $100 business lunch would be entirely appropriate and deemed acceptably lavish, but for other companies, due to the nature of their business and spending personally and professionally, $100 would not even cover the cost of what they would call a good bottle of wine.

Essential Elements

Every business function comes with its own basic set of objectives and essential elements that must be met in order to bring about the desired results. Tactical planning must go into essential elements, such as the requirements necessary for the optimal:

- location
- transportation
- accommodation
- room
- room layout
- meeting (handouts, promotional material, etc.)
- audiovisual
- staging
- lighting
- translation
- food and beverage

- entertainment
- decor
- floral
- group activity (golf tournaments, etc.)
- off property (dine arounds, venue rental, etc.)
- guest safety and security
- protocol
- legal (permits, insurance, fire marshal, etc.)
- communication
- promotional material (invitations, printed material, etc.)
- teaser campaign
- staffing
- meeting or show content
- speechwriter
- MCs
- show production
- show flow
- call sheet
- meeting or show books
- technical director
- stage manager
- dry technical run (test equipment, sound checks, etc.)
- TelePrompTer
- recipient award
- gift
- live event and industry media coverage
- professional event planning management
- move in
- setup
- day of
- move out
- teardown
- timing and logistic
- shipping (custom, duty, shipping, handling, etc., for goods being sent)

- couriers
- work visas
- expense accounts

With each of these areas, attention must be given to their intention. What purpose will they serve? Are they required or not to produce successful execution of your event as well as meet your company goals? How will they be set up and orchestrated to ensure that they are all targeted at meeting the needs of the attending audience as well as the company?[1]

In order for an event to be designed to meet and exceed both company and guest expectations, a working knowledge of event planning logistics and timing is essential. There are several ways companies handle events. It could be you or your assistant organizing them yourselves, an event team in the company, with suppliers only, or with professional event planners. In all cases, you need to have a clear plan, objectives and process, be alert to red flags and have an understanding of what you are about to undertake.

The investment of money, time and energy to fully understand the event planning principles, philosophy and psychology behind each essential element is the first return you bring to your company. Being in a position to make informed decisions about logistical requirements can mean hundreds of thousands of dollars in both expenses and growth over the years to even small companies. As one cautionary example further on in this chapter will show you, not knowing an event's logistical requirements for one event made an executive's company come in $100,000 over budget, and they were contractually obligated to pay.

If you are handling your event in-house, someone will need to be assigned the role of lead event planner. It is advisable to have them read the entire *Event Planning* series of books so that they can guide your team into informed spending decisions and successful

---

1   The how-to's and examples of the related charges to expect for each specific area are covered in detail in *Event Planning: The Ultimate Guide* (Wiley, 2000) and *The Business of Event Planning* (Wiley, 2002).

event execution. And if this is your company's first venture into event planning and you feel that you cannot afford the services of a professional event planning company, you could supplement your knowledge by doing what many professional event planning companies do—hire an independent event planner or freelancer who can pull in and out of your event as required and who can take an in-house staff member through and teach them the steps all professional event planners move through, as detailed in the *Event Planning* series of books.

If you place your department in a position of producing events that deliver outstanding results, you will strengthen your stand on handling events from beginning to end under the direction of the department holding the event. Ultimately you will be responsible for the results as opposed to having procurement departments assigned to secure space, which will be discussed later in this chapter, and having to deal with their decisions, which are not based on meeting the same objectives as yours—to deliver company growth but contain spending.

If you want to make a case to the company, senior management or the board to have all event decisions go through sales and marketing as opposed to procurement, you have to deliver results and be able to clearly define where and why procurement will not work as an effective means of producing an event that will deliver the same level of long-term growth results to the company. One way of doing that is understanding the complexities of event planning and how they can be successfully orchestrated to meet layers upon layers of company objectives with the right components.

Going in to plan your business function, realize that each and every essential element bears a hard financial cost that must be carefully reviewed as to what is necessary and what is not. The dollars and cents being spent must make financial sense and lend themselves to producing a return on the investment you are making. In order to do so, you need to have the full picture in the form of a proposal from your suppliers in front of you that outlines every conceivable cost related to your requirements. This vital information should be compiled into a master budget spreadsheet—cost summary breakdown[2]—before you sign a single contract.

Once you have a clear idea of all proposed costs, outlined and hidden (that have been pulled from contracts and other related material that will be outlined in the contracts, e.g., charges as per the food and beverage menus, which can include surcharges for chefs or room rental charges if your numbers drop below your guaranteed numbers, etc.), some essential elements may need to be moved into another category, which can be billed as enhancements. Enhancements are wonderful to have if you can afford them but they are not the essential elements that are necessary to guarantee the overall success of this particular event or business function.

Essential elements and enhancements can be interchangeable depending on how they are being used to meet objectives. For example, flying everyone first class to your meeting program could be deemed an enhancement in most cases. Business class or economy might be more in order so that you have money left over to spend where it matters most. In other cases it may be deemed an essential element, such as in the case where it is part of the reward and incentive experience.

Your essential elements require consideration and care in selecting them at the planning stages, otherwise you leave meeting your objectives to chance, open the door to possible meeting chaos and mixed messages being sent, leave yourself wide open for overspending and lose the investment of time, energy and money no matter how large or small the function. And you can never afford to become complacent—company objectives and the essential elements that will contribute to bringing them about will change and grow with each and every business function you hold. It is important that they not become cookie cutter in style or predictable or they will lose their effectiveness. Each business function should pave the way forward for the next and become a solid foundation to build on. Once the essential elements are in place, strategic planning can be brought into play in order to achieve maximum results.

---

2   Should you require a cost summary breakdown example, one can be found in *Event Planning: The Ultimate Guide* (Wiley, 2000) and *The Business of Event Planning* (Wiley, 2002).

Requests for Proposals (RFPs)

It is important that your requests for proposals from your suppliers be as detailed as possible and your expectations and objectives be clearly stated. With regards to proposal or quote expectations, in order for you to make informed decisions about your essential elements you will need to request that all proposals submitted to you be broken down by line item—"menu style"—as opposed to one lump sum, with all applicable costs shown, such as taxes. These may just be noted as "plus taxes and gratuities" that will be included at final reconciliation and not detailed in dollars and cents. In some locations, gratuities are taxed and in others not, and depending on the number of participants and types of inclusions, these can add up. You need to know exactly what you are spending going in so that you have no surprises at final reconciliation.

Hidden costs can abound. For example a group room delivery in a hotel can have a delivery charge, a gratuity and a hotel administrative charge, all taxed. It is your responsibility to read the fine print in the proposals and contracts that are received and protect yourself from any misunderstandings with regards to costs. What can look like a $5 charge for a beverage can run well over $10 by the time all taxes, service charges and gratuities are added on. You need to know that in advance because that could make the difference between choosing a flat open bar rate or being billed upon consumption at your function, and you could use the savings elsewhere. Total cost transparency is what you are looking for from your suppliers and those that are working with you to come up with creative cost-saving options to help you maximize your budget.

Request that your suppliers break their quotes into two main areas. Have them prepare a breakdown of your inclusions and costs for what they feel would be the event essentials you require to meet the specific objectives you have laid out and, in a separate section, cover program or event enhancements that, budget permitting, you may wish to add in. As well, have them explain their reasoning as to why they are recommending a particular inclusion or event element.

Always remember that while your suppliers may be presenting to you and your event team, there will be times when you will then be presenting what they have submitted to others on your committee and chief executives in the company. You need to have a clear understanding—an executive summary—of what has been included and why in order to help you explain various charges and costs so that you can make your final decision.

Along with buying your suppliers' services, remember you are also buying their years of experience and event expertise. It is important to make the time to listen and learn from them. Your suppliers can provide valuable training that will aid you in future endeavors and help you sell your colleagues on your final choices.

Information Your Venues Will Require on Your RFPs

- the date your event is scheduled to take place
- the time your event will take place
- how long your event will be
- what time you would need access to the room for move in, setup and rehearsals
- what time your event will end and how much time your suppliers will require for teardown and move out
- how many guests will be in attendance
- if you will be bringing anything else, for example, decor, music, entertainment, audiovisual and so forth into the room
- how you would like the room laid out
- if you will require any additional space to be held, for example, additional rooms, storage and so on, and if so what type of space, room capacity and time duration you are looking at
- if you will have any food and beverage requirements or if you are just looking to rent the site
- if you have any other special requirements

Information You Will Require from Your Venue

- all the room rental charges (move in, setup, rehearsal, day of event, move out, etc.) that could apply

- all the taxes that could apply
- all the service charges that could apply
- how the taxes and the service charges are calculated (i.e., are they both charged on the room rental rate or is the service charge taxed as well?)
- any costs involved for staff
- other services you could conceivably be charged for, for example, parking attendants, coat check staff, site security and so on
- walls color and material
- flooring color, pattern and material
- ceiling height
- sightlines
- acoustic quality of the room
- type of in-house sound, lighting, audiovisual, piped in music systems they have
- additional charges to use their system, such as power charges, and so forth
- type of seating they provide and if there are any charges associated with this, for example, chair rental, labor for setup and so on
- other charges that could be billed at final reconciliation, such as power charges, room cleaning, and recovery charges (staff and cherry pickers) for retrieving escaped helium balloons from the ceiling and so forth.
- the legal room capacity of the rooms being looked at
- if there is a bad weather backup for outside events that will be on hold
- any additional costs you need to be aware of if it is necessary to move the event inside
- parking capacity
- handicap accessibility
- other events that may be going on in the facility at the same time
- any special permits that will be required and who will obtain them

- insurance coverage in place, and if you or your suppliers will be required to obtain special occasion insurance
- fire marshal requirements you would need to comply with, for example, candles
- facility requirements you would need to agree to with regards to fastening items to the walls, tables, chairs and so on
- if the venue is unionized, and how could this affect your costs, as well as when labor negotiations are next taking place (possible concerns regarding strikes)
- when renovations were last done
- when renovations or construction are next scheduled to take place
- other events of this nature held at the facility before
- letters of reference or people you can call
- preferred supplier list that you must use, if any
- information on access to your facility for supplier move in and move out
- a quote in writing, a full sales kit, room layouts, a sample contract, cancellation and payment schedule, and the space placed on tentative hold

Emerging Trends

Sales and marketing executives around the world are beginning to see new corporate buying trends emerge. This is having an effect on how they are having their event planning companies and suppliers prepare their proposals as well as structure their event and program inclusions.

Traditionally, sales and marketing staff have met with suppliers and event planning sales executives to solicit a request for proposal on their corporation's upcoming programs. This is no longer the case.

Today, corporations are having their procurement departments— not sales and marketing—solicit requests that have been prepared by sales and marketing and review proposals from event planning companies and suppliers. This can have a limiting effect on creating events that are strategically structured to meet company objectives, as decisions are being made based on a hard cost and not on the cost of excluding something or doing something in a manner that will bring about a better return. Procurement works well when you are buying office supplies and equipment such as a desk but not when you are undertaking an event to produce event energy, event emotion and the like to create momentum and help, not hinder, company growth.

Procurement—not sales and marketing—is determining who wins the business. Once the proposed event has gone to contract, only then does the procurement department turn the event over to sales and marketing to be managed and live with the results.

This trend, plus another emerging trend—RFP online auctions, which are explained later in the chapter—are changing how business is done. Sales and marketing departments are concerned that the event planning dollars being spent make sense and will ensure a return on their company's investment of time, money and energy and meet all company objectives. Procurement departments' main focus is often just on the total dollars and cents being spent. The winning bid could be based entirely on price.

Company executives have to make sure as they are preparing their requests for proposals that their suppliers know they are now being required to meet the needs of two very different departments and that they are presenting to two very different mind-sets. This will need to be spelled out to them in proposal requests. Let the suppliers know that procurement—not your department—will be making the decisions, and ensure that they know exactly how procurement will need to see their proposal laid out. Take them through any areas that they need to consider in order to help them select the right elements that will meet procurement's dollars and cents requirements and make sense to deliver a return on the company's investment. It will be important for you to fully understand the workings and requirements of your procurement department—and every company's is different—to help your suppliers through this transition of buying power.

Meeting the Needs of Both Procurement and Sales and Marketing Departments

The meeting planning and event industry is all about service. Reputation, word of mouth and their relationships with sales and marketing executives mean everything to its members.

Procurement is the direct opposite of this. The representatives of one large pharmaceutical company found that while they had saved money by using their procurement department, their lowered costs did not reflect their return on investment. Their people were not happy with the meeting. They were not organized efficiently. It appeared to all attending that no care had gone into the meeting and it was just cookie cutter in format. Procurement is not trained to assess a cost on how well it will deliver a return on company objectives.

Procurement is based on getting the best bottom-line cost, regardless of service or experience. It works well when working with products where you are comparing apples to apples, but for a service such as event planning where there is a human element, it is very difficult to compare companies without first experiencing their services.

If sales and marketing want to produce results they can live with, they need to either invest time in training the procurement department as to what to look for, be prepared to justify to company heads why their company should not go this route when it comes to their business functions and how the desired results can be placed at risk and business growth jeopardized by going this route, submit better requests for proposals and work closely with their suppliers to ensure that all needs are being met.

Your suppliers need to know that procurement people have a very serious job to do and that it is important to develop mutual respect with them as well as sales and marketing. They need to ensure they understand procurement's needs, but also must deliver creatively to the end user—sales and marketing. It is imperative that you are available to have open dialogue with your suppliers about their objectives and work with them as they walk the fine line of how to meet them within your budget. It is a constant juggling act to be able to successfully balance both budgets and meeting overall corporate objectives, but it can be done.

It is extremely important for both departments to work closely together at the proposal stage to ensure that everyone's needs get met and for your suppliers to develop strong relationships with both. Many corporations are finding that procurement's involvement works best for internal meetings where it is important that costs are kept to a minimum. However, in events where a company is looking for a WOW factor or trying to impress clients, and where it is important to remember the value of meeting the objective and not just controlling costs, events are best left under the direction of sales and marketing from beginning to end. Sales and marketing will need to continue to produce desired results. If they fail to do so they could very well find themselves having to live with and be judged on the results procurement has contracted.

TIP

The more groups are involved in the event, the stronger your communication and organization will have to be.

How Procurement RFPs Work

Procurement departments often put out an RFP that is quite ambiguous. That's why sales and marketing departments must get involved at this stage and help them prepare a better submission. Third-party suppliers and planners are asked to submit the quote most often in a line-item manner.

Usually, the procurement department that sends out the RFPs does not allow suppliers to personally contact them if they have questions. They will instead suggest that suppliers e-mail any questions by a certain date, at which time they will share the answers with all bidders. Therefore, if one of your suppliers, for example, a hotel, has come up with any questions that the other hotels submitting a bid hadn't thought of, the other hotels would now be able to include it in their quotes so procurement is not making their selection based on who had the knowledge or expertise to address an important issue. In the past, the hotels not raising the question would have been a red flag regarding their level of experience but now that is no longer the case because everyone has access to the same information.

Once an RFP is submitted, quite often the top bidders are not even asked to make a presentation; the decision is based strictly on price. Or, the top two or three bidders are asked to "resharpen their pencils" and lower their costs in certain areas based on what the other bidders have proposed. There will always be companies that are either willing to work for nothing or will lowball and then hope to add in other items later, but will they be of the caliber that your company requires in terms of creativity and execution? Gambling on that can be dangerous and damaging to a company. Short-term gain in the dollars and cents area may prove to be very shortsighted and a costly mistake that will have long-lasting effects on company growth and direction.

Value versus Price RFP: Proposal and Presentation Adjustments

Preparing proposals and presenting to procurement departments is very different than doing so for sales and marketing. There can be a learning curve that can be costly in terms of money, time and business. It can be very beneficial if the suppliers you are soliciting quotes from have the technical know-how to change their proposals to meet the requests of costing templates for the procurement decision-makers, because each company template can be quite different. Suppliers have to be extremely flexible in their spreadsheet applications.

While procurement is all about the bottom-line costs, it is still important to request that your suppliers submit creative concepts as program enhancements or options in order to meet the fixed budgets. It's key for all suppliers having to submit to procurement departments instead of sales and marketing that they be as detailed as possible so that they can make the procurement decision-maker's job easy.

It is important that they provide in-depth information as well as explain the budget assumptions in a much more detailed manner, since some of the people now reviewing budgets are not familiar with the whys and do not necessarily understand the rationale behind what could appear to them to be an unnecessary cost, such as early arrival guarantees for those arriving from overseas at 8:00 a.m., 24-hour hold on meeting space and so on.

It is also important that your suppliers understand and accept that your colleagues in procurement are not the enemy, but rather allies in obtaining the best possible outcome for the company and their clients. They are professionals whose objective is to obtain the maximum value for each dollar spent. This is very different from just cutting costs. Sales and marketing departments have the same objectives, but it is up to them and their suppliers to educate procurement professionals about what constitutes quality and value in a meeting or business function. And internal staff knowing and clearly articulating objectives can help to educate procurement staff. Suppliers know where they can tighten up the dollars being spent and where they need leeway to produce the results that will provide a return on the money being spent. If the procurement people understand this, the dialog is much easier, and sales and marketing will get more of what they require in the end.

For companies electing to go the procurement department route, it is extremely important to assess the results of your event with both sales and marketing and other departments that may have been holding their own events, and it is essential that the procurement department be a part of the findings as well. If the results other than financial were not realized, that is, if company objectives were not met, changes need to be made quickly before other events are contracted.

One of the dangers of using this method of supplier selection is that events can be planned and contracted years out. The only way of limiting the danger is by being on top of your final reconciliation and findings and comparing them to past results. If you can prove—with factual documentation—that there is a significant downside to having procurement handle the buying based on results, then company heads may be open to new suggestions. If it is determined from events that have taken place that mistakes are being made in using procurement in supplier selection, contracts may need to be cancelled and charges would apply. It is less costly to pay cancellation charges and change suppliers and the selection process than to proceed with an event that will not give you a return on your investment today and build toward your future growth.

Online Auctions and Other Emerging Buying Trends

A new bidding and buying trend taking place that executives should be aware of is meeting planning online auctions. Online auctions have come about as a means to provide the client with more transparency, the lowest possible rate and the most concessions. Companies are being set up specifically to handle online auctions and develop customized online RFPs for group hotel and meeting room contracting for corporate in-house meeting planners—and potentially involving procurement department staff—and sales and marketing, as well as professional event planning companies working on behalf of their corporate clients.

Companies select up to 10 properties that meet their needs from their database and these hotels or meeting venues are invited to take part in the bidding process. The online bidding for the business runs until a specific time and date. The corporate client or the planner looking to block and contract the space will know exactly which property is which but the competing venues do not; they can only see what is being offered from their competition. Room rates, meeting space and concessions are all a part of the bidding process.

The company hosting the online auction receives a fee from the property, not the corporate client or event planner. Event planners must build their management fee into their client proposal to corporate clients. Dollars are saved on basic costs but the creative elements that work to bring about the returns on investment are handled separately, either by sales and marketing or procurement.

Again, an assessment must be made to see how costs compare at the end of the day. If companies are looking at several destinations, the danger in doing online auctions is that you will be committing to and contracting to space without knowing the full costs of all essential elements, such as air costs. Costs could come in conceivably higher for some types of events using this buying method.

Care should be exercised as to when and how online auctions are used. You may find they are best used for very simple meetings as opposed to other types of events. Auctions can be appropriate/ effective for straight meetings or in-house conference programs where the location does not necessarily matter as much because the main context of holding the event is delivering the meeting content and not the facilities amenities or social programs and so forth. The only purpose of the hotel is to meet and sleep in it.

Another trend being seen is suppliers becoming proactive in looking for new ways to secure business, promote their customer loyalty and increase value to their clients, and introducing air miles in return for business booked through credit card companies or as something that they have negotiated. Air miles are awarded to anyone specified by the company, and the air miles earned could be incorporated to reduce event costs (such as flying in the speaker, for example). It is very important to establish clear guidelines as to whom the air miles are assigned and how they may be used so that no company ethical breaches occur. For example, if the person planning the event had all the air miles assigned to their personal credit card, not company credit card, that could be—depending on company policy—an ethical breach, especially if they chose to use the miles for personal and not company benefit.

It is important for corporate executives to be aware of and prepare for changing buying times. Staying ahead of new buying trends helps you to be proactive, and be able to know if a passing trend is one that will have lasting benefit to your company and how best to utilize it without compromising your event success. Change can be, but isn't always, for the better. You don't want to be caught today for an event taking place a year or more out in a buying that proves to deliver little or no return on your specific company objectives, all because the decision was based on dollars and cents alone rather than on the dollars being spent making sense.

How to Assign the Allocated Dollars

Once quotes have been received and a master cost summary prepared listing only event essentials and all related costs, not enhancements, you will be able to gauge how close or far you are from your assigned budget. It will be important to find out exactly how your budget figure was arrived at. In many cases, budgets are based on the last year's projected budget for an event, which may or may not have run yet. That's when it is important to go back and carefully look at your company's history of spending and pull the final reconciliation figures for similar business functions that include all applicable expense report items as well in order to get a true idea of total costs. This is your starting point. You will be able to see if the prices quoted are in line or if serious negotiations and concessions need to take place before you can consider contracting.

A supplier quote and contract are not set in stone and you will find that your suppliers will work with you to help you find a way to cut costs and still meet your objectives once they know exactly what you need from them. But what is paramount to remember is that they are a business, too. They have overhead and have company bottom-line objectives to be met, and they should not be nickled and dimed to death because it will show up somewhere. Your suppliers cannot be expected to run your event at a loss. Cutbacks that could result in less-than-stellar quality in goods or services should not be risked, such as not having sufficient staff on hand to run your event smoothly.

Your suppliers, carefully interviewed and with referrals checked, are experts in knowing what they can take out without affecting the overall performance results and helping you to bring your budget in line. And if you have dollars to play with, they can also advise you as how best to spend them on what will have the most impact.

Remember, sought-after event professionals, suppliers and venues are doing events 365 days a year for a variety of clients—including your competition—in all types of industries, but they should never divulge who did or is doing what. Rather, they should offer creative cost-saving ideas to be considered, and all with different budgets. It is their job as event strategists to guide you through the pros and cons and advise you as to what will best lead you to the desired results.

In the end, though, it is your decision as to what to include and how to move forward. You must actively take on the role of investment strategist and event strategist for your company. What you produce will be the building block for your next event and your company's business growth, and you must keep that in mind. Due to location or other factors, the suppliers you are working with today may not be the suppliers that you will be working with on the next. Only you will be privy to what else is taking place in your company, so you have to look at all the angles to see if what they are suggesting has merit or not to you. Their primary concern is making the event they will be contracted to do an outstanding success for you and your company. Yours is much more far-reaching.

As you carefully review your cost summary proposal, look at each expenditure with an eye on which company objectives it will help you fulfill. Prioritize them. Fireworks to produce a WOW finale may be warranted or you may choose to keep those dollars intact and spend them elsewhere. Just make sure that you are not "burning" more money than is required in order to achieve your desired outcome. One company had their employees raving about a dessert they served at a company employee appreciation event that cost a fraction of a more traditional one. It was the creativity and the caring to take the time to find something unique that created the WOW effect for just $2 a person.

Innovation does not have to be expensive. Creating business functions that are meaningful, memorable and magical is an art and one that can deliver a powerful company message that will deliver a multitude of rewards. And it begins with making sense of the dollars being spent.

Conclusion

You can spend your budget in a million different ways, and get different results every time. That's why it's important to be able to successfully assess how to structure your events and choose the elements that will ensure that you receive the maximum return on your investment and meet all of your objectives.

This knowledge will enable you to determine how budgets should be spent for optimal return on your investment, and help you to set reasonable and responsible standards for corporate expenses. It also enables you to be savvier when it comes to reviewing proposals by peers and by event planning companies.

CHAPTER SIX

IDENTIFYING POTENTIAL LANDMINES

SOMETHING AS SIMPLE AS A MENU faux pas can make or break a career in business and put an executive's reputation on the line. For example, a group of New York congressmen traveling with the President on Air Force One had an embarrassing moment thanks to a frozen fruit bar served for dessert. The frozen treat was served very cold and their tongues became stuck to the fruit bars. Being the person responsible for okaying a menu selection that caused guests to lose face as they struggled to free their tongues in front of the leader of the free world is not the situation any executive wants to face.

A seemingly innocent choice can result in an executive being perceived as not thinking ahead, not paying attention to detail and having bad business judgment. These types of labels can and do carry forward and affect careers. This particular blunder was covered by radio stations and other news outlets and flashed across the Internet. Being the person responsible for signing off on decisions and expenses and producing results is not a career move to take lightly, and company executives cannot leave the decision-making up to their in-house, hired event planning staff or contracted suppliers.

What to Be Aware of When Planning Business Functions

The idea to hold a business function usually begins in the boardroom or executive offices with a discussion of how best to meet a new or ongoing company objective or how to move forward with planning a long-standing company event, such as the next incentive program, product launch or appreciation day. A committee is formed and someone is asked to step up and take the responsibility of running the production from beginning to end. For many executives it is a sought-after position, viewed as an opportunity to shine within the company and possibly the industry, enjoy the perks that may come with the position and add something of value—if the results are outstanding—to their professional résumé. They give little or no thought to the time, energy and effort required on top of their daily workload and the consequences if they should fail to deliver a return on the company's investment.

Often, executives undertaking this project on behalf of their company do so without having run an event before, and if they do not take the time to familiarize themselves with the process and the requirements they can easily run into problems that can have serious career and company repercussions—financial, legal and otherwise. The time invested to learn what needs to be done, how it needs to be done, why it needs to be done, when it needs to be done and where it needs to be done can pay tremendous dividends for their present function and future endeavors. The skills learned— strategic planning, budget management, operations, on-site event orchestration, timing and logistics, negotiations, business ethics, business etiquette, establishing and setting codes of conduct, business protocol, event marketing, time management, media and public relations management—are transferable to many other company management projects and are very valuable in the business world.

The planning of business functions can be divided into four main stages and each comes with its own set of challenges, areas to be aware of and red flags to be wary of, and they apply to events of all sizes. The same exact steps are required regardless of how big or small your event. A seemingly low-key event can trip you up as much as a full-blown event extravaganza if you let a step slip through the cracks. Because the event you plan goes through numerous changes of hands and who is on-site running your event may have only been apprised of what is taking place a week or less before your event takes place is exactly why all i's must be dotted and t's crossed as you go along:

- planning
- operations
- execution
- final reconciliation

Planning

The planning stages of business functions will take you through design concept to contracting. Within the planning stage there are seven steps that you will move through regardless of if you plan and execute your event on your own working directly with your suppliers and use company in-house planners or committee members to do the work or if you contract professional event planning services.

These seven steps include:

- theme or event design
- request for proposal
- presentation
- cost summary breakdown preparation
- contract negotiations
- site inspections
- contracting

Theme or Event Concept

The initial business function concept or category that the type of event falls under is generally decided on by the corporate executives who will be handling the event. If a theme name will be required, it can be decided on in advance by the planning committee to give suppliers an idea of the direction to move in or be left open for discussion and input from your business function suppliers. Also included in this step is a discussion of the type of event, the date, past history and present events that are already booked. Event concept is the time when all company objectives should be identified.

Request for Proposal

Once the type of event has been decided on, the date has been selected, past history and present events that are already booked have been reviewed and company event objectives have been set, the next step is preparing a formal request for proposal from various business function suppliers.

Before the requests for proposals are sent out, you need to determine how the company wants to handle the event. You also must choose between being hands on from beginning to end and handling the myriad of details and demands yourself using either in-house company meeting planners and/or committee members, and contracting the services of a professional event planning company to handle your event from beginning to end, including the day-to-day operations, with the company's involvement still being hands on with regards to overseeing the event details and in-house staff assigned to provide the event planning company with all that they will require. Large-scale events that have complex components, for example, multimedia stage shows as part of the event; events that involve intricate theatrical special effects, such as indoor or outdoor pyro; or that have numerous moving parts may require additional event planning expertise and the services of a professional event planner unless your company has an in-house event planning staff available to work with you on your project.

There are many pluses to using the services of a professional event planning company. While they do charge a management fee for their services, often what they provide in terms of your staff hours saved, preferred rates they are able to negotiate based on their ongoing supplier relationships and the professional execution level they can raise your event to more than makes up for the fee.

There are several different types of event planning companies. Some event planning companies are proficient at handling everything that will be taking place in the room and onstage, either by having their own in-house sister communication company to design your audiovisual components or by working in partnership with one of their preferred audiovisual companies. Having them involved in both can bring continuity to your event that you might not have if hiring two separate companies one for event planning and the other for audiovisual—and having both work on their separate agendas that may or may not blend together seamlessly in the end. Some audiovisual companies that are working directly with the corporate company as opposed to working in partnership with the event planning company have been known to bar all event planning staff from the room while their part of the show is taking place, which can cause difficulties and areas of conflict if your event planning staff need to be in the room orchestrating their own portion of events that will directly follow the stage presentation.

It is important to find out the exact type of business the event planning company you are considering using handles. There are professional event planning companies that specialize in corporate business events that are designed to meet your company objectives, and they are masters of their craft. There are caterers and decor companies that bill themselves as event planners when party planners may be a more accurate description. They may be skilled at social events but not necessarily adept at strategic planning to bring about business results and they may have their own in-house props, decor and so forth that are simply reused, as opposed to a corporate event planning company that does not have a warehouse of goods to rent but has flexibility to custom design exactly what you need from an army of suppliers. It is very important to qualify the type of event planning company that will best meet your needs for a specific event.

Before you make the decision as to which route to take, it is important to assess your internal staff's workload as it is now and what will be required of them in the future to see if what you are proposing they take on is manageable. Remember to factor in vacations, business travel and holidays, as well as work deadlines and peak time demands.[1]

Once you have decided on your preferred route with regards to who will be handling what, a detailed request for proposal will need to be prepared. The more information that you can provide for your suppliers, the better quote you will receive back. If, in the end, taking the time up front to prepare and submit a very detailed request for proposal will save you time, energy and money but lessen the amount of back and forth in working toward coming up with a submission from your suppliers, that will work toward meeting your company objectives. Your suppliers cannot provide you with an accurate projection of costs unless you provide them with your exact specifications and expectations. Your suppliers will also need to know your total budget parameters so that they can tell you if what you are proposing is feasible or not within your allocated spending. What follows is an outline of what they will need to know.

Participants

The more information you can provide your suppliers with, the better your program or event will be. They will be able to tailor it to fit your target audience's needs. More information takes away the risk of having "cookie cutter" events.

- How many participants will be taking part in your event?
- What is their relationship to your company?
- What are the group demographics, for example, ages, gateway cities (if flying in from across the country/world), employees, marital status, level of sophistication, interests, special requirements and so forth?

Location Requirements

Location is an event element and must be treated as such. It can also use up major dollars so the return has to be there.

- Will your event be held locally, nationally or out of country?

---

1   Detailed information on event planning timelines and time management
    requirements can be found in *Time Management for Event Planners*
    (Wiley, 2005).

- Are there any locations or destinations that should be ruled out, for example, no destination that requires more than five hours of flying time or poses a safety concern?
- Are you looking for destinations that will provide your guests with an historical or fun/sun (or ski) experience?
- Are there any destinations that tie into the type of work your company does that could provide a tax benefit or other desirable benefits?
- What is your past history? Where have you held these events before and when?
- Are there any locations that should definitely be considered?

Transportation Requirements

Your company's transportation requirements can limit where you can and can't go. It is important to know your requirements up-front so that time is not spent researching destinations that do not meet your company's travel criteria.

- How will your participants be arriving at your event?
- If flying, what class of service will be required? Your suppliers will need the number of passengers traveling from each main gateway city as well in order to provide you with an accurate costing.
- Will everyone be traveling on the same class of service, for example, will company heads and executives be flying in business and first class with the group traveling in economy? A breakdown as to who will be traveling in what class of service and from what departure cities will be required for costing purposes.
- Will everyone be flying to and from on the same date or will some guests be arriving in advance of the group or departing after the main group has left?
- Is there a company policy on how many employees can travel on the same aircraft?
- Is there a company policy on how many company executives can travel on the same aircraft?

- Will the company be picking up the cost not only for necessary overnights en route but overnights for guests that will be required to travel long distances to the airport?
- Upon arrival at the destination, how will guests be transported to the hotel? Will you require private limousine transfers or shared? Group motor coach transfers or private shuttles arranged? Taxis? A combination, for example, limousine for company executives and motor coach transfers for your guests? A breakdown of numbers will be required.
- Will refreshments, entertainment or other amenities, for example, cool cloths, hot cloths, movies and so on be desired during transportation?
- If driving, will each of your guests be coming in their own car? Or will they be sharing, as in the case of a spousal event but not necessarily if your event is scheduled to take place on a weeknight and both partners may be coming directly from work? This could affect parking requirements. Will guests be responsible for their own parking costs or will the company be prepaying parking?

Accommodation Requirements

Not all hotels and resorts are created equal and, as such, will deliver different results. You need to know all your possible room requirements in order to know which properties to rule out. For example, one company had a policy that their president must stay in a separate tower from their participants. Right there single standing resorts were ruled out, unless on a property villa there was a suitable alternate.

- What caliber of hotel or venue is required?
- If guestrooms are required, what is the breakdown? How many single or king rooms (for couples)? Twin bedded rooms (for shared accommodation)? Suites (how many and what level, for example, presidential, luxury, oceanview)? Any special requirements, for example, handicapped accessible and so forth?

- Dates required including pre- and post-event dates for any company executives arriving in advance of the group or staying on after the group departs.
- Can senior management be housed on the same floor? The president of one Asian company required the best suite in the hotel but no one in his company was allowed to be on the same floor or a higher floor. If the selected hotel had one or more towers, this was an easy demand to work around, but careful planning and room assignment had to take place if there was only one main tower.
- Must all guestrooms be booked in the same category, for example, all oceanview, or can they be booked run-of-the-house, where the caliber of room types assigned could vary greatly and egos can become bruised?

Room Requirements

It is not enough for hotels to know your meeting requirements over your in-house dates. Move in, set up, rehearsal, teardown and move out must be factored in as well.

Meeting Room Requirements

Find out from your suppliers their time and logistical requirements.

- How many meeting rooms will you require?
- What days and times will you need each meeting room for?
- Will move in be intensive, for example, in the case of setting up a product launch?
- Will you require 24-hour hold on all your meeting rooms?
- Will you require meeting rooms that can be locked?
- How many participants will each need to accommodate?
- What style of seating will you be utilizing?
- Will meals or coffee breaks be served in the same room or will additional space be required?
- Will staging, specialty lighting or rear-screen audiovisual be required?

- Will you require rehearsal time?
- Do you have any other special requirements, for example, air conditioning, kitchens?

Function Room Requirements

Again, to ensure the property can handle all your needs, you must determine in advance all your function room requirements.

- How many function rooms will you require?
- What days and times will you need each function room for?
- Will move in be intensive, for example, in the case of setting up theme decor, staging or product?
- Will you require 24-hour hold on all your function rooms?
- Will you require function rooms that can be locked?
- How many participants will each need to accommodate?
- Will additional space be required for a pre-function event, for example, a cocktail reception?
- What style of seating will you be utilizing? Will you require tables of eight? Or of ten? Will there be food stations or buffet setups that will need to be accommodated?
- Will anything else be taking place in the room, for example, entertainment, dancing, awards presentation and so on?
- Will staging, specialty lighting or rear-screen audiovisual be required?
- Will you require rehearsal time, for example, band rehearsal in the same room as the meal will be served in?
- Any other special requirements, for example, air conditioning, kitchens?

Room Layout Requirements

Provide as many details for requirements for each meeting and function room as possible. A sketch or grid is very helpful to show exactly what you are visualizing.

- What will be taking place in the room?
- Where will the stage be located?
- Will you be having rear-screen or front-screen projection?

- Will rigging from the ceiling be required? If you are doing a stage show that requires specialty rigging from the ceiling and special flooring, you will need to make this known in advance, as labor costs could soar in a union facility if proper calculation of setup requirements are not factored in (which you would obtain from your supplier handling the entertainment or stage production elements for you).
- What are the seating arrangements?
- How much electricity will be required, and how many plugs will be required? Depending on the venue, backup generators could be required, and location and availability of electrical outlets would be a concern. Both could bring additional costs that will need to be factored in.

In order to get the most from your RFPs, you need to have everyone working from the same page so that you can compare costs. What will set your suppliers apart is how they take your list of requirements and design an event that features elements strategically planned to meet your objectives, and if the recommendations they make show a clear understanding of how to best meet your requirements and deliver a business function that will meet and exceed your expectations.

Be sure to specify how you would like your quote laid out, such as menu style with all applicable charges and the date you will need to receive it by. Have potential suppliers note on the proposal if space is or is not being held on a tentative basis. Or if you would like them to place it on a tentative hold for you, request a sample boilerplate contract so that you can review their company terms and conditions and ask them to submit to you all related material that may detail cancellation charges and surcharges that are just listed in their contracts, for example, food and beverage terms and conditions may be laid out in their stand-alone brochure, and not spelled out in the contract but listed as "per terms and conditions." It is also important to have your suppliers list charges that are not included and that could show up at final reconciliation, such as power drop charges. Request that they also include a list of all required permits, insurance and other legal, safety and security requirements, with costs and notes as to who will be responsible for acquiring them. Also note how many copies of the quote and backup material will be required for presentation and/or submission.

Special Note: Having multiple suppliers bidding on the same business function does not guarantee obtaining better rates, terms and concessions. It often has the reverse effect. If a hotel, venue or business function supplier realizes that there are many people bidding on the same piece of business, they know that regardless of the outcome, there is a good possibility it will be held at their facility or the planners will be using their services, and therefore they may not be as competitive in their rate offerings as they might have been if they knew they were going up against different destinations and so on with one or two main bidders. One car manufacturer had 19 event planning companies bidding on its product launch to be held in a destination where only one possible hotel could accommodate them. All the planners knew who was bidding—the hotel had advised all that there was multiple bidding going on—and they all received exactly the same rate and terms. This would not have been the case had the hotel not been as certain about the outcome. The automobile company was setting itself up for higher rates from the onset.

Presentation

There are two ways to conduct proposal presentation meetings. The first is to request that detailed quotes be sent in by a specific date so that you can take time to review them with your committee members, narrow your suppliers down, prepare your questions and then call in the finalists for a formal presentation. The second method is to start with the formal presentation, where your suppliers will walk your committee members through each step of their proposal, be on hand to answer any of your questions as they arise and leave copies of their presentation and all collateral material behind for your in-depth review.

There is a great deal that you will be able to tell from your supplier's proposal. You will be able to determine if they have an eye for detail, how accurate they are—you will be able to pick up any glaring omissions from other proposals—and clearly see cost differentials. Their transparency will be apparent to you, and both their creativity and how it will meet your business objectives will either set them apart or it won't.

Never cross the ethical boundary of giving one supplier's proposal to their competition or taking someone else's creativity and running it in-house. Confidentiality agreements have been the exception rather than the rule in event planning, but steps are now being taking to protect creative intelligence and you could conceivably be asked to sign one. Just as you need to be careful with whom you are doing business, so do the suppliers you are working with. There is a bond of trust that once broken is hard to repair, and some companies who have violated that code of conduct have found it difficult to find suppliers to work with them on future events. And it works in reverse. One corporation was incensed that a supplier their event planning company used, with whom they had an excellent long-term relationship, contacted them directly, trying to cut the event planning company out of the business. The company forwarded what had been submitted to it, and their event planning company no longer used the services of that supplier— nor did the rest of the industry—and the supplier eventually went out of business.

Cost Summary Breakdown Preparation

Once you have narrowed your options down, it is time to prepare a master cost summary breakdown to capture all estimated supplier charges and all applicable in-house company charges as well. Before contracting, have a clear understanding of all possible expenditures, make sure that there are enough dollars to produce your desired results and decide if any suggested enhancements are warranted and/or affordable. If you start to contract piecemeal before you have the full financial picture, you could find it to be a very costly mistake. If you are being pressured to contract, request that the space be placed on tentative hold for you so that the space is protected while you review where you stand financially.

Contract Negotiations

Remember that contracts' terms and conditions are not set in stone. If you require changes, such as having payment schedules adjusted to meet your check runs, or need additional concessions worked out, do not hesitate to request them before you sign on the dotted line. Make sure that everything has been detailed on your contract, including the time you have access to the meeting room and the time you are required to move out by, meeting room charges, and the type and number of guestrooms blocked. Review your contracts carefully and have any changes put in writing and signed off by both parties.

Site Inspections

Site inspections should take place before the contract is finalized. The event planning companies or suppliers may stipulate that, should the contract not move forward, your company would be responsible for all related expenses for the inspection. This is done as a measure of protection from unscrupulous staff taking advantage of suppliers using site inspections as a vacation and even requesting bringing their partner along.

Site inspections are generally incorporated into your quotes and should appear as line items. In most cases the amount is based on one member of your staff taking part and one member of theirs accompanying them. Depending on how intricate your arrangements, they may need a second person to advance the site as well, but that should all be laid out for your review. If you need more than one company representative to go on the site inspection it is important to advise your suppliers in advance in your request for proposal so that they can include the costs for additional personnel. It is also important to find out from your company how to handle a request made by your representatives as to whether or not they can bring someone with them if it is permitted, and who will be responsible for the cost. In some cases, senior executives have said that their spouse's input is valuable, especially if spousal programs will be a part of the program, but it is important to make sure than no unethical company breaches are taking place and to let your suppliers know how your company would like site inspections handled.

Contracting

Make sure that whomever signs the contract with your suppliers has company signing authority and is in a position to authorize company expenditures. Any and all amendments to contracts must be in writing and signed off by both parties. Hospitality industry professionals do move around, and the person you are dealing with today may not be there when your event takes place in the future. All you will have is your contract as proof of what has been agreed to.

Operations

Once your event has been contracted there is a very good chance that you will no longer be working day to day with the sales representative that you contracted with. Once contracted, sold business is often transferred to operations staff to handle the implementation of all that has been agreed upon. It's very important that all terms, conditions, inclusions and concessions are in writing so that there are no gray areas and nothing gets dropped. Schedule a meeting with all key personnel—both internal and supplier—so that they can meet and establish working guidelines and timelines.

Suppliers will also need to be advised of company policy and how to handle any requests that may come in directly from employees and/or guests. For example, requests for upgraded air seats and rooms are often received, as are requests for extended stays on out-of-state or out-of-country events. If your airfare has been based on group airfare rates, which require "x" number of participants to fly on the same flights, permitting guests to deviate from arrival and departure dates could affect airfare costs—not just for the person requesting the change but for the balance of the group on the same flight—should numbers drop below those required. Establish who will be responsible for additional charges or even if they will be permitted. Knowing in advance how you wish these special requests to be handled will allow the operating staff to address the issues with finesse and avoid ruffling any participants' feathers by being able to explain refusals as due to a company directive or policy.

Critical Path

It will be important to prepare a master critical path that has been compiled from supplier contracts, proposals and suppliers' own individual critical paths so that you can stay on top of pending deadlines and no unnecessary charges are incurred. This would happen if you missed submitting approved copy by the printing deadlines and rush charges applied, or numbers for attrition dates were not reviewed and your company ended up paying cancellation charges. The onus will be on you, not your suppliers, to meet contracted deadlines, and you cannot depend on your suppliers to remind you of your upcoming commitments.

It will also be important to assign specific dates. For example, your supplier contract may say that food and beverage guarantees must be called in 15 "business" days not 15 days before your event, and you will need to make sure that the proper date is noted so that you do not end up paying for more than is necessary.

Function Sheets

Business functions are live stage productions and, as such, "scripts" are written that contain a detailed breakdown of all that will be taking place and when. If you are using the services of a professional event planning company, they will be preparing what is called function sheets[2] for their suppliers that will lay out your event from beginning to end in time order. The suppliers will review the sheets and sign off before meeting with the company for a final review. A copy of the function sheets should be prepared for your review and sign-off as well.

If you will be handling the event in-house, it is advisable that your staff prepare function sheets for your suppliers because they are your only means of ensuring that all will be done exactly as you specify. If you leave it to each individual supplier to do their own sheets without input, then their stamp and style, not your signature company style, will be on your event. For example, for coffee breaks,

---

2   Samples of function sheets can be found in *Event Planning: The Ultimate Guide* (Wiley, 2000).

some hotels as a matter of course will do a setup with a stack of saucers and a stack of cups, packages of sweetener and tiny containers of milk and cream, which may or may not be fine. Your company may prefer a more gracious setting, with the cups placed on top of each saucer to make handling easier for your guests, silver sugar bowls with cubed sugar or brown sugar and silver containers of milk and cream. This may be more in line with the image you want to project, but unless you put that in writing—in function sheets—that may not happen. That is just one tiny example; function sheets deal with each and every aspect of your event.

Your cost summary budget, which should be continually updated, should be reviewed as well. It is important to always know exactly where you are with regards to spending, and you simply cannot wait until final reconciliation to do a revised costing. As final costs come in, estimated expenses must be updated. If you go into your event knowing exactly where you are with regards to spending, sometimes there are very pleasant surprises and you may find that you will be able to add in an enhancement or two. Or, if real costs have far exceeded projected costs through ongoing event changes, additions and subtractions, depending on cancellation clauses there may still be time to make adjustments to keep costs in line.

Supplier Pre-con

Once function sheets have been prepared, reviewed and signed off, a final version will be compiled incorporating any changes. A supplier pre-con meeting is scheduled to take place in advance of move in. At this meeting, you will review your event with all who will be on site on the day of your event. Once an event moves from operations to on-site execution, a whole new group of people may become involved, and for many it will be the first time that they are familiarizing themselves with your event. This is one reason why detailed contracts and functions sheets are vital to the success of your business function.

Execution

The execution stage begins the moment the advance team arrives on site. Depending on how intricate your event and setup is it could take place days or even up to a week in advance of the actual event. All the costs associated with advance, move in, setup, day of, teardown and move out should be included in your original cost summary from your suppliers, and costs for your staff should be added in as well. You will know from your supplier proposals and contracts what you can do yourself and what the union requires that they do, and this must be adhered to even as far as to what crew break you will be picking up the cost for and providing.

Move In

"Move in" refers to the arrival of your various suppliers and their goods that have to be off-loaded and transported from the loading docks to your meeting or function rooms. Move in must be carefully orchestrated. It is important to make sure that all is in order for a speedy and timely off-loading. For example, specialty equipment may be required and union staff may be needed. Costs can skyrocket if timelines are not adhered to and everything that is necessary to expedite the move in is not in place.

Setup

"Setup" is what takes place in your meeting and function space. Again, this is an area that must be tightly scripted. There is an order to what must be set up first and it has to be followed. Each supplier will have outlined their setup timelines and requirements in advance and laid them out in the function sheets so that everyone involved knows exactly what to expect and by when. Crew meals could be part of setup costs; these arrangements have to be made in advance to ensure they are looked after.

Day Of

"Day of" is the day of your event. On-site orchestration takes place. It is important to advise all of your suppliers that any additional charges on-site must be approved before taking place and be signed off on by a signing officer of your company.

Teardown

Depending on arrangements, "teardown" may or may not take place immediately after your event finishes. The costs to do so must be weighed against the expense to do so the next day, for example, overtime charges could apply that could be more expensive than waiting, or noise restrictions could prohibit teardown from taking place at a certain time of day or night.

Move Out

"Move out" is the loading up and moving out of supplier equipment and goods. Again, special equipment and additional labor may be required and all must be in place for a quick move out. Costs for move out should be included in your budget.

Final Reconciliation

A final reconciliation meeting is advisable once your suppliers have prepared their final billing. Costs can be reviewed and an overview of what worked and what could be done differently next time could be done at the same time to help you with the preparation of your executive summary history. Your final reconciliation should reveal no surprises.

Conclusion

A great deal rides on your ability to identify potential landmines when planning and executing your event elements. Make certain you give adequate time, energy and effort to ensure you deliver a return on your company's investment.

The planning of business functions can be divided into four main stages. Each comes with its own set of challenges, areas to be aware of and red flags to be wary of, and they apply to events of all sizes. These areas must be considered, regardless of how big or small your event:

- planning
- operations
- execution
- final reconciliation

CHAPTER SEVEN

PROTECTING YOURSELF AND YOUR COMPANY FROM RED-FLAG AREAS

SHOULD COMPANY EXECUTIVES and their team members make the wrong choice and fail to deliver what the company was seeking from their venture, they sometimes find their livelihood, chance of future promotion and professional reputation on the firing line. And if the corporate event they are in charge of puts the company in peril—financially, legal or otherwise—executives can no longer plead ignorance to company heads or to judges if they end up on trial. Corporate events and business entertaining can damage a company's image and put the company and its management in potentially high-risk situations.

Bringing red-flag areas of concern to the executive level, and getting sign-off from the company lawyers, insurance company and the chief financial officer, is a must in today's litigious society where corporations and individuals are being held liable for company indiscretions and failure to adhere to social host legal responsibilities.

Two red-flag areas to pay close attention to are:

- event insurance
- fire marshal permits, licenses, social host legal responsibilities and so forth.

Event Insurance

Hurricane Wilma, the 2005 season's 12th record-tying hurricane (billed as the most intense Atlantic storm ever, with winds of 175 mph and lowest minimum pressure ever observed in the Atlantic Basin), coming on the heels of the devastation caused by December 2004's tsunami and August 2005's Hurricane Katrina, is causing corporate clients to take a closer look at hotel terms and conditions, event insurance and proposed future bookings at severe weather watch locations and disaster-prone areas.

Hurricanes and natural disasters such as earthquakes, tsunamis, storm surges and flooding are seemingly on the rise. The 2005 season tied with 1969 for the record number of hurricanes and with 1933 as the busiest storm season on record. Many hurricane-prone regions are popular meeting and incentive travel destinations, so it is now more imperative than ever that the ABC principles of event planning—Anticipation, Backup Plan and Crisis Management[1]—be applied to destination and hotel selections and contracting. Florida alone has been hit an unprecedented six times between 2004 and 2005, and that can't be overlooked.

Many companies are now becoming proactive and looking for ways to protect their programs and deposits. Those in charge of planning events are now finding themselves facing weather or health advisory warnings against travel to specific areas; re-routed aircraft; shutdown of local airports; mandatory evacuations; moved locations; the rebuilding of entire city infrastructures and even double event disaster hits.

One company executive was told "Your hotel is no longer there" when he called to find out how the hotel he had booked for their upcoming event had fared in a hurricane. The hotel was totally wiped out and everything was moved to Florida. Florida was then hit badly the following month, and they were not sure the event would take place.

---

1   For more details on the ABCs, read *Event Planning Ethics and Etiquette* (Wiley, 2003).

Event Insurance Coverage and Application

For a number of reasons, savvy company executives are now making sure that they are familiar with event insurance that covers event cancellation. Event cancellation/postponement insurance and event liability insurance (which covers bodily injury or accidental death of attendees, property damage caused to venue by participants and suppliers and so on) are two types of insurance that are offered. Event cancellation and event liability insurance cover a number of corporate events, including trade shows, conventions, exhibitions and sporting events. The policies protect companies against unforeseen problems such as damage to their venue, extreme weather conditions, strikes by third-party employees, non-appearance of a large number of participants, late arrival of necessary equipment, national mourning and many other unpredictable events.

Cancellation insurance is a specialized insurance. It is becoming increasingly popular where there could be potential financial loss. Cancellation insurance offers protection for financial loss associated with an insured event that is cancelled for reasons beyond the control of the insured, promoter or organizer. Some examples of the type of incidents that might result in a loss of revenue are power failure, damage to a leased or rented venue, damage to surrounding venues resulting in lack of access, failure of public transport facilities, natural catastrophe (e.g., earthquake), failure of TV transmission, satellite breakdown and any other previously unforeseen cause. There are also policy extensions such as non-appearance, which applies to keynote speakers and performers; adverse weather, which applies to outdoor events; and terrorism coverage.

It is important to be very specific when discussing event cancellation insurance requirements. Ask your insurance provider whether or not custom coverage can be arranged if their standard policy does not offer you the full protection you need. Areas of event cancellation coverage consideration should include:

- severe weather, for example, hurricanes, typhoons or tornadoes
- natural disasters, such as earthquakes and tsunamis

- physical damage to the premises where your event is to take place
- uninhabitable accommodation at your destination
- no access to your hotel or venues
- complete cessation of your airline
- complete cessation of your arrival airport
- complete cessation of your travel suppliers
- mandatory evacuations due to weather, natural disasters and other (terrorism threats, etc.)
- mandatory relocating
- mandatory rescheduling of your event due to conditions beyond your control
- strikes by contracted suppliers, including airlines, hotels and venues
- withdrawal by authorities of obtained licenses and permits
- late or non-arrival of items essential to your event
- infrastructure rebuilding delays

When contacting insurance companies regarding custom event cancellation insurance, executives need to be sure to address all possible financial liabilities, including:

- planning costs
- site inspection expenditures
- travel deposits (air, rail, motor coach, limousines, etc.)
- hotel deposits
- venue deposits
- destination management company (DMC) deposits
- decor deposits
- entertainment deposits
- travel and technical rider financial commitments
- food and beverage deposits
- staging, lighting and audiovisual deposits
- on-site staffing deposits
- speaker fees
- print and promotional costs
- rescheduling costs

- communication costs
- any other fees that may be charged in the event of cancellation that have been laid out in supplier contract terms and conditions

Only a few companies specialize in this type of insurance and it is important to find one that has offices all over the world so that they can cover almost any event anywhere. Check with your venues and suppliers to see who they have used before and how well they were looked after if a claim was filed. You can also check with event planning associations and industry resources to see who they recommend. Ask for references and be sure to check them out. Worldwide claims assistance may also be very important, depending on where the event is taking place.

Examples of Damage from Adverse Weather

Good weather can never be taken for granted. Weather patterns are changing around the world. Examples of extreme weather conditions that have impacted events include:

- freak snowfall causes curtailment at trade show exhibition
- rainfall affects sporting event
- freezing weather conditions affect outdoor event
- gale force winds cause tent to collapse
- severe fog on motorway causes disruption of event
- freak hailstorm causes cancellation of event
- flooding causes grandstand seating to sink
- fire damage
- fire destroys venue
- forest fires cancel event

Examples of Damage from Structural Damage

Structural damage can take place pre-event or during your event. They can be caused by weather construction and other elements. Samples include:

- temporary pool structure partially collapses and the show is curtailed
- roof collapse causes cancellation of product launch

Examples of Damage from Utilities Failure

Cities have been blacked out for over a week. This can affect events moving in, in progress, moving out or about to take place. Utility failures that can impact an event include:

- power grid supply failure causes shutdown of venue
- water supply failure causes shutdown of event
- gas leak causes denial of access to event location

One-Off Concerns

Risk assessment for all your event components is critical. Examples of what can and has occurred include:

- performer attacked by audience member
- crash of jet causes death of a performer resulting in cancellation of their tour
- golf event injury causes police to restrict access to golf course
- failure of stage hydraulics cause stage collapse
- sprinkler leakage at event venue causes flooding and damage to space and venue
- sprinkler leakage at venue causes depletion of water reservoir; venue forced to close as sprinkler system unable to operate until reservoir replenished

Weighing the Expense of Event Insurance versus the Cost of Not Taking It

It is important that executives look at an area's history during the time of year that they are proposing traveling. If it is a high-risk location at that time of the year, it is important to know the financial risks should their event be canceled and to research cancellation insurance options. Event planners handling events for corporate clients are making sure to cover themselves legally and include mention of event cancellation insurance in their letter of agreement to their clients to show that insurance coverage has been offered and discussed. You will find yourself being asked to sign off on the fact that insurance has been recommended and declined.

The cost of the policy will vary depending on the event cancellation inclusions you may require. The cost depends on the size of the budget, duration, location of the event and risk involved. It is very important that you know the policy's ifs, ands and buts. There can be very tight guidelines. It is important to request that all exclusions are stated in the quote sent to you. You then have to weigh the expense of taking insurance against the possible cost of not having insurance in place should something go wrong. Pay careful attention to cancellation clauses in contracts with venues and suppliers and look for areas of concession.

Event Cancellation Terms and Conditions

It is important to find out whether or not, under an insurance company's terms and conditions, it insures only local domiciled companies if you are planning an out-of-state or out-of-country event (corporation, event planning companies, clients and all relevant suppliers) and to find out coverage status if a corporation, event planning company or supplier's head office is domiciled elsewhere.

The first step will be filling out an insurance application. After receiving the completed application, a quote will be generated within one to two business days. Along with the non-binding quote will be all the wordings for the policy. This will include general conditions, conditions precedent to liability, and exclusions. The period of insurance should commence as soon as event organization begins, and immediately if any contracts have been signed. The cost of this insurance tends to increase if taken out nearer to the scheduled dates, and some coverage may be restricted.

Making a Claim

Before purchasing insurance, you should know the proper procedure, timelines and requirements, for example, backup material that needs to be obtained, in order to make a claim. Each insurance company will have its own precise requirements that companies will need to comply with. For example, one insurance company states that the insured must notify the underwriters or appointed representatives within 72 hours of an event claim.

Other Event Cancellation Safeguarding Measures

Executives can also negotiate event cancellation insurance and cancellation contract terms and conditions with their selected hotel, venue and suppliers. It is important to find out what a hotel's position and legal responsibility will be in the event of a disaster such as a hurricane. Executives have to make sure that they have a backup plan if the situation warrants that their event cannot go on as scheduled. Will the hotel or their suppliers refund deposits without penalty? If so, it needs to be stated in your contract.

You also need to consider whether or not the property you are booking your event at will be able to step up and assist your group in time of need. Is your hotel part of a chain or an independent property with links to other hotels? Will they be able to move your event to another location, and what will happen if no space is available? Again, what the hotel is prepared to do needs to be outlined in your hotel contract for it to be legally binding. The executive whose company event suffered two encounters with hurricanes found that everything was on tentative hold as far north as Chicago, and that it was next to impossible to secure space.

Many hotels and suppliers have clauses in their contracts that reference "acts of God," "force majeure" and "impossibility," and you need to know exactly what will and will not be covered under those terms. Practices differ from hotel to hotel and supplier to supplier and they are not always consistent within hotel chains (some may be franchises). You need to find out who will be held accountable should something unforeseen take place. Amendments can be negotiated and addendums added to standard contracts with regards to how your group will be accommodated in the event of an emergency situation. You may arrange to have the hotel re-route your guests to another property if is available or perhaps the hotel will offer your company a full or partial refund. Another condition that should also be covered is what will happen if the infrastructure doesn't support the hotel by the time your event is scheduled to take place. If the infrastructure—everything from electricity and water to staffing and restaurants—is not in place, your event will likely fail to meet its objectives.

Event cancellation and event liability insurance are areas that executives must become well informed about so that they can fully protect their company—and themselves—from financial loss and liability. It is important to understand the costs and benefits of event cancellation and event liability insurance and be familiar with what would be required to fully cover your event in case emergency situations arise. Crisis situations are becoming more and more prevalent and should be prepared for at the time of contracting.

Discuss your company's insurance requirements—event cancellation, personal liability, special occasion and so on—with your company heads and lawyers to make sure that they are comfortable with what is in place. Be aware that your venue may have its own set of specific insurance terms and conditions that have to be met not only by your company but by all the suppliers that you are bringing into their facility as well.

Fire Marshal Permits, Fire Watch, Licenses, Nursing and Ambulance Service, Personal Liability/Waivers, Social Host Legal Responsibilities and So Forth

Both your venue's insurance policies and the law can require an on-site nursing service and fire watch officials in order to obtain a specific permit. Your company's insurance coverage may require it as added protection against possible lawsuits should anything go wrong.

Providing and ensuring guest safety and care is an important part of event planning, as is protecting your organization from possible legal liabilities. This applies to events of all sizes. For example, you should always consider adding nursing services, even when it is not required by the venue or your insurance policy, when doing a team-building activity where there could be chances of injury (and have all participants sign a legal waiver, as well). Accidents—no matter how much care is in place—can happen within minutes of taking part in a fun event activity. Something as simple as a fall can potentially leave a guest or participant on crutches for six weeks, impact their day-to-day lives and leave your organization or the venue at legal risk if waivers have not been signed. Should something go wrong, having immediate assistance available helps to demonstrate "duty of care" and that reasonable thought went into planning for guest safety. Remember, injuries—even deaths—have occurred during special events.

As one of the terms and conditions to issuing an event permit, fire marshals can demand that fire watch officials are on duty. Fire watch officials may be standard policy for a particular venue—again, part of their insurance requirements—and not based on the type of event you are holding or what you may be bringing in. And in the case of a product launch for a car company or a gala fundraiser where a new car may be part of a giveaway and on display, in addition to having fire watch officials, extra fire precautions may also be required, such as having a specific amount of gas in the tank, having additional fire extinguishers, posting fire exit signs and so on. The same applies when pyrotechnics—indoor and outdoor fireworks—and other theatrical special effects or decor are involved.

Everyone involved in the on-site orchestration knows exactly what role he or she must play. Crisis mode management needs to be reviewed in advance and discussed not only with your staff but also with on-duty nursing services and fire watch officials so that event disruptions are minimal.

Major mishaps have taken place at events with no one but those in the immediate area any the wiser because everything was handled smoothly and efficiently. For example, during a confetti burst, a hole in one of the air hoses caused the confetti (professionally treated with flame retardant) to come down heavily on the small votive candles (permitted by the venue) on one table and catch fire. The fire was quickly and quietly put out and the tabletop freshened in minutes because everyone knew exactly what to do. In this case, while there was a fire watch official on duty, it was actually staff that spotted the problem and alerted the fire official about the incident.

At another event, proper attention was not given to all the potential fire hazards that could take place using pyrotechnic centerpieces. The pyro centerpieces were to be a surprise to guests, and because the guests did not know what they were or what would be taking place, many items on the tables were moved around and placed too close to where the flames were going to shoot out. The staff was prepared for this and before the charger was set off they took care to make sure that every table was safe. At some tables, however, guests had accidentally disconnected the wiring, which was something that had not been planned for. It was also not anticipated that once the charger itself was set off that it could catch fire. The charger was set up in a seldom-used back hallway, and once it had been activated, the person manning the charger went to the ballroom to see the effect and rejoin the party in progress. Luckily, waitstaff passing through saw the flames and took action, but not before the fire alarms had been sounded, causing stress to guests since they could smell the smoke but the staff had not yet discovered the source. The talk of the evening was not how wonderful the event was, but how careless the company had been about guest and fire safety.

It is also important to remember that your event could be immediately shut down if the fire department does a random inspection and you do not have a fire watch officer when one was required, or have the proper permits, insurance and licenses in place.

In a recent business function tragedy, a boat a corporation had chartered for a private dinner cruise celebration for some of their top executives was found, after it tipped over in calm waters, not to be licensed to be used in that capacity. Fifty of its senior executives died in the boating accident. There was concern that the boat was top-heavy from the moment guests boarded it and in fact, 16 participants refused to sail and stepped back off of the boat before it set sail.

The company that chartered the boat, as well as the boat owners, have now left themselves wide open for lawsuits by grieving family members. Had they protected themselves by checking licenses to make sure that they were up to date, confirmed the legal boat capacity and so forth, they would not be in this position. By their own lack of providing guest care and safety measures, the company has lost key members of its executive team and devastated family, friends and the company.

You cannot afford to be lax in areas that can have serious legal, personal and professional ramifications to yourself, your company and your attendees. Ask to see and receive copies of permits that suppliers are obtaining on your behalf to ensure that they have in fact been actioned. The same applies to supplier insurance that may be required. Check that the venues you are using are up to safety code and licensed. Never exceed room or venue capacity because if you violate it and an accident occurs, you and your suppliers will be held liable.

And remember, it is not the size of your event that determines what you can be held responsible for or the dollar amount your company can be sued for. One company that was putting on a street festival with clowns was sued by someone who was injured by a clown's juggling, and that could easily happen at a small store opening where a clown has been hired to provide entertainment. Nightclubs hired for an exclusive event and related companies and suppliers have been sued for allowing too many people into their event and been responsible for injuries when a fire broke out or when decks collapsed because of too much weight. Companies have been sued because the transportation vehicle they provided was in an accident.

Conclusion

Ensuring your company's event delivers a return on investment is not limited to the success of your event and your event execution, but encompasses many areas such as guest security and safety. Working your way through the series of required event planning steps will serve to bring red-flag areas to the front before they become potentially explosive landmines that will threaten your company's well-being

CHAPTER EIGHT

BENEFITING FROM
A COMPETITIVE ANALYSIS

MANY COMPANIES JUMP INTO holding business functions without considering what their competition has done, is doing and will be doing, and the caliber the business functions will take on. It is important that companies don't repeat what others have done or they risk coming away being professed as second best, as followers, not leaders, in their industry. Not knowing what your competition has done and how well it was received can have an adverse effect on the success of your own business entertaining venture.

For example, in the financial industry, automotive industry or pharmaceutical field there are a number of manufacturers or companies trying to encourage the same pool of potential customers to do business with them and only them. Companies want the top stockbrokers, dealers or doctors in their individual areas to attend their event—and hopefully only their event—and not be enticed to attend their toughest competitors'. They want to create, through their strategic event design, the opportunity to spend quality time with these individuals one on one and devise a means to secure their future business upfront.

In order to do this they need to look at what type and style of business function will hold the most appeal to their target audience and sway their customers to spend their time with them exclusively, especially since a number of these events take place around the same time. If the company representatives cannot convince their customers to attend only their event, at the very least their function will outshine their competition's. This is why it is essential not to risk duplication of destinations and event elements.

If two companies are offering their customers an incentive program to the same destination in the same year but using two different calibers of resorts or inclusions, the one that holds the most cachet is going to win out and the other company's will run the very real risk of failing to meet its company objectives. The chances of the same customers wanting to take time out of their personal life to go to the same destination twice in a matter of weeks or even within the year is minimal. They most likely will head off on another company's incentive jaunt to somewhere that offers them something they haven't experienced yet.

But if faced with a decision as to whether or not to go on a company's one-week combination incentive meeting on a South Pacific luxury sailing cruise or another company's shopping and sightseeing first-class getaway to exotic Bali, chances are that if the desire is high enough and the customers can afford the time, they will do both. If both companies were offering the same trips in relatively the same period the customers would choose to go on the one that held the most personal and professional interest to them. And if another company used the same destination the following year, the company would most likely find that the attitude they will be facing is "been there, done that." Their targeted guests will be off on someone else's more advantageous program.

The same thinking applies not only to destinations and your choice of resorts, but also to key event elements such as top entertainers and speakers. If your customers have already enjoyed seeing them it could be dicey as to whether or not they would make the time to do what in their eyes is a repeat performance, while placing themselves in a situation where they know they will be solicited for sales. They will weigh their options very carefully, as must you when you are coming up with your master business function plan. Not only do you have to anticipate what will draw your audience, but you also need to look at your competition's past and present history and foresee what they might be coming up with next, so that both of you do not end up offering something fairly close in design.

What sets your business function apart is not the amount of dollars you have to spend but how creatively you tap into your customers' senses. For one company, securing the rights to hold an exclusive golf tournament on a course many of their participants had only dreamed of playing, with the added bonus of being able to play with several top celebrity golfers, was the pièce de résistance that had their customers signing up immediately. The company had strategically designed a once-in-a-lifetime business function that would give their customers a life experience they would long remember and one that they could not put a price tag on. They added layer after layer of creative appeal and had their industry buzzing with the golfing coup they had pulled off.

Another company's representatives decided that low-key sponsorship for a new event that appealed to families in their market area would bring them the brand awareness exposure they were looking for, be something their competition had not done and tie into the innovative image that was a fit for their company. Sponsoring an event such as WaterFire, a free public arts event, would accomplish something similar. WaterFire is an experience that began in Providence, Rhode Island. It combines water, fire, music and performance and is set up on three rivers. It takes place several times each month from May to October and draws crowds of up to 60,000 per event. The fires are lit at sunset and are put out at midnight. Gondolas can be rented to provide a closer view and add a romantic air to the event. A corporate sponsor could invite families on a private boat charter to enjoy the magic spectacle and have a captive audience, or if the area permitted, set up a tent and hold a private dinner followed by the performance show.

Offering something different draws people to your event. Sponsoring or holding a private dinner boat cruise to view fireworks is nice, but the fireworks may not hold the same pull if they take place over a long holiday weekend or if many of the people you are inviting have experienced the event before. A private dinner boat cruise to watch an international fireworks competition could possibly have more appeal, as this is something not everyone will have done and the displays will be new and fresh. Simply holding a private dinner cruise and not building in something special may have guests carefully considering their attendance. Do they want to be somewhere where they cannot leave when they want in exchange for a steak dinner that they could enjoy in the comfort of their own home without the hassle of rush hour traffic, parking and so forth? But for guests who have seldom had the opportunity to enjoy a dinner cruise with their partner or family it could be a wonderful event for them to experience.

It's all about knowing your target audience and what they may have experienced in life or through your competition's events. Extending an invitation to a casual cruise when your competition is offering something unique, such as WaterFire, may not bring you the return on investment you are looking for to meet your company objectives. This same philosophy can be applied to the smallest events and the largest, most extravagant ones.

Driving business growth today—and this applies to all key business development areas, including business functions and business entertaining—is creativity, not knowledge. High-end technical knowledge and skilled industry know-how can encompass software, accounting and other left-brain thinking activities, and is being easily outsourced from around the world, giving competing companies an equal business footing. But creativity, which is right-brain thinking, is what is setting companies apart from their competition and sending sales soaring. Creativity will get you noticed in the marketplace, generate brand awareness with consumers, help you to attract new business, foster company loyalty and drive your business growth. Knowledge will get the job done right, help you keep your customers happy and acquire referrals, but you first have to use your creativity to be imaginative and innovative and display ingenuity in order to capture your customers' attention, commitment and business.

Customers today are looking for custom—not cookie cutter—life experiences and products and services that enhance their lives. Consumers are seeking companies that can connect with their emotions and anticipate their evolving needs by offering products and services that make their day more easy, efficient, entertaining or enjoyable. By strategically designing your goods to be innovative and creative, you are targeting and selling to your clients' senses. This can set you apart from your competition and earn you the reputation of being a leader in your field. By strategically designing your business functions to showcase your company and products in this light, you are reinforcing this cutting-edge image to the public and to your peers. If you want to stand out from your competition it is important to become known for making and setting trends, not following them, and in order to do that you need to be on top of what your competition has done, is doing and, where possible, is planning to do next, and this applies to goods, services and business functions.

The Value of Driving Trends, Not Following Them

One of the main benefits of successfully setting and executing new business function and business entertaining trends is how it can fast-forward the positioning of your company and product in the public's eye and within your industry. Being known, your innovation and creativity can take you from the middle of the pack, move you into a powerful leadership role and set you apart from your competition. It can open the door to new opportunities and business growth and change consumers' and colleagues' perspectives. Invitations to your business affairs will be eagerly anticipated and sought after.

If you and your competitors are all going after the same target market, if you settle for doing what is tried and tired, you will be setting your event up for limited attendance and attention. You can't afford to be last out of the gate when it comes to creating consumer interest in your product if you are looking not only to maintain but to increase your market share. You must tap into your consumers' senses, target their emotions, get close to understanding and anticipating their needs and reframe how you have been designing your business functions so that they drive sales and customer perception of the higher added value your company brings to them.

In order to become a leader in your industry, maintain your position and become a driving creative force, you must stay on top of what your competition is doing, become knowledgeable about successful events other industries are holding and be well aware of hot destination and event planning trends. You can accomplish this by creating a competitive analysis checklist that is custom built to your company requirements around the D.R.I.V.E. event design program I have created.

D.R.I.V.E.

If you want to propel business growth and outperform your competition, it is essential that you don't allow your company functions to become stagnant and sluggish. Make sure that you transcend past results by continually fueling your event designs with new creative energy. In order to drive results and get to where you are going and growing through bold, inventive business functions and business entertaining, you first need to map out your directional route (past, present and future for both your company and your competition) and keep the D.R.I.V.E. creative design organizational process principles in mind:

D Define
R Research
I Innovate
V Visualize
E Execute

Define

Define what has been done and is being done with regards to business functions and business entertaining in your industry. Also define your business function and business entertaining creative design style that will lend itself to meeting your company objectives and the public and professional image you want to project. Industry publications, the financial pages and even gossip columns are a good source of what types of business events are currently taking place. Note if the events taking place in your industry and in others are receiving favorable feedback. You can set up both Google Alerts and Google News with specific keywords or company names to keep you apprised, or hire the services of a clipping company to monitor news and magazines for you. Sales representatives can also be a wealth of information, not divulging names of who is doing what but sharing what is being done in a general sense. Keep a record of your findings.

One company's representatives, in an attempt to stand out from their competition, moved away from following their industry's overdone trend of showcasing scantily clad models next to their product at their major exhibition to pull customers in and moved to having models dressed in business suits, billing them as product specialists and making sure that they were well-informed on the product they were selling. Other companies are now following in their wake—combining beauty and brains with professionalism and personality—as a marketing tool to help sell their product. They are making sure to retain the same staff to travel with the show as it moves across North America to maintain the level of quality of the knowledge being provided to their consumers. They are positioning themselves as having elevated understanding of their potential customers' needs, and companies that are still using swimsuit-clad models to draw crowds are offering their clients a very visibly different experience. Now that a shift has taken place and others are following, it is time for someone to step up the design strategy game again and take it to a new level to once again drive business in their direction as they continue to set new industry standards.

Research

Research what other industries are doing. Event planning trade publications and trade shows are a wonderful place to begin. Magazines such as *Special Events* (www.specialevents.com) can be read online or through subscription and they will keep you on top of current and coming corporate entertaining trends. BiZBash (www.bizbash.com) is another example of a site you can visit to keep abreast of what other companies are doing, both in your industry and in others, from which a concept can be taken and adapted to your field.

A professional event planning company's clients could be your competition and many times, with their corporate clients' permission, their events are displayed in industry magazines, featured online and showcased in industry award-winning competitions. All these resources are available to you as a corporate client doing events and many of them can be accessed for free online.

Professional event planning associations also have educational seminars, trade shows and monthly meetings that members and guests can attend.[1] Hotels, venues and event planning suppliers are also an excellent basis of knowledge. While they will not tell you who has done what, they will share creative concepts with you that they feel could work in your industry. And it is acceptable to ask them if they have handled others in your industry and if any of your competition—kept nameless—will be in the same facility at the same time or immediately before or after.

Two major competitors were dismayed to find out that they had booked the exact same venue over the same time period. Both spent the week trying to make sure that neither side was able to have one of their staff members sneak into the other's meeting and product launch. The customers they had targeted were divided among the two camps. Both companies would have had a better chance of achieving maximum attendance had they not held their event during the same time period. It was a stressful period for all involved.

---

1   A list of top event planning publications, associations and resources can be found in *Marketing Your Event Planning Business* (Wiley, 2004).

In future, both companies made sure to ask about competing events before contracting and requested that notification of competition bookings be written into their terms and conditions, with the right to be able to move dates without penalty should competing events arise.

In some cases it pays to work with properties that are known to handle your industry (e.g., in the automotive industry, a property's ballroom doors must be wide enough for your product, and the property must be familiar with your specialized needs, etc.), but not over the same time period or even same year. And the same applies to all of your event elements. If your competition has staged a product launch featuring Cirque du Soleil–style performers, that is the last thing you want to repeat. You want to make sure that you do not follow in anyone else's footsteps within your own industry.

Innovate

Work with professional event planning suppliers and special effects experts who have a proven history in delivering outstanding results and can help you to design and deliver your vision. Remember that you are producing a live stage production and there are no second chances to get it right. Don't be afraid to try something imaginative that you know will delight your guests and help you to realize a return on your investment. Sometimes, this means breaking into new frontiers, such as space, but now, even that has been done in several different manners and by very different companies. If you are going to take on such a challenge, then you have to do it well and work with those who can help you create and pull off your vision.

Visualize

Always keep your objectives top of mind as you work your way through your event elements. Look at how each will serve to meet your goals and how you can layer them to produce better results. Visualize the business opportunities you can create through your business functions and always be prepared to be proactive and switch gears when it is critical to your company's future growth and success.

One fast-food company's representatives about to be hit with a less-than-flattering book and a movie coming out on their industry took immediate steps to use product launches and public relations as an offensive move to block any negative press and customer backlash. They had missed this critical visualization step when a movie came out addressing the same issues a couple of years earlier and at that time had not been as proactive as they might have been to circumvent loss of sales by introducing new products that would address the concerns of their newly informed customers.

Another company, number two in their industry, visualized how to become number one the minute its main competition announced a public apology for a product that was being recalled. Company executives did not waste any time before beginning to look at how they could use business functions to get the word out about their own product, address any safety concerns that customers of their main competitor would be having, and position themselves to step into being number one in their industry.

Visualize how changes in your company's product line or services can make news, and be brought to consumer attention through the media and business functions for maximum effect. For example, one car rental company now offers hopped-up classic cars to rent. They teamed up with a car manufacturer and together they launched their new venture at a major product launch event. Media coverage was extensive and effective, timed just at the beginning of spring. Desire was created for leisure car renters, as only five hundred of these models would exist for rent and none were available for sale in dealerships. And they had the perfect tie-in theme event for press conferences.

As you visualize your concept or your competitors', ask:

- What will this function say about the company to the consumer and to those attending?
- How will it help to sell the product, service, objective or message the company wants to convey?
- How will it meet the participants' needs and the company's requirements?

- Will it boost present averages and sales?
- Will it have a long-term reach that will produce results?
- How will it serve to attract new business?
- What are you bringing to the table that is new?
- How will holding this business function boost company image?
- What would be the perfect timing for maximum results?

Execute

Execute your event using everything in your arsenal. In business, creative thinking (right-brain thinking) is visual, and required in sales, marketing, research, business development and planning. Knowledge-based thinking or logistical thinking (left-brain thinking) is more linear and verbal and a major part of day-to-day business operations, customer service, execution and delivery.

The crafting of business functions and business entertaining to produce desired results requires mastery of both creative thinking and logistical thinking from the planning stages onward. Make a misstep at the beginning and you can create a domino effect that you may not be able to recover from. The quality of polish and professionalism displayed when executing your business functions will directly determine the level of return that you receive on your investment and affect to what degree your company objectives are met. Do not place your results and your reputation in jeopardy by placing responsibility and accountability in untrained and unskilled hands without proper preparation, guidance and direction. You will be setting yourself and your company up for failure.

One company's executives were publicly embarrassed after it was discovered the junior they had placed in charge of handling their biggest event of the year had booked the wrong person for their annual benefit gala. The company thought that they had booked a very sought-after A-list entertainer and had announced this with great fanfare. Invitations were printed and sent out, tickets sold, sponsors solicited and signed up...only for everyone involved and invited to find out that a person with a similar name had been booked—a D-list sports figure that no one had ever heard of. Monies had to be returned, the event cancelled and contract penalties paid. The company had found out about the error just days earlier when the media had tried to obtain an advance interview with the actual A-list celebrity, only to discover who had actually been booked.

Learn to create visibility. That includes wooing and welcoming the media at your event and making sure that they have everything that they need to help you achieve your company goals through exposure in the press. Here are a few key steps:

- Before you set out to shower the press about your event, know the message that you are looking to convey through your proposed business function.

- Learn who you need to be targeting in the media to cover your event and keep an up-to-date list of editors, writers, television and radio producers and other key industry players.

- Have professional press releases prepared that will have reader appeal for the media's target audience and be sure to keep the focus on the benefits of what you are doing, not on selling to the media or to their readers.

- Be on top of editorial calendars and make sure that your copy and any required photographs with names, positions and so on arrives at the publisher's on time, and always supply the media with correct spelling of names and titles.

- Become a source of information for the media and provide them with valuable news about your company, product or industry that their readers can use on an ongoing basis.

- Take the time to develop a long-lasting relationship.

- At your event—if they are invited to cover your function— treat the media with respect and assign a staff member to make sure that they are properly looked after.

- Decide in advance if you want to do a pre-event press conference, if you will be having the media take part in your event as an invited guest and how much access you want them to have unsupervised with your attendees—bearing in mind how your guests will feel about having the press around covering their every move. Work with the media to make sure that the photograph groupings that you want to showcase get taken, even if it means hiring your own professional photographer to cover your event so that you can have control and sign-off on which pictures are submitted for publishing.

As part of your competitive analysis, track the results both you and your competition are receiving in media play, who and where exposure is coming from and the results the media coverage has produced. Always bear in mind that while you are doing a competitive analysis of your rivals' business functions, they will be performing one on yours, as will your customers, both existing and potential, your employees, your suppliers, your industry peers and the media.

You want to do all possible to leave a lasting impression in everyone's minds so that they will be eager to attend your next business function and give you their full support. Each event that you do is the foundation for the next one. It is essential that you build a solid foundation by engaging and captivating your participants' attention and senses through creativity and following through with meticulous execution, because each event that you do speaks volumes about who you are as a company and how you conduct yourself in business.

Conclusion

Doing a competitive analysis will help you to track what works and what doesn't work in regards to event styles, event elements and how successfully they all came together. It is much better to read about your competitors' mishaps in the morning papers and learn from them as opposed to having your company's name splashed across the headlines as a prime example of what not to do. If you learn your competitor had run a particular style of event and had received unfavorable results, you could ensure you didn't make the same mistake.

Take the time to study not only the business sections of your newspapers but the social and entertainment sections as well. If you don't personally have the time to do this yourself, assign someone on the planning committee or hire a clipping service to keep you informed. And pay attention to the general public's perception. It can help guide you as you begin to design and produce your event for maximum results.

There are valuable lessons to be learned—and cognizant of—pre-event, during and post-event as you map out your next and future events. You can identify them easily when you use the D.R.I.V.E. creative design organizational process principles.

D Define

R Research

I   Innovate

V Visualize

E Execute

CHAPTER NINE

EXCEEDING EXPECTATIONS THROUGH EXECUTION

A RETURN ON INVESTMENT, OR ROI, is the value or the measure of the benefit a company receives for the money they spend doing business. But companies need to factor in more than financial expenditures when calculating an event's ROI, because time and energy are other major operating costs that should not be overlooked. Some events' ROIs will be immediate and you will see measurable financial or other met company objective returns. Other events' ROIs are intangible because you are planting future growth seeds, and they could take years to develop and mature.

Earning the Highest ROI

In order to receive the highest possible present and future ROI on your company's investment of money, time and energy, you want to do everything possible to ensure that you not only meet your participants' expectations but also exceed them. Uncommon efforts produce uncommon results. Produce a mediocre event and the mediocre results you get will end up being your ROI. Always remember that one of your event objective goals is to create a business function that is not only effective in the now but also is capable of delivering long-lasting and long-reaching benefits.

To strategically design a business function that will exceed expectations—both company and attendees'—and bring the highest return on the company's financial investment, company executives must learn to assess each event element and how it will work for and against them in meeting their company objectives. While business functions are a financial investment, the returns received in exchange come in many forms.

Choosing the wrong style of business function and sending the wrong message can impede components and a company's stature and growth. For example, one major New York newspaper reported that the dress code was strict at the two-day pajama party a real estate company threw for 75 of its executives at a mountain resort. Attendees had to wear pajamas and slippers and remain in their pj's for the course of their stay. The red flag that should have been raised at the planning stage for an event of this type is, does this corporate theme event cross the line by asking executives to attend wearing pajamas? Could they be leaving themselves open for sexual harassment or other lawsuits, such as over stress from being asked to do something against a personal belief? Attending a two-day meeting in your pj's may seem like fun to some, but to others (perhaps if they are married or in a serious committed relationship) it may be offensive and cause problems at home. The executives should have asked themselves:

- What company objective was being met by choosing this event theme?
- How does attending a meeting in pajamas and slippers bring about a return on our investment?
- Is there a better way to create a casual tone throughout the meeting?
- Would we be able to achieve what we want—and lessen any signs of suggestiveness—if we limited the pajamas and slippers to an optional pj, pizza and movie after-dinner event instead of strict pajama dress code enforcement for two days?

- If the press picks up the way we conduct this company event, will it hurt or help their company's reputation, and turn clients and potential customers on or off?

Every aspect of a business function needs to be addressed and questioned before contracting takes places. Every event element has an effect on the next, and in order to meet and exceed company objectives and receive a return on investment, each element must be carefully examined as to the role it will play and if it will add or detract from the message and return you are expecting.

It is important that corporate executives know how to analyze and accurately predict the outcome of a proposed business function and determine how many of their objectives it will, in fact, meet if it is structured as it is. Before moving forward with their specific event, they need to look at it objectively, as it is currently designed, before spending capital that may not be recovered. They must examine their event elements to see if they are laid out in a manner that will produce their desired results. There is a rhythm and a flow to events, and by mapping out your event elements on a grid you can clearly see if the event energy produced by your proposed inclusions—in the order they are scheduled to unfold—builds to a grand finale or sputters and burns out midway through, thereby limiting the return on company investment.

Visualizing your event and the emotional energy it will return from beginning to end will also help in the preparation of requests for proposals, as it will enable you to clearly convey your desired outcome from your participants' perspective as well as the company's.

Meeting and Exceeding Your Attendees' Emotional Needs

It is important to remember that going into any event, attendees are looking to be either (or a combination of two or all three of):

- educated
- enlightened
- entertained

And coming out, they are anticipating spending their time at something that was personally either one or a combination of two or all three of:

- meaningful
- memorable
- magical

As you are mapping your event elements and inclusions, keep asking if these emotional needs of your participants are being met. Identify the where, when and how, and then as you lay out your grid, carefully assess the peaks and valleys of the energy that will be received by your guests. Ideally, you are looking to build to a crescendo—the WOW factor—and then send them home on an emotional and energetic high. Skilled event designers and executives are able to physically feel the journey, through visualization, that they are about to take their guests on, and as they lay out their design grid, they feel exhausted or exhilarated at the end.

Events are live stage productions that are carefully designed to produce emotional responses—that fact should never be forgotten or left to chance. Emotion must be built into every event you do to give it energy and deliver a life experience, either personally or professionally, and a message that your guests will not soon forget. Otherwise your time, money and energy will have been ill-spent. Whatever is being conveyed to them has got to be wrapped in having their best interests, not just your company's, at heart. And if you cannot afford to do it right, you need to either revise your event design or move the date to a time where you can meet the expense required to do all possible to ensure the return you are hoping to achieve.

Event Element Considerations

The appendix contains a discussion of possible event elements. The elements can be adapted to both large and small events held locally, nationally or around the world. Understand that the same level of care, attention to detail and innovative creativity is required no matter the size, location or budget.

Take, for example, the event element of transportation. No matter where you are holding your event, whether it is a store location opening you are celebrating or an incentive trip halfway around the world, your attendees share in common that they have to get from point A to point B. Sometimes transportation will be included and other times attendees will be making their own way to the event, but your responsibility is to make sure that every detail has been attended to for their comfort and safety. You, not them, need to be thinking about transportation glitches that can occur. At every turn, if they encounter your foresight into making the experience of getting them to your door more pleasant for them, it will start their event experience off on the perfect note.

Sample local scenario:

Gala fundraising theater premiere followed by a hotel reception at a separate location scheduled to take place mid-week.

Transportation considerations:

- If couples are coming, there is a higher probability that they will be arriving in two cars as opposed to one than if we scheduled our event to take place on a weekend, as they could be coming from different locations, i.e., home or work. Can the local parking lot handle that number of cars?

- How far is the parking lot from the theater and will this pose a problem if the weather is inclement?

- How many attendants are on duty at that time of night and can they handle an influx of cars arriving at the same time?

- What time does the parking lot close and will this pose a problem if some guests leave their cars parked there and taxi to the reception, i.e., will they be able to access their cars or will the lot be locked by then?

Continued

- Is the area safe late at night?

- Is the parking lot well lit?

- Does the lot have any problems with vandalism, and should we hire additional security?

- Where is the next closest parking lot if this one is filled?

- How much is parking at the theater parking lot?

- How much is parking at the reception parking lot?

- How much parking is available at the reception area? Can it be reserved due to the location being trendy and our guests are not arriving until later?

- How much is a taxi ride from the theater to the reception area and back?

- Is parking an expense that we need to consider picking up so that our guests do not feel that they have their hands in their pockets the minute they arrive?

- How does the cost of picking up the parking compare to where we want our guests to be spending money? For us, it will mean finding a sponsor whose logo can be printed on parking passes and thanking them as a contributor in our program in order to enable our guests to spend their money on silent auction items.

- Do we need to consider getting a sponsor to pick up the cost for private motor coaches to shuttle guests between the theater and the reception so that guests are not inconvenienced by having to move their cars twice and potentially pay for parking twice?

- Will we require off-duty police at either location to direct traffic, since hundreds of cars will be arriving and departing at the same time at each location, and the reception location does not have a traffic light?

What you are producing is an outstanding live performance experience and a life experience that you want to produce outstanding results for you in return. Your role in this production is event designer, producer and director and you are responsible for staging your show event for success.

Sample national incentive travel scenerio:

Couples traveling across the U.S. and connecting in Chicago and Dallas.

   Airport transportation considerations:

- How many company and professional representatives should we have on hand at major gateway cities to welcome our guests, and ensure that all have arrived and encountered no problems at check-in or otherwise?

- How many professional representatives should we have on hand to oversee connecting flights in Chicago and Dallas to handle any difficulties with flight delays, make sure that our attendees do not face a situation of overbooking and being bumped from their flight, and help them with any difficulties they might experience in a busy airport at peak travel time?

In both sample scenarios, guest comfort, care and consideration are an important part of the event element of transportation and part of a company objective to show guests the company's attention to detail in all that it does.

Restraining Expenses Is Part of the Equation

Seek out suppliers who are open to negotiation and actively help you find creative ways to meet your budget objectives as well as your event objectives—they can contribute to the success of your events. Be up front with your suppliers regarding budget limitations. They need to know your budget in advance so they can adhere to it and look for ways they can bring costs down. They can work with you to design the core elements your event requires to be successful, stand on its own and stay within allocated funds.

It is important to remember, when looking for cost-saving, budget-conscious ideas, that every single aspect of the event you are planning should be reviewed. In order to assess which areas offer the most cost-saving possibilities, you must first look at the overall event components and work through them one by one. Look for areas where a supplier may have profit margins that will allow them to maneuver and be open to negotiation.

If you encounter an event element where the revenue will not allow for flexibility, determine if there are cost-saving areas from a secondary source. For example, a hotel may not be able to greatly lower their guestroom rate but they may be able to change a net rate to a commissionable one or include breakfast daily, offer a welcome and farewell cocktail reception or waive health club charges using funds from one of their other budgets.

Always be on the lookout for new ways to reduce costs so that you can effectively bring about your desired results and maximize the return on dollars being spent. Remember that a little saving here and there, in each event element area, can quickly add up based on the number of guests. These savings can help to bring your budget in line and help you to meet your financial expectations and your guests' expectations in producing and executing an outstanding business function.

If you meet your guests' event expectations—whether the event is pure business or business social—in terms of caliber and style, content delivery and their emotional contentment (how well they perceive that you have anticipated and met their event, personal and professional needs), you will have strongly positioned yourself to reap rewards on the return on your company's investment of time, money and energy spent. If your guests leave on an emotional energy high, they will be taking with them the feeling of having totally connected with your event and your company. A business function successfully designed and executed, targeted to the senses and to bring about specific company objectives will produce long-lasting, meaningful memories for your guests and work well into the future to bring desired results back to you and your company.

Conclusion

In order to receive the highest possible present and future return on your company's investment of money, time and energy, do everything you can to ensure that you not only meet your participants' expectations but also exceed them. And in order to strategically design a business function that will exceed expectations—both company and attendees'—and bring the highest return on the company's financial investment, company executives must learn to assess each event element and how it will work for and against them in meeting their company objectives.

Remember that at any event you hold, attendees are looking to be:

- educated
- enlightened
- entertained

And they are anticipating spending their time at something that is:

- meaningful
- memorable
- magical

There are several elements common to both large and small events held locally, nationally or around the world, including arrival, dinner and departure. Understand that the same level of care, attention to detail and innovative creativity is required no matter the size, location or budget.

CHAPTER TEN

ESTABLISHING CODES OF CONDUCT AND SETTING COMPANY STANDARDS

CORPORATE BOARDS AND CHIEF executives are now seeing how company scandals played out in the headlines can estrange customers, sink stock prices and end careers in a matter of minutes. And many of the transgressions that have been made public have been linked to corporate events and business entertaining. For example, the recent firing of a married CEO of a major airline manufacturer came about because of an affair with another company executive that began at a corporate meeting in Palm Springs. The fact that the company asked the CEO to resign—and accepted the subsequent resignation of his partner—became national news. This took place after the CEO was brought in to replace another resigning CEO who was being charged with a contracting disgrace that went on under his watch. The contracting scandal cost the company a $27 billion contract, resulted in jail time for the CEO and had an impact on the company's business reputation. The second scandal in the press was a double whammy the company needed to rebound from. Their subsequent actions showed that displaying a lapse of business judgment in any form, which could impair an executive's ability to lead the company or its employees, would no longer be condoned, and the company wanted the world to know it.

Today, with the advent of cell phones that can capture every action and word, you never know when the world is watching, listening or recording. Inappropriate behavior ends up flashed on the Internet and making headlines globally at warp speed. For example, at a G8 conference, President George W. Bush gave a spur-of-the-moment backrub to German Chancellor Angela Merkel. This, and the Chancellor's startled reaction—with her hands thrown up in the air—was posted on YouTube (www.youtube.com) and became one of the most popular clips on the Web. The President's actions then became the main topic of what is and is not appropriate etiquette for world leaders. And this was not an isolated incident captured at one event. President Bush's use of a profanity at the same summit, caught both on film and audio, was also transmitted around the world. It can happen to anyone, anywhere, even at an event such as the G8 surrounded by the utmost of protocol and with a team of experts in charge of making sure that microphones are turned off during casual moments. A slip of the tongue, an inappropriately placed hand or undesirable behavior can easily become a company's undoing. It is important to put policies and procedures in place to safeguard personal, professional and company reputations.

Company policies regarding employee conduct attending company, industry or professional functions—business and social—must be mandated, formally presented and carried out. It is also important when hosting company events to clearly define your company employees' business function hosting responsibilities and assign them. The role that corporate executives should be playing at business functions should be outlined as well. There is a time to be shown rolling up your sleeves and pitching in and a time to step back and manage what is taking place. Knowing when, where and why to step into a designated role is imperative. For example, it should not be hired event planning staff that greet your guests on arrival. Yes, they should handle the registration desk, but they should not meet and welcome your guests. As a matter of good business protocol and business etiquette, a senior company executive should be on hand to welcome attendees to your function.

Your employees and hired suppliers need to be familiar with your company standards and expected codes of conduct from them and your attendees. Formal guidelines need to be established and a policy reviewed with your company lawyers to make sure that you have not left yourself or the company at risk. The policy should include how to handle emergency situations, such as if your staff can, legally or not, physically lay a hand on another employee or guest should they spiral out of control from too much overindulgence. And what is the company's legal responsibility if someone has too much to drink during an event? Are they responsible for making sure that the guest gets safely back to their room? Are they putting themselves at legal risk if they step into the room with the inebriated guest to make sure that they safely make it to the bed? Or to protect themselves, should they always have another company person with them so that they are never left alone with the guest? Does the company have a responsibility to make sure that the guest is okay and have someone from their staff or hotel staff sit with them or check in on them? Employees and hired staff need to know exactly where you stand on legal matters and how they should conduct themselves.

One sales meeting included a car rally as a team-building event. The sales force was young, very competitive and all male. Because of the nature of the event and the participants, the company did not provide alcoholic drinks during the rally or over lunch—they were only made available at the clock-in party. But at checkpoints it became obvious that several of the participants had been enjoying liquid refreshments, as spirits were becoming extremely high.

One of the stops along the way was at a small laundromat, where they were to find a clue. As part of the rally, teams were being awarded prizes for creative photojournalist pictures tied into clues, and a team decided this location would be a perfect picture opportunity. They decided to strip naked and pose behind boxes of detergent and in the machines. This was not a checkpoint, so no staff was on hand to monitor guest behavior, and the poor girl on staff at the laundry was ill-prepared to handle the out-of-control actions of the group when they descended on her shop. She had been pre-warned by her store manager that teams would be coming by, but had no idea they would be stripping off their clothes in front of her and customers.

Their antics were laughed off by company executives, pleased that their sales force was having a good time, and adopted an attitude of "boys will be boys." Later in the week, this same group of "boys" were stopped by hotel security as they were trying to put bubble bath in the hotel's fountains and swimming pools, and later trying to rent chainsaws in town in order to rearrange the resort's landscape because the hotel stopped them from having their fun with the fountains. Luckily, the local hardware store where they tried to rent the chainsaws alerted the hotel security and they were waiting for them when they returned. In this case, the company was aware of bad guest behavior and had done nothing to stop it. Had damage been done to the resort property, the company would have been held responsible. The laundromat employee and/or customers using the facility could have laid sexual harassment charges, especially if there were any underage children present or a teen employee was on duty. The cost of having someone stationed at a clue point or monitoring the route would have been minimal compared to a lawsuit.

Accidents can and do happen at events. Deaths happen as well. On one European incentive program, participants were given their dream cars to drive themselves from point to point. One car crashed and a death resulted. Companies need to think carefully about how they structure their programs, the liability they leave themselves open to and what they need to do to prepare their staff to handle any crisis situation, such as a death taking place during an event out of country, or even something such as an emergency operation being required.

When time is of the essence, employees need to know who to turn to, what their role is and how you want them to respond to any given situation. On-site codes of conduct need to be discussed in advance. For example, are employees allowed to drink on their own time? Or is no drinking permitted because staff that are assigned to work the event need to be available 24/7 in case they are needed to handle a critical situation?

Codes of conduct—expected and accepted behavior—from employees, hired staff, suppliers and guests should be set and discussed with all involved going into an event, and company lawyers should be apprised so that they can give their input. Your company employees and your hired event planning staff must know in advance how you want worst-case scenarios handled. The time to work out a plan of action is in advance. The ABCs of event planning (A—anticipation, B—backup and C—crisis management mode) and codes of conduct must be in place.

When Your Guests or Employees Spiral Out of Control

At corporate events, the line between proper business behavior and pursuit of personal pleasure can often become blurred, with caution being thrown out the window after a couple of drinks.

One company executive was literally sent packing—fired on the spot, moved out of the hotel the group was staying in and put on the first flight home the next day—when his drinking got out of control at an event and he tried to physically attack one of the senior VPs and push him through a window. The out-of-control guest was tackled by coworkers, restrained and taken away by local authorities.

The assault came seemingly out of nowhere, but the event planning staff on hand were poised and prepared to quickly take charge once it happened. They worked with their client to make sure that what the client's company lawyers required from a legal standpoint was carried out. They did not want the person being fired to be placed in an out-of-country jail, but they did want him removed from the hotel property and moved to another location. The hired security held the guest in custody until the hotel security had packed his room and moved him to another location. His partner was given the option of moving with him or staying at the hotel in another room and having their name taken off the hotel list so that they would not be harassed during the night. The fired employee was then escorted to the new hotel and his partner back to their old hotel.

Arrangements were made to have the employee fly back the next morning, but the flight that was selected was the flight that had a connecting flight the furthest from the destination so that the employee could not get off the plane, rent a car and return. Staff were also in touch with company lawyers so that they were kept apprised of the situation and made sure that they were doing all that they needed to in the way that they needed to. The hotel security team were also instructed to keep the now ex-employee from returning to the hotel. During the course of the evening, events did escalate when the ex-employee began calling the hotel and threatening to commit suicide, but all was handled and resolved in a peaceful manner.

The airlines were alerted to have security standing by in case of any behavior problems at the airport the next day and were given clear instructions regarding the airline ticket that the company had purchased for the ex-employee to return home on to ensure that the routing was not changed and so forth.

A company employee or their invited guest being fired or reprimanded for displaying inappropriate behavior is not uncommon and is not limited to staff. Even senior company executives can get caught up in the moment. A crew of top senior-level executives, after a romp in the desert on ATVs and a BBQ lunch with plenty of liquid fuel, decided to commandeer their "return private transportation to the hotel by motor coach" and drive across the border to continue their party in Mexico, which was in driving distance from where their afternoon excursion was being held in Arizona. The staff member, who lost control of the event and the company's top executives she was overseeing (and the motor coach driver), was reduced to tears and refused to board the bus, so the guests set off without her on board for a night of revelry. The motor coach was not insured to go into Mexico and was only contracted and covered to go from point to point. Had anything serious happened en route, the company would have been left financially responsible.

It is extremely important to be fully prepared for any kind of behavior at any event. The best way to be prepared is to know your audience, understand the scope of the event, and brief your staff—in-house and hired—accordingly. You must make sure that the staff understands the audience and the event as much as possible. You want them to respect the people and the event and not just use one mind-set when judging behavior. You don't want to ruin anyone's fun, but you do want to make sure that everyone is safe. The more information you can give to people, the better prepared everyone is for any outcome.

You need to ensure that your guests also come to the event with an understanding of the event. If appropriate, clearly communicate to all staff and guests any corporate policies regarding behavior expectations. They need to be aware of what is viewed as inappropriate with regards to your internal business code of conduct and what is allowed by the venue. Your staff needs to know how to properly handle any situation that will arise—through company directives and guidelines—and your attendees should understand in advance what behavior is expected of them.

Today, companies must prepare staff on what to expect and how to handle the unexpected with business finesse, as well as legal responsibility and accountability. There are very strict liquor and other laws in place that impact events, and liability repercussions extend beyond principal companies such as the venue, client and suppliers; individuals can be held personally accountable as well. For example, an employee who was asked to drive a guest home from an event was involved in an accident, and both the employee and the company he worked for ended up being sued. In another instance, the company that constructed a deck that collapsed at a venue is being sued for personal injuries, as are the building management and party host for allowing the deck to be filled beyond capacity.

Make sure your staff working the event know, before your event begins, what is acceptable and unacceptable behavior from staff, suppliers and guests. Educate them on the warning signs that a guest may be getting out of hand and provide them in writing with a process to follow if this scenario does occur. Should they intervene directly or wait for assistance? Who should they contact? What is an appropriate method of handling the situation? Discussing these issues in advance and reaching agreement on them is an important part of the planning process. Having a disorderly guest policy or procedure allows everyone to act quickly and cohesively to ensure that any disruption is minimized for the remainder of your attendees. It also protects you legally by demonstrating that you'd planned to mitigate the risks to your guests, venue and other interested parties.

In the matter of handling with business finesse any guests gone wild, there is also the aspect of saving face and reputations to consider. Company employees on a site inspection had to deal with one of their company heads becoming drunk and incapacitated before midday. They put him to bed but were directed by their head office not to embarrass their company head by calling in hotel staff or doctors to help and to stay with him, as the individual was becoming physically ill. The head office wanted the employees to watch over the top executive and assist with any cleanup that was necessary. Part of the job? Above and beyond duty? Or were the employees putting themselves and their company at personal and professional legal risk? Consider the legal ramifications if the company head suffered serious complications, for example, he slipped and injured himself on his way to or from the bathroom, or choked or suffered from alcohol poisoning, and appropriate assistance is not given in an attempt to cover up bad behavior.

Prepare your staff in advance for contingencies. Discuss potential difficulties with all your "front line" staff and make sure they know who to go to in an emergency and how to make sure that they and others are not placed in any jeopardy.

Frequently the out-of-control difficulty is inappropriate sexual behavior. Staff running events are often targets of innuendo, flagrant passes, harmless flirting and occasionally physical touching. Staff—both the women and men—should be advised not to go for drinks alone with another individual and to be very careful about meeting anyone in their hotel rooms.

It is essential that staff assigned to handle your event are capable of maintaining their cool when handling disorderly guests. It is important for them to remain emotionally distant and to not get heatedly engaged. Everyone around them depends on calm and effective lead. The ultimate goal for all concerned is prompt and pleasant resolution.

It is also important that you act swiftly for credibility and results on behalf of the corporation and your guests. Your most important resources are the skills and commitment of your team, so designate specific people who are authorized to respond. The key is to exercise due diligence to be sure that your team is competent and prepared if something goes wrong.

You are obligated to have valid insurance coverage and be very aware of legal issues. You do not want to be found culpable for someone else's behavior or negligence. With liability laws, you need to ensure that all involved are very aware of proper procedure and handling.

Stay alert. Be prepared and aware of what is going on with your people attending the event. Trust your instincts. Don't wait for trouble to happen—act before it does. Take troublesome individuals aside, but not on your own, and do not discuss (if possible) their unacceptable behavior in front of others.

Ensure that your suppliers understand that they are your eyes and ears at the event. Let them know that they are to tell you if they notice anything untoward. Make sure that the bar staff are empowered and will limit any alcohol intake if need be, as well as let you know if someone is overindulging excessively.

Once an offending party has been removed from the scene of the party, the responsibility does not stop there. It may be necessary to make sure that the guest is not re-admitted, provide hotel rooms if appropriate to the event or provide alternative forms of transportation to and from the event—taxi chit, shuttle services, designated drivers—and know the legal implications of each option.

Never send a staff member out alone to handle any problem areas. You want to ensure their safety, and witnesses may be required.

Always provide backup and enlist the services of site security as well as your own. Discuss possibilities with your legal department to make sure what you are doing is in the best interests of the impaired guest, the individuals involved, and all companies involved.

ABC (Anticipation, Backup, Crisis Management Mode) Checklist

✔ Have a written policy on dealing with unruly participants and communicate it to all staff, volunteers and suppliers in advance of your event.

✔ Outline an alcohol control policy and assign a specific person to monitor consumption at all events. Controlling alcohol in many cases controls disruptive behavior. Hire washroom attendants to ensure that drugs and even sex do not become a part of the mix.

✔ Anticipate controversial or emotionally charged topics or issues included in your meeting or event that might result in disruptive behavior, and plan for staffing and security appropriately.

✔ Discuss the possibility of disruptive behavior and reach agreement on appropriate actions to be taken, up to and including the removal of participants from the event or legal action. Communicate clearly the type of audience and event to everyone working the event.

✔ Establish everyone's respective role in handling an out-of-control situation. Prepare staff in advance on company and client procedures for when they must handle an out-of-control guest.

✔ Make sure your staff know key contact people to go to who are familiar with potentially troublesome people/situations for additional insights on possible issues, for example, emotional instability, alcohol problems, illegal drugs and so on.

✔ Make sure that event staff do not drink at the event or even on a night off. They need to always be prepared to be on call to handle the unexpected.

✔ Know liability laws and legal issues you may have to deal with.

Guest Safety

Company executives planning events cannot afford to be lax in areas that can have serious legal, personal and professional ramifications to themselves, their company, employees, attendees and guests. It is important to ask to see and receive copies of all required licenses and permits that your contracted suppliers are obtaining on your behalf and to ensure that they have, in fact, been actioned and are up to date. The same applies to supplier insurance that may be required. Always check that the venues you are using are up to safety code and licensed, and don't just take someone's word for it. Ask to see written proof. Your guests' safety depends on it. And never exceed room or venue capacity—it is in place for a reason. If you violate it and an accident occurs, you, your company, your client and your suppliers could be held accountable.

In today's litigious society, corporations and individuals are being held liable for company indiscretions and failure to adhere to social host legal responsibilities. Making certain that guest safety and security needs have been addressed is an essential event planning element that no one can afford to overlook—and this applies equally to guests simply attending a business function at a venue, during their hotel stay and taking part in group activities. In recent headlines, deaths have occurred in venues due to fires, people have died or been seriously injured while taking part in group activities and team-building events, murders have been committed in resort destinations, people have disappeared without a trace while staying abroad at top hotels and onboard cruise ships, and guests have been charged with raping staff that are in their hotel rooms. Concerns over guest safety are being raised by both attendees and those hosting events around the world.

The venues, event planners and suppliers you choose to use must be proficient in this area so that you can put your participants' minds at rest. They need to know that all possible has been done to not only create a memorable event and stay but one that will have been designed with their safety and security in mind, regardless of whether they are in their hotel guestroom, attending a function at the hotel or chosen venue, taking part in a scheduled activity or out and about on their own in a recommended event location.

Company executives should ensure that their venue and suppliers have a solid crisis response plan with regards to guest safety that covers key emergency situations, and that all the staff are trained to execute on this plan. Ensure you are given a key contact list for both external and internal contacts. The external list should include the closest hospital, walk-in clinic, police station, and possibly a store or shopping mall for any last-minute supplies. The internal contact list should include hotel key contacts that can quickly act on the needs of the guest. A 24-hour emergency contact number should be clearly identified, with the names and extensions clearly noted. Have a floor plan that generally identifies the room assignments, elevators and emergency exits and ensure the hotel representative walks these areas with the person overseeing your event so that the layout is clear. It is important to ask the size of the security team and whether or not they operate on a 24-hour schedule. Also, question whether or not the hotel or venue has a fully integrated fire safety plan.

If there is no documented emergency plan or general security procedures in place, this red flag will tip off decision-makers and tell you that personal guest safety/event security is not a major priority of a hotel or off-property venue you are considering. Confirm basic hotel safety and security procedures; for example, callers must identify the guest's name prior to being transferred to a room, and providing only a room number is not acceptable. Should a guest lock themselves out of their room, what are the requirements to allow them room access? Do they require that the guest present picture ID to gain access? If a special name for a group is provided for safety reasons, but the hotel does not use the name, instead referring to the public name, that is another red-flag tip-off that security measures are lax.

Should company executives make the wrong choice and fail to deliver what their participants are seeking from a guest safety and security standpoint, their and their company's professional reputation may be put on the firing line. If the event they are in charge of putting their guests' well-being at jeopardy, companies can no longer plead ignorance to judges if they end up on trial. Bringing guest safety and security red-flag areas of concern to the executive level—documenting and if necessary obtaining sign-off from the company's signing officers, lawyers and insurance company—is a must in today's litigious society, where corporations and individuals are being held liable for a company's failure to adhere to social host legal responsibilities and demonstrating duty of care when it comes to providing guest safety and security.

Codes of Conduct

Codes of conduct can encompass many things. They are not limited to how to behave in public, what to wear, and what can and cannot be said to a supplier, client or guest, which are all essential elements to address when defining company standards.

It is important to communicate what is right and what is not in all areas from proper dress to business decorum, whether your staff are attending your event as a guest, are attending an industry or professional event or helping to host a company event. One common problem at events is employee and supplier dress code and appearance. Another is making sure that employees, suppliers and entertainment understand your meal and beverage standards, for example, that meals need to be taken discreetly and always away from the guest and never interfere with the program delivery, no drinking while on duty and so forth. One company had a strict rule of "family eats last"—family being company employees.

Another area is on-site conduct. Emotions and stress must always be kept under control in public during an event, and it is imperative that the behavior displayed and the way in which you deal with issues is reflective of your company culture and values. Codes of conduct need to be established for events both in and out of the office.

One major newspaper made a major business faux pas with Asian-Americans after publishing what readers said was a racial slur on its front page. The offending headline "Wok This Way" was a word play on "walk this way" and the traditional Chinese sauté pan, and ran with a photo of President Bush tugging at the sleeve of Chinese President Hu Jintao at a White House event. It was billed as a clumsy, offensive attempt at humor and did not display the respect that the occasion warranted. But this example shows us again how inappropriate actions, such as tugging on a dignitary's sleeve to pull them in the direction you want them to go, are a poor way to handle a situation.

Unfortunately, that was not the only business breach of etiquette that was displayed during this event. The meeting between the American and Chinese presidents began with a business protocol blunder about a sensitive issue when an announcer used the wrong name for the country, referring to China by the formal name for Taiwan in association with the country's national anthem, billing it as the national anthem of the Republic of China (the formal name of the island 100 miles off the mainland) as opposed to what China is known formally as: "the People's Republic of China."

Human error happens but safeguards should be in place to make sure all possible is done up front to avoid it. If it does happen, those who have been affected will be watching to see how it is being handled and what is being done to make amends. This is what happened when a new cruise ship tilted without warning and 240 people were injured, with 116 being treated in hospitals. The findings were "human error" and letters of apology went out to all passengers. For some that may have been enough, but for others it may not have been. Human error can cost a company future business, set them up for lawsuits and have customers lose confidence in how a company trains their employees.

You want your company employees and staff, and suppliers you hire to work your events to present a poised, polished and professional reflection of your company image no matter what is taking place around them. An incentive group or company meeting could easily have been being held on this ship when the accident took place and your participants would have turned to your staff for calm direction. It is important to take the time to train your staff as to what you expect from them. Achieving your highest level of return on your investment is dependent on meeting and exceeding your guests' expectation in all areas.

One hotel invested in having their front-line staff trained by an artistic ballet director to teach them how to open doors and present keys and luggage with style and finesse. This is a company taking that extra step in bringing the ordinary to the next level. And if the attention to detail is that careful on the small things, it serves to put customers' minds at rest that any event they are holding at the property is going to receive the best of care, as will guests attending the event.

While not all events that companies orchestrate are televised or written up in the news—with an employee's bad behavior, poor judgment or lack of preparation flashed around the world in a matter of minutes—inappropriate company comportment can still become industry news, whether it takes place in the office or in a public arena in front of colleagues, suppliers, clients and guests, and can have a profound effect on your business and your personal and professional reputation. As you conduct day-to-day business, others will be watching for examples of acts of grace under fire and determining, if a breach of conduct has occurred, how it was handled and whether or not it put them or their company at business risk. Your clients are looking to see whether or not the company they are considering doing business with has codes of conduct safeguards in place or if its staff exhibit a lack of company standards, with unacceptable codes of conduct and professional lines being crossed. The line they draw may be deciding not to do business with you.

The Value of Outlining Expectations

Many companies, busy dealing with pressing day-to-day issues, have not taken the time to set out company responsibilities and office policies and procedures, let alone review or update them. Today, that is no longer acceptable and more and more companies have discovered the value of clearly outlining their expectations and setting company standards to move their companies forward.

In order to have a lasting benefit and bring about positive change, codes of conduct and company expectations must be established, clearly outlined and reviewed. When setting up company guidelines and standards, it is important to set them in writing, review them with staff and have them signed off, as it is vital to have this framework to fall back on in case of violation. Having clearly defined codes of conduct lessens the margin for misinterpretation with all parties involved.

In today's economic climate, companies and customers are all looking closely at who they choose to do business with, as they know it could reflect directly back on them and their business and put their professionalism in jeopardy. Knowing that a company has codes of conduct in place and that their employees are well versed in proper correctness is crucially important today. When things go spiraling out of control, guests want to be secure in the knowledge that the people around them are skilled at keeping it together under pressure, that rude and discourteous behavior is not permitted and that those responsible for overseeing their well-being are well trained and know the expected code of conduct in any circumstance.

Areas to Consider When Setting Up Codes of Conduct

Your company's employees reflect your company's standards and image in all they say and do—consistency is important. Areas to be reviewed and polices and procedures to set up include:

- *basic in office procedures*
  - ✔ How telephones are supposed to be answered, for example, answered before how many rings; company greeting when answering the telephone; company policy on returning calls to customers, for example, within 24 hours; how clients are to be addressed—Mr., Mrs., Ms.—or is first-name basis permitted; level of familiarity with customers, such as banter, jokes and so on.
  - ✔ What is and is not permitted to be displayed on desks, in cubicles or as computer screensavers.

✔ Company rules with regards to use of the Internet during the business day, for example, blocked sites, personal use time, company IT monitoring policy and so forth.

✔ Company templates and standards for all business correspondence, for example, e-mails, letters.

✔ Company policy regarding personal telephone calls and personal e-mails.

✔ General comportment, for example, eating at desks, listening to music while working, gathering to talk in main work areas (disturbing others around them) and so on.

• *dress codes—in office, client meetings, supplier meetings, on site (on duty and off duty)*

✔ Is casual dress permitted in the office on a regular basis? If so, clearly define casual dress. For example, are flip flops allowed or just dress sandals? Shorts or capri pants during summer months, or should all pants be down to the ankle? Will belly shirts or low-rider jeans or pants be acceptable?

✔ Specific dress policy for client and supplier meetings, both in and out of the office. For example, will jackets or long-sleeve shirts be required for men, or will covered legs or skirts worn to a certain length be required for women?

✔ Required dress code for attending and working company events.

✔ Expected dress code during leisure time on hosted company events or when attending events as a representative of the company. For example, if the hotel or resort has a pool, will thongs or other revealing casual wear be permitted to be worn?

• *site inspection accepted behavior*

✔ The responsibilities as a representative of the company, for example, some employees on site inspections forget that it is a business trip and not a paid vacation.

✔ Both on- and off-duty expected behavior.

- *on-site guest and supplier interaction*
  ✔ Firm boundaries. Is employee and guest/supplier interaction to be professional at all times? For example, some events may include dancing. Are employees permitted to dance with the guests if asked? On their off time on location, are employees allowed to date guests should a personal relationship or attraction take place? Are employees allowed in guests' hotel rooms, and vice versa?

- *per diems/meals on site/expense reports*
  ✔ What is and is not covered on a business trip, whether working the event or attending an event as a company representative? For example, mini bar charges, in-room movies, personal calls home when out of town.
  ✔ If the company has a set policy with regards to a maximum dollar amount for breakfast, lunch and dinner.
  ✔ Policy regarding the consumption of alcoholic beverages during meals and the ability of these costs to be billed back.
  ✔ The requirement to keep receipts.

- *drinking (on site, professional events, client meetings, site inspections)*
  ✔ The number of alcoholic drinks permitted during meals.
  ✔ How to report drunk behavior.
  ✔ Detailed consequences should employees overindulge when attending a business event in the capacity of a company representative.

- *company expectations*
  ✔ Company image and professional standards, including business ethics as well as expected business etiquette. For

example, is there a company ruling on accepting gifts from suppliers looking to do business with your company?

- *company confidentiality*
  - ✔ What is and is not off limits to talk about to coworkers, industry peers, customers, suppliers and so on?

- *guest confidentiality*
  - ✔ What is and is not off limits to talk about to coworkers, industry peers, customers, suppliers and so on?

- *appropriate language*
  - ✔ The company policy on swearing. Develop guidelines for employees both when in the office and when away on company business.

- *appropriate comportment*
  - ✔ What is and is not acceptable behavior in office and out of office?
  - ✔ Any consequences should they cross any company lines, such as when during one out-of-country event, guests decided to hold a moonlight nude pool party at the resort they were staying at and one company employee decided to join them in their antics.

Conclusion

Company-endorsed codes of conduct and company standards need to be clearly defined and firmly established. There must be no room left for misunderstandings, misinterpretation or misbehavior. Your colleagues, employees, suppliers and clients will be watching to see how your company conducts business and how individuals are comporting themselves and interacting with others in and out of the office, during company events and when acting as a company representative. When setting company codes of conduct and company standards, it is time for "plain speak," ensuring that there is no room for confusion. How your employees act and react at business functions put on by your company and at events where they act as company representatives can affect the level of return that you receive on your investment, reflect back on the company and impact company growth.

CHAPTER ELEVEN

TRACKING AND ANALYSING YOUR RESULTS

WHILE THE REASONS FOR HAVING particular corporate events, event styles and structures may vary from business to business and industry to industry, corporate business functions done right can help fast-track a company's business growth and success no matter what its size. As a business grows in size and stature, so does its need for corporate events.

An important step in being able to predict which type of corporate functions will best meet future company objectives and to build in event elements that have a proven history of producing powerful returns on your investment is to evaluate your present business function and prepare an executive event summary at the same time that final event review and reconciliation is taking place.

Preparing an executive event summary will serve to create a company business function history, enable you to measure the benefit of past business functions and help you to design effective future corporate events with ease and efficiency. You need to be able to access the final reconciliation of dollars and cents that were spent and determine if what was spent made sense. While your participants should not be able to put a price tag on their experience, you are in a position to do so and judge both the value of your endeavor immediately after your event and the impact on sales activity, financial returns and performance six months, one year and so on, down the road. If you do not prepare both—a final reconciliation and an executive event summary that is updated as the year goes on—you will not have a way of measuring your return and foreseeing future outcomes.

What typically happens post-event is that a final financial reconciliation is prepared by each of your suppliers or compiled by your event planning company if you are using one. This is reviewed, paid and then packed away with all the other related material in a "dead file," never to be opened, read or referred to again. All that is discussed post-event is not recorded and lessons learned and insight gleaned is forgotten. And in some cases, companies that are working directly with suppliers miss another very important step—assembling a master final reconciliation budget that includes all expenditures and compares projected costs against final expenditures. That can be a very costly mistake. A year or more can pass before doing the same type of event again and people that worked on the project may have come and gone, taking with them all the knowledge that was acquired. Many company executives find themselves back at square one, encountering the same learning curves all over again.

An executive event summary should be started when your initial request for proposal is going out and you are setting company event objectives so that you can capture all of your goals—monetary and otherwise. It should be updated at final reconciliation post-event when your executive event review takes place, but it should not stop there.

Measures for post-event tracking should be put into place and your executive event summary updated at scheduled times to see if long-term objectives as well as short-term goals were met. And to make this as easy as possible, a company executive event summary reference manual or binder should be set up so that all department heads can benefit from what has taken place and see the results produced from past events.

Don't make the fatal error of forgetting about your event summary once it's completed. If you file your executive event summary away in your "dead files," that is where it and all the valuable analytical data and planning information it contains will remain.

Your executive event summary should include the following information:

- *date planning commenced*

Timing is everything when it comes to successful execution. Note the time that planning for the event started and if there were any unforeseen problems that slowed down the planning process, for example, planning started over the summer months but follow-up was delayed because many of the committee members were away on vacation at the time, or because a major sales promotion divided your attention and insufficient time was allotted to handle the demanding needs of both. If, in the end, things ran down to the wire, note that "x" more weeks of preparation would have better served the event.

- *date of event*

Discuss how the selected date worked for or against your event. Was attendance minimized in any way by your choice of the day of the week, the time of day, or the season the event took place?

- *assessment as to whether or not sufficient time and manpower was allocated for successful event execution*

Could the committee have used more members? Were there times that additional hands would have been a benefit, and if so, when were they? Was your event handled entirely in-house or did the company bring in professional help? Capture as much as possible of how the planning and operating of your company event affected all who were involved in primary work responsibilities. It is important to know for future events exactly how the event planning affected internal staff loads and projects.

- *type of event*

Identify the type and style of event that you chose to use to meet your targeted company objectives. Rate the success level of your event. How was the feedback from those who attended? What were the measurable results on present and future business? Be sure to address the issue of whether or not you would recommend this type of event again as a fit for both your company and your attendees, and explain why.

- *number of participants*

It is important to track not only the number of guests that attended your event but how this final number compared to your original projected guest number. If numbers were down, include your reasoning as to why. If numbers were up, note what this could have been attributed to. Another important area to note underparticipation in would be guest demographics—who attended your event, for example, age group, sex—and list any observations about likes and dislikes. For example, the group was mainly seniors and many left early because insufficient seating was on hand. A stand-up reception was not the right fit for this guest list. Also pay attention as to whether or not your event was attended by your A-list of preferred guests or if you had to reach into your B-list to fill up the guaranteed numbers. If you did not get your desired targeted audience to come out, be sure to include your findings as to what would have better served to draw them to your event.

- *event day-by-day overview/grid*

Provide a history in the form of a grid and include days required for move in, setup, rehearsals, event, teardown and move out so that you can reference your time and space requirements for your next event.

- *proposed budget*

Keep a copy of your initial proposed budget and event inclusions with your final reconciliation.

- *contracted budget*

A copy of your contracted budget should be available, as well. What would be of great future value is to include—while the event is still fresh in everyone's minds—any major changes from your proposed plans to your contracted plans and why the decision was made to amend or enhance your proposal. Include your reasoning as to why changes were made, because this will give you added insight when it comes to planning a similar style event.

- *final reconciliation figures (attach copy of the final reconciliation to the report for easy reference of inclusions, costs, venues and suppliers)*

Note differences between your contracted budget and final reconciliation. Look closely at your suppliers' final charges. Did you have any surprises? Start to compile your own master preferred event supplier list, one that is available to the company as a whole, and include your findings. Did the supplier deliver more than expected? Is the supplier one that you would strongly advise working with on future projects? Are there any suppliers that you would recommend that your company not do business with?

- *cost analysis, for example, did spending stay on track with the original budget, and if not, why did spending increase/decrease?*

It is important to prepare a critical cost analysis and understand why and where costs increased and decreased and where dollars spent would have made better sense—while all who were involved are still in place and when details are clear. Also include what you would do differently if you had the chance to do it all over again. For example, would an event element you took out have been a winner if you had proceeded as you originally had planned?

- *assessment as to whether or not funding was sufficient to bring about desired results and return on investment*

Did you go four stars when five stars was required to bring about a higher return on your event investment? Upon reflection, was the cost of not doing something that was deemed too expensive too costly? Did you make your event about dollars and cents, not dollars being spent making sense? Were there areas of spending that delivered no return on investment?

- *proposed event objectives laid out in priority order*

Include a list of all of your proposed event objectives in priority order and note which ones were realized. Did you meet all of your objectives? Just your top objectives? Only your bottom objectives? A mix of both? And to what do you attribute your success/failure ratio? Did some of the event elements not deliver as expected and did some wildly exceed expectations? Knowing how you did will help you to define future objectives and create the means to deliver them.

- *short- and long-term event objectives realized immediately following the event, six months after the event and so on*

Update your event objectives periodically throughout the year. Don't invest the time, money and energy to do an event and not make the time to track your results. What you learn will work toward helping you to choose and use events to their maximum benefit and yield you the highest return on investment.

- *what unexpected company objectives and goals were achieved by holding this event*

There can be many hidden surprises that reveal themselves post-event...things that you never imagined can come about. You never know who may be in the room or who will read something about your event that spurs the idea that opens the door to new possibilities. Take time to connect the dots and record your findings of unexpected bonus objectives that were met as a direct result of holding your event.

- *unexpected problems/damage due to the event*

Make sure to capture any adverse effects that any event elements had. For example, did something take place that cost your company business or damaged your business reputation?

- *overview of value received from holding this type of event to meet specific company objectives*

What was event feedback? Did you follow up to see how the event was received by those who attended? Make sure to include the good and the bad reviews, as both will serve as learning tools for your next event. Listen carefully to what is being said and what is not being said.

- *findings as to what other type of event may have delivered the same or better returns*

Upon reflection, what other events would have served the same purpose? For example, if your event was a hit, what other style of event do you now think would hold equal or more appeal? What elements were your guests raving about? What did they remember as the event highlight?

- *the competition and their events*

Never lose sight of remaining on top of what your competition is doing. You have done your event and they have done theirs and now is the time to compare how the two stacked up. Whose event produced better results? Remember, you will only be privy to perception because you will not have access to your competition's set of objectives. One nonprofit organization held a sponsored event that ran at a loss, which to outsiders could have been judged a failure, but the publicity they received delivered a multiple of rewards to their cause. This is what had been their main objective all along, not the fundraising.

- *whether or not everyone's expectations were met, that is, company expectations, employee expectations, participant expectations and so forth*

It will be important to weigh in with total honesty on whether or not expectations—not just those of the company—were met. If so, where, and if not, why? Holding a post-event meeting to record impressions is imperative for future direction.

- *the overall emotion taken away from the event*

How did the emotion you wanted your event to leave behind compare to what was taken away? Where did you go right and where did you go wrong? Note what you would include next time and what you would lose.

- *short-term and long-term exposure—both internal and external*

Where were you able to receive brand awareness and company marketing public relations? Was it effective? Through what mediums? What could you have done differently to produce better results?

- *key team members and qualities*

Conduct an informal performance review on those working on the event team. Did some members display hidden talents or expertise that contributed to the success of your event? Note the roles that people would be open to taking on in the future that are a fit for their talents.

- *critique of key event elements*

Go through your event elements one by one and do an audit on them. Did they help you meet your specific objectives? What feedback did you receive? Was travel time too intense? Did the hotel or venue meet the needs of your event? Not only will this exercise help you understand your results better but what you will take away will be of great value when planning your next event.

- *impactful event elements*

Determine your WOW moments. Were they what you anticipated or did something unexpected produce an impact you never imagined? For one company, a very creative and fun $2 dessert was being talked about throughout the next day. Attendees were trying to find out where they had been purchased so they could serve it at home for their next special get-together. Elements don't have to be costly to be effective. In this case the attendees were impressed by the company's innovation.

- *event elements to potentially repeat*

You don't necessarily want to repeat the same event element in exact duplication, but in the above-mentioned surprise hit, for example, that company knew that in future their attendees would anticipate something unexpected for dessert, and in order to not disappoint, they would not take that event element for granted but rather take that element up a notch. If they were being perceived as being innovative, then that is exactly what they would strive for. An event element bar had been set and they were prepared to meet it.

- *event elements to avoid next time*

There will always be hits and misses. Pay attention to what these were. For example, if, at the end of your event, no one took home the gift bag offerings, then this would be an event element that you would need to carefully examine. Was it that the item held no appeal? Or were your guests the type who did not want to be burdened down—or seen—carrying a gift bag?

- *unexpected learning curves*

Did you get tripped up along the way? Were there red-flag areas that were missed and caused setbacks? What can you do now to put yourself in a better position for next year, for example, courses to take, pre-event planning research to be done?

- *recommendations to produce better results*

Professional event planners will always come away from an event, no matter how successfully executed, with one thing they would do differently next time. Each event is a learning and growing experience and by carefully examining yours you will end up producing even more outstanding results from your next event.

- *venue review*

Analyze the part your venue played in your total event experience. Did it meet the expectations of your guests? How was service? Was it a match for your corporate image? Would you use it again for another event? Did your venue selection add to the success of your event? Did the location work? How was the function space? Note the good and the bad for future reference.

- *supplier review*

Take the time to do a performance review and event review with each of your suppliers. Note their observations as to how they felt the event went. Record how well they interacted with your team and the part they played in creating an event that delivered results.

- *competing or comparable business functions*

List any contributing factors—internal (company-wise), industry, local and worldwide—that may have limited the amount of returns on your event investment. Were there other competing or comparable business functions taking place at the same time that contributed to the success of or took away potential value from your event? Determine if the decision to hold the event at a certain time of year was beneficial or not.

- *the performance level of the event as a whole*

What part did the event play in increasing brand awareness, developing new business, nurturing company loyalty and driving growth? The more detailed you can be, the better your executive summary will be as a planning tool for your—or your colleagues'—next event. It becomes a valuable time-saving report that will save you from future missteps and help you create events that meet and exceed the expectations of all involved.

Conclusion

Ensure that after investing time, money and energy in producing events, you don't stop short of taking one more step—creating an executive summary and performance review—that will guarantee you the means of taking your next event to a higher level. Your executive summaries become your company's instructive guide to choosing and using corporate functions that are tailored to your exact needs and are a teaching tool to build upon. To design an event that will yield your company the highest return on investment by meeting a myriad of company objectives and drive company growth, it is not enough to just get to and through your event; each event must become the solid foundation on which to provide the framework for the next, and the way to do that is to invest the time to track and analyze your results in a post–business function executive event summary. It is a vital step that will help you create winning events and keep you ahead of your competition.

CONCLUSION

KNOWING HOW TO CHOOSE AND USE corporate functions to increase brand awareness, develop new business, nurture customer loyalty and drive business growth is critical in today's competitive marketplace. The time you spend mastering this valuable business skill will not only help move your company forward, but you as well, personally and professionally. Developing a track record for designing and successfully executing company events—that under your expert leadership deliver outstanding results with high-yield returns on your company's investment of time, money and energy— is an important business talent to have on your career résumé as you move up the corporate ladder within your company or elsewhere.

Remember that every event and every event element can produce multiple rewards and can be used to meet a number of company objectives. It is all about the dollars being spent making sense, not just dollars and cents. Keep in mind what has been done in the past, what is being done now in your company and in your industry and how you can position your event today as a building block for future events by working backwards from your long-term company goals and objectives. For example, if one of a company's long-range plans is to take on the competition and move the company from where it is into the number one spot in the industry, the company would need to take part in an innovative future event that would foster the competitive edge atmosphere. This might mean the company CEO taking part in a "CEO Challenge," which could be golf, fishing, Ironman, cycling and so on (www.ceochallenges.com), and company events leading up to this can be built on the theme of forming a better, stronger, fitter company and workforce that is committed to giving their personal and professional best in all they do.

Take the time to review and record your event history. It will become an invaluable tool to help you stage events that are targeted to your specific audience. Look for the learning. Post-event reviews are not about assigning blame, but rather about taking the good from what was produced and going and growing forward with your newly acquired knowledge. And never lose sight of the fact that an event is a critical marketing tool in business today and one that should be maximized at every level. Every corporate event—large or small—can be an incredible opportunity to deliver a return on your own and your company's investment of time, money and energy.

An Executive's Event Planning Checklist

✔ Define your event

✔ Traditional business function:
- board meetings
- business meetings
- client appreciation events
- conferences
- conventions
- corporate shows
- employee appreciation events
- trade shows

✔ Advanced business function:

- custom training seminars involving emotional and physical challenges
- executive retreats
- gala fundraising events
- incentive travel and premium programs
- award presentation shows
- naming rights
- product launches
- product placement
- special events

✔ Set your event objectives

✔ Qualify your event objectives

✔ Prioritize your event objectives

✔ Review past, present and future events of your company and your competition

✔ Structure your event design for maximum effectiveness

✔ Determine your essential event elements

✔ D.R.I.V.E.

D   Define
R   Research
I   Innovate
V   Visualize
E   Execute

✔ Establish if your event design will:

- educate
- enlighten
- entertain

✔ Decide how you will help your attendees to leave your event feeling that their event experience was:
- meaningful
- memorable
- magical

✔ Establish how your event design will deliver results and meet company expectations

✔ Ascertain how your event elements will work to meet and exceed participant expectations

✔ Review and update event codes of conduct and company standards

✔ Prepare an executive event summary

APPENDIX

Event Elements for Any Kind of Event

Events must be strategically designed to meet specific objectives. Each event element has its own set of considerations that you need to review and carefully consider the return you will be receiving in exchange. Taking a look at them one by one will help you to make sure that the dollars being spent make sense.

Destination

Your destination is the foundation you will be building your event upon. Destination can be both a:
- location
- venue

Your end destination, which can be a location or the venue you are holding your event in—whether is it local, national or out of country—will set the tone for your event and can be an important attendance factor. Does the destination excite your guests? Will it pull them in as part of the emotional hook? Is it the right setting for the message that you as a company are looking to put across?

Choose Your Venues with a Company Image in Mind

Headlines in the business section of a respected national newspaper asked, "Should business execs meet at strip clubs?" Designated client appreciation events and business meetings are taking place in private rooms in strip clubs, complete with $400 lap dances being provided by nearly nude dancers. *USA Today* reported that "Adult entertainment is enjoyed by men—and some women—in most every industry in the USA, and it's a tax-deductible business expense allowed by the IRS (but there are proposed changes). Investment banks and brokerage firms are taking the lead in cracking down on the practice. The NASD [National Association of Securities Dealers, Inc.] and the New York Stock Exchange both recently proposed rules that would force firms to adopt business entertainment policies that cap amounts and specify appropriate venues. The move is expected to rule out company-paid or work-related strip club jaunts at the more than 5,000 brokerage firms in the USA."

Booking meetings and client appreciation events in venues or destinations that are known for their red light districts with the intent of visiting them on company time and money is a dangerous thing. While they may excite some of your guests, such areas are better left for clients to explore on their own. Choose your destinations and venues carefully. Always keep potential company- and career-damaging headlines in mind, and don't leave yourself open for potential lawsuits from inside the company or outside.

Look for event destinations and locations that are open and hold appeal to both genders and to both staff and guests. That doesn't mean limiting the fun, but the question that must be asked is whether or not the destination or venue is an appropriate place in which to conduct business.

Creative client appreciation events and destinations that are suitable for both genders are readily available. The Inn at Manitou (www.manitou-online.com), for example, specializes in them. The Inn at Manitou is a luxury, five-star, award-winning resort with 35 rooms perfect for a company takeover. A weekend spousal client appreciation event featuring a hot new trend—Texas Hold 'em

Poker—can be custom designed, with guests of both sexes learning the finer points of the game under the direction of a leading expert, with poker clinics, games and nightly tournaments set up for novice through expert players. This type of activity, created in a destination that also offers a stunning private golf course right in its backyard, a spa, customized fly fishing lessons with top instructors on the lake—with freshly grilled fish to be savored for lunch out in the open—will give company executives ample one-on-one time with their top clients in a setting that will allow them to enjoy themselves and be more business-appropriate. And top clients and their partners can be assigned the resort's luxury junior suites and enjoy guestrooms with private saunas, skylights and whirlpool baths, private sundecks, log-burning fireplaces and spectacular lake views, leaving them to make their own fun.

Educational. Enlightening. Entertaining. Meaningful. Memorable. Magical. This style of event hits all the emotional buttons, is business-setting appropriate, gives attendees a personalized life experience that they could not have enjoyed on their own, feeds the senses, lends itself to meeting a number of company objectives and provides a positive return and reward on investment, and avoids financial repercussions that can be costly personally and professionally to the planning committee and the company. A quality event that is designed to deliver quality one-on-one time with your company's top investors with no distractions—such as strippers—is far more beneficial in the long run and one that is not fodder for newspaper and television news headlines that could alienate potential and existing customers from doing future business with your company.

Documentation

Documentation as an event element is all your promotional material, which can include:
- event invitation
- trip itinerary booklet

Your invitation and trip itinerary booklets set the tone of anticipation for your upcoming event. Displaying a touch of class, creative flair and style is important, and so is attention to detail in the documents and invitations you send. You don't have to give away event surprises, but you do have to ensure that your guests have no surprises waiting for them in regards to what will be expected from them in terms of attendance, dress and expenses. Make sure copy is proofed and proofed again by fresh eyes, the spelling and titles of your guests' names and those of their partners are cross-checked, and any special requests, for example, meals, medical and so forth, are accurately recorded.

Arrival

Event elements that fall under arrival take into consideration all areas of getting your participants to your destination with ease and comfort. They include:

- *overnights*

If your event is being held out of town and airport overnight accommodation is required, your guests will be looking for a location that offers them convenience with regards to parking and transferring to the airport. At this point, they will not be expecting a welcome room gift or group dinner. Guests are generally at leisure to arrive and check in on their own.

It's important that everything has been looked after for them in advance regarding prepayment, where applicable, of the guestrooms, parking, bagging handling, airport shuttle transfers (private or hotel), dinner and breakfast. Your guests should have been fully informed in their itinerary booklet as to how these will be handled, for example, what the company has paid for, what they will be expensing and what will be at their own personal expense, such as mini bar purchases. As well, they should have been made aware of the times for shuttle departures, check-in and checkout, and if arrangements for a late arrival have been guaranteed for them.

Your attendees will be counting on an easy, effortless and expected—by the front desk—check-in and checkout. If meals are not being provided for them, they will expect there to be facilities on the property for either room service and/or restaurant service. Fail to deliver on any of those counts and their expectation level will immediately drop, which starts your event out on the wrong note. You can count on anything that has been overlooked being the subject of your guests' conversations at the airport when they leave for home.

Your care for their comfort will come across if you budget into the cost of your business functions overnight accommodations for those who may have a distance to drive to the airport, especially if your business event is planned to take place during a time where they could face inclement weather or other travel difficulties. One top company producer always felt richly rewarded for his hard work by his company remembering that driving in the dark at the time of the year their company traveled posed safety concerns because of the number of moose out at night on the roads where he then lived. When he first called in to remind them, he was told that that had already been noted on his file and a hotel room has been booked for the night so that he would not be forced to drive in the dark. For minimum dollars and remembering his needs every year without him having to ask, they got maximum returns from their employee. They exceeded his expectations and in return he met and exceeded theirs in sales numbers continually year after year.

- *airport check-in—meet and greet*

If the group traveling together from one gateway city is large enough, a comforting and caring touch to add is to have staff on hand to welcome them. This also serves a dual purpose in reconfirming who has arrived and who hasn't, and staff already in place in the destination can be apprised of any missing guests in advance. Depending on the destination, the airlines and security requirements in some parts of the world, it is possible to either negotiate or pay for added touches, such as private group check-ins, lounges, refreshments and so forth. Anything that can be added to make their airport experience and flight more comfortable will be appreciated by your guests, and that translates into feeling cared for and valued by your company.

It is important to remember that your event does not start at the welcome reception. Every step of the way leading up to that can add a layer of warm fuzzies—caring, excitement or other emotions that you are targeting to bring you closer to meeting all of your different company objectives. Staff greeting your guests can be professionally contracted event planning freelancers just handling airport duty and who are experienced in handling airport check-in requirements, part of your event planning team, and/or staff who are scheduled to fly with the group.

TIP

Due to security-conscious times you may or may not wish to have the name of your group or company logo displayed on jackets, luggage tags and so on, but you may want to have something that will discreetly identify guests to your staff and each other but is not necessarily apparent to others. This can have other benefits as well, such as in the case of too much celebration during flights and potential and existing clients witnessing high-spirited behavior that may not be in keeping with your company's image.

Focus on in-flight comfort. Headphone, movie, drink and meal vouchers may be thoughtful add-ons to think about including for your guests. Group seating, depending on your numbers, may be something else that you may wish to consider. Give your participants added time to begin to bond and give thoughtful care to ensure your guests don't talk loudly or stand in the aisles, disturbing and annoying fellow passengers. After all, your fellow passengers could be existing or potential customers. If your guests' spirits get too noisy, the other passengers will know, or make it their business to find out, which company the participants are representing.

Remember that egos can easily become bruised on business trips. If some company employees and/or participants are flying in first or business class while the rest of the group is on the same aircraft but situated back in coach, they will remember being thought of by your company as not deserving of better seating and being relegated to "the back of the bus" with the rest of the pack. It is far better to send any company executives or other guests that you want to provide upgraded air transportation service to on alternate flights. The only time that having some of the group upgraded to first class or business class on the same plane would be advisable is if it was part of your planning strategy around rewarding top company incentive winners with first-class service and it was something that all of your participants could aspire to attain. In that case it is not a matter of the company favoring one person over the other but rather a company promotion where some qualified and others didn't, which is entirely results-based. It could, depending on your participants, serve to stimulate sales next year and create the desire to be one of those who had obtained preferred seating due to their status of being best of the best in productivity

And if you have the budget, consider the possible return—motivational impact and desire payback—of chartering your own private aircraft (company policy permitting "x" number of employees to travel on the same flights) or flying as part of a select group aboard Eos Airlines, which operates daily commercial flights to Europe in addition to chartering their planes to North American and European destinations that can handle Boeing 757s. This would create the opportunity for your top incentive winners to give their partners, as well as themselves, a once-in-a-lifetime experience of being one of 48 people being pampered on board a luxury aircraft that was built to hold 220.

Eos Airlines features 21 square feet per passenger, with seats that convert to 6'6" flat beds when fully extended and become more of an airline suite than an airline. They come complete with turn-down service, lambs-wool and cashmere blankets, sheets with high thread counts and Bose noise-canceling headphones. During the day, seats can be configured so that two passengers can sit facing each other using a convertible ottoman/companion seat. A conference table can be placed between the two facing seats so that passengers can dine or work together if they choose. Their in-flight meals are gourmet restaurant quality and other features include curbside pickup and escort through security and pre-flight lounges.

Premier air flight service for your premier award-winning salespeople and their partners sets the tone of the reward from the minute they arrive at the airport, and hints of a life experience they will long remember and talk about—one that could have your industry buzzing about how well top performers are looked after and attract the level of employees you are looking to add to help grow your company sales.

When it comes to choosing your destinations, consider how many hours your guests will have to spend in the air and how many hours they will sit in different airports. Requiring your guests to take five planes to get to a destination, no matter how wonderful the site may be, shows a lack of consideration for comfort in these trying days of meeting maximum security requirements at airports. No one wants to be put through more than they need to. One company upset their incentive winners by booking their air seats for a cruise as a package deal as opposed to booking their flights with the group departments of the airlines directly or through an incentive house. As opposed to being able to fly non-stop to the destination, their guests were required to change planes multiple times and the group was spread out over many different flights. There was no guarantee of direct flights, and they faced plane changes and milk-run flights (multiple stops en route).

If you are purchasing tickets through a package for scheduled air flights, not private charters, your guests could end up spending more time than was necessary sitting in airports. They will not be happy and you will be starting your event on a bad note. The money being spent on the company's top "winners" will not make sense to them if they feel they are running an endurance race just to arrive at the destination. You would be better served by selecting another location and waiting to take the cruise at a time when you can afford group airfares on scheduled aircraft where you are in charge of which flights and times your guests will be flying.

Air Cost Considerations

Air savings should be looked into so that your dollars are spent on event elements that will bring higher returns on your investment. Opportunities include:

✔ avoiding peak travel seasons, and if unavoidable, steering clear of peak travel days of the week (i.e., midweek is usually cheaper than weekend)

✔ looking at moving meeting dates to accommodate a Saturday night stay to take advantage of lower airfares if this is a viable option for the company, employees and guests

✔ negotiating with the airlines to waive the minimum Saturday night stay requirement if the best hotel rates are available during the week at the hotel/destination of your choice (this has been done successfully with a number of airlines)

✔ reaching a deal upfront for VIP upgrades to business or first class, site inspection tickets, and staff travel tickets, because savings in each of these areas can work to lower your total airfare budget

✔ putting the quote out to multiple airlines when possible

✔ using the services of travel management companies and corporate travel agents as opposed to booking online, since experienced professionals will usually do better on your behalf (they have probably negotiated for that route before and have developed good working relationships with the airlines)

✔ negotiating two-for-one tickets with the purchase of any full-fare ticket in any class with the airlines

• *airport arrival—meet and greet*

While your guests may not be expecting you to meet them in their departure city, they will be anticipating that you look after them from the minute they arrive, unless they have been instructed to make their own way to their hotel or resort. Guests will expect to be greeted by a company representative—professional destination management staff or event planning staff—who are on hand to oversee baggage handling and their transfers, and help them with any missing luggage claims.

Your guests will note and comment on any other groups' meet and greet arrival, comparing it to their own, and if yours falls short, for example, if another group is perceived to be better cared for, then that will reflect back on your company. Dealers attending one automotive manufacturer's product launch were thrilled when their competition—who were number one in the business and who arrived at the airport at the same time—had to walk past their waiting transportation to get to theirs. The group that was striving for the number one position felt like their company was treating them as winners. Baggage handlers were ready to assist them with their luggage and their motor coaches were all lined up, waiting in the prime pickup location, while their competition had to struggle on their own with their luggage and walk a fair distance to get to their transportation. And the caring treatment that was being displayed toward the group did not go unnoticed by their competition, who were heard loudly remarking and querying why their company hadn't taken the time to ensure that they were better cared for. You just never know who will be taking note of what you do and how you do it.

- *transportation*

Transportation from the airport to the hotel or resort can come in many forms, such as motor coaches, limousines, taxis, private helicopters, luxury cars with drivers, car rentals, boats and so forth. It is important that the transportation is on time, clean and easily found. It is important to know the caliber of transportation you are contracting. For example, not all motor coaches or limousines are the same in terms of comfort, cleanliness and amenities. Never assume that air conditioning is included or even available. Ask. And make sure that your contract stipulates exactly what you are agreeing to.

Special touches that can add to your guests' enjoyment include refreshments pre-boarding, hot or cold towels, refreshments and snacks on board, movies or live entertainment and pre-arranged comfort stops. Again, attention to detail and your guests' well-being are important from beginning to end.

The same rules apply with regards to transportation as they do for flights. It is best to have all of your guests that are arriving and departing for their hotel or resort at the same time transferred in the same level of style. For example, do not have limousines waiting for company executives in visible sight of the participants you are transporting via motor coach, taxi or private shuttles. That visibly points out to them that some people are regarded more highly than they are, and that is never an advisable tone to set at the beginning.

Handling Your VIPs with Finesse

As you move into your event, there are ways to impress VIP company executives discreetly without offending those whom you are wining, dining, wooing, treating like winners or valued company employees, clients, suppliers and so on. Be very careful and remember that actions do speak louder than words. Your participants will be taking careful note of and experiencing the layers—positive or negative, peaks and valleys—that you as a company are choosing to build into your event.

Again, the only time that having different classes of transportation could be a plus is when upgraded transfers are part of the reward that everyone could have obtained had they met company objectives. And if those who didn't meet the objectives can see that the company did deliver on what they promised in terms of reward, this plants the seed that they will want do all they can to ensure that they are in the position of being pampered next year.

It's key that the upgraded transfers live up to guests' expectations. A standard limousine may not create the strong desire you are looking for; it may be a wise investment to spend a few dollars more to make a very powerful statement.

- *welcome check-in*

Many hotels will tell you that they cannot do satellite private group check-ins. That is not necessarily the case. It is easier for them not to, but it is not as convenient or as pleasant for your guests to be lining up with other hotel guests. You may be able to make a private group check-in one of your terms and conditions of contracting. Registering at a private check-in setup in a function room or area to the side tells your guests that you are doing what is necessary to make them and their comfort a priority. Your guests can mingle and chat with one another, enjoy refreshments upon arrival—these can also be negotiated with the hotel—and be escorted to their rooms in a relaxed state of mind, feeling they are valued.

As part of your contract negotiations, ask the hotel what they can provide on a complimentary basis. In Texas, one hotel offers complimentary cookies in the shape of a boot and serves them with sweet tea (iced tea) or lemonade. Light local background music is always a nice, relaxing touch upon arrival as well.

Make sure that your guests are never placed in the position of being embarrassed at check-in. In their itinerary booklets, let them know what type of credit cards and so forth. will be required from them. If some of your guests have problems, for example, do not own a credit card or are close to exceeding their limit, they can come to you discreetly in advance to see what can be worked out. Their gratitude for making them aware in advance and helping them to avoid a potential loss of face in front of peers, depending on how it is handled by hotel staff, will be long lasting.

- *hospitality rooms*

Depending on check-in time and your guests' arrival, it may be necessary to work with the hotel to make hospitality rooms available to your participants. This will be a place where they can leave their hand luggage under supervised care, change into casual clothes, enjoy a snack and a beverage and set out to explore and enjoy the resort until their rooms are ready. Extra towels and supplies for the bathrooms will be required, as will be service to refresh the hospitality suites.

It is very important at time of contracting to stipulate on the contract that assigned rooms will be clean when turned over to guests. There are some hotels that are known to give out keys to dirty rooms so that guests will immediately go out and play in their casinos as opposed to settling in, unpacking and perhaps taking a nap after a full day of travel. Walking into a dirty room is not what you want your guests to experience and would cause an emotional dip.

- *accommodation*

There are business function pitfalls when it comes to meeting your attendees' accommodation expectations versus meeting company objective opportunities within the approved budget. If your event is non spousal or your participants are not permitted to bring a guest to this specific function, one of your first decisions regarding contracting guestrooms will be whether or not your delegates will be having single rooms or will be asked to share a room.

Sharing a room is not necessarily a cost-saving ploy; it can be a strategic planning move to bring key company staff members together to spend time one on one, where the rooming list is carefully orchestrated. Sharing rooms only works with company employees for the most part and is not advisable for other business functions unless you are comfortable that your guests' knowledge that they are to share a room will not decrease attendance or have your guests demanding separate rooms on arrival. In advance of your event, you must advise participants if they will be expected to share guestrooms. If shared accommodation is what has been decided on, you will need to decide if your participants will be permitted to request who they would or would not like to be roomed with.

Hotel check-in staff will need to be aware of exactly how you would like requests for upgrades, roommate changes and so on handled. They can refer all such requests back to your point person if instructed. You need to make them aware—in your contract and in your function sheets—that upgrades are not permitted at the hotel's discretion and that they must be approved by you first, for example, if they wish to do something special for the group and upgrade some but not all of the rooms. because such changes could cause internal friction and hurt feelings. Your guests will be in and out of each other's rooms and will note any differences. That is the reason many companies do not opt to take "run-of-the-house rooms." Run of the house means that your participants could receive any level of accommodation and the levels could vary greatly. In a tropical resort, some run-of-the-house rooms could end up being magnificent luxury ocean view rooms, while others could be standard rooms that overlook the parking lot. It is better to contract one level of guestroom with the provision that should upgraded rooms be available for the entire group, then the entire group will be upgraded at no additional charge.

Savvy planners make sure they work with the hotel's front desk manager the day before the group is scheduled to check in to see what accommodation is open and determine if that group can be assigned an upgrade. They do not leave this important step until the group is arriving, as it may take time to get approval. Some hotels are more than happy to upgrade guests if their upgraded rooms are going to be sitting empty. It can be a successful marketing tool to help them obtain repeat business. And if the group's guestrooms are already sitting empty and have been cleaned, the hotel can start preparing express check-in key packets in advance of the group arrival for their private satellite check-in.

Early check-ins and late checkouts are two other areas of negotiation that you can discuss with your hotel sales representation at time of contracting. To demonstrate guest care and meet the expectations of those guests arriving before the hotel's standard time, you may wish to negotiate early check-ins. If the hotel cannot agree to that provision for any reason, such as they are already close to being fully booked, then weigh the costs versus benefits in meeting your guests' expectations and look at other options: booking their rooms for the extra night or having the hotel provide complimentary hospitality rooms (that are shared) for the group. It can be necessary to book and pay for rooms the night before group arrival and have them sit empty so that they are available to your participants immediately upon their arrival at the hotel or resort.

Placing top winners in suites is acceptable if it is something that was part of the reward or promotion. While participants usually do accept that senior company executives will have the best accommodation, some companies have chosen as part of their strategy in meeting company objectives to do the exact opposite and have held draws on site or devised alternate means to give others the chance to be spoiled.

Asking your guests their preferences when it comes to smoking or non-smoking rooms, two double beds or one king (in spousal or partner business functions) and so forth shows care and attention to detail and your guests' comfort. Again, you are displaying anticipating, meeting and exceeding their expectations, which in return emotionally opens them to being receptive to meeting and exceeding your company objectives.

Always assign a staff member to walk through the VIP guestrooms to make sure that everything is in order before your VIPs arrive. As well, have them visit any guestrooms that have had a special request, such as handicap accessibility. Many times you may be faced with a surprise. At one top resort, the room assigned to a top company executive winner was absolutely empty of furniture, dirty and filled with spiders. It had not been used in quite a long time. Had the company executive walked in and found what the advance staff fortunately had seen first, it would have been an extremely poor beginning to their stay.

On some corporate business functions, top company executives have been known to bring their spouses, children and even their nannies where all others have not been allowed to bring their wives, partners, guests or children. One company head brought his entire family down for a six-week stay at an upscale resort while the company's weekly incentive program went on. Each week's incentive winners wondered who was picking up the cost for their stay and why they hadn't been given the same opportunity. It left a bad taste in the delegates' mouths and the talk was focused on the company head and his family, not on meeting company objectives.

There are ways, for the same financial cost, that this could have been more professionally handled. A nearby private home could have been rented and the family tucked discreetly away, with the company president retiring there each night, as opposed to having his children running into the meeting room, interrupting private discussions or taking part in company events that were not geared to having small children around. Company executives and hotel managers were later placed in an ethical dilemma when the company head requested that the cost of bringing his family down be billed under fictitious meeting room charges. The company president's actions were the main reason his company did not receive a return on its investment. The industry buzzed about how inappropriate their actions were. People's professional perceptions of the company head, his lapse of business judgment and the corporation were changing, and that affected the development of new business, customer loyalty and company growth.

Accomodation Cost Considerations

Here are some opportunities to save costs on accommodation. They will free up your dollars so you can spend them where they matter most.

✔ If you are planning events in the U.S., substantial savings can be found over the American Thanksgiving and Memorial Day long weekends. Hotels are open to negotiations during this time period, as hotels are generally not operating at full occupancy because most Americans are home with their families. Another good time to travel in the U.S. and benefit from savings is during election week. In the Caribbean, May and November are excellent times to travel and take advantage of good weather and good off-season rates.

✔ For affordable accommodations and meeting space, you may want to consider universities. Several universities offer hotel-style rooms as well as apartment and dormitory bedrooms.

✔ Work with your hotel to find their "need dates." One company was able to negotiate complimentary buffet breakfast for every day, in addition to a one-hour cocktail reception with hot and cold appetizers, in exchange for moving their dates to accommodate the hotel.

✔ Some hotels are open to providing complimentary hospitality rooms and late checkouts for guests departing on evening flights; they can earn corporate bookings by helping clients save dollars by not having to pay for an additional night.

✔ Corporations and professional planners are often able to work with hotels to pay for one type of room for the entire group instead of booking run of the house, and receive as a return concession an upgraded room category.

✔ Look for destinations that offer quality hotels and meeting space, and good air and transportation choices for attendees, but that also can provide an overall less expensive option in which to hold your meeting. For example, book in outlying towns that have appeal as opposed to holding your event in a major city center's downtown core.

• *in room welcome*

Your guests will notice whether or not anything has been done to welcome them. A welcome gift, note or welcoming telephone message always adds a touch of caring class for minimal cost. And if you have the funds, having local snacks and beverages waiting is always nice. One company that ran numerous programs in Tuscany found that a creative display of salsa, tortilla chips, local beer and juices on ice, and a welcome note always put their arrivals in a good mood when they walked into their guestrooms. Cost was minimal and the return was maximal.

Welcome Reception and Dinner

A welcome event can be informal and does not have to go on for an extended period of time. Your guests will need time to relax, settle in, unpack and recover from their travels. Event elements to consider include:

- *welcome reception*

Welcome receptions are not the time or place to invest major dollars and should be held at your resort or hotel, not off property. Your guests may be arriving after a full day of travel and in some cases may be dealing with jet lag as well. The last thing your guests will want to do is get back onto a motor coach or into a limousine and be transported somewhere. The same applies to booking a private boat for a welcome function. Your guests will react more favorably to a welcome event that is staged with their comfort in mind and gives them the freedom to retire early if needed, so that they can be refreshed and ready to go the next day.

Spend your money on a plentiful array of appetizers, rather than on decor and entertainment, to ensure the effect of your spending is noticed. For some, this may be the first main meal they have eaten that day. If you want your guests to mingle with one another, do not request that your canapés be passed and drinks be served or your guests will likely remain rooted to one spot, not speaking to anyone else, and you could miss an opportunity to meet a company objective. Set up interactive food and beverage stations as well as entertainment around the room as innovative icebreakers. Provide topics of conversation and require your guests to go to these stations as opposed to allowing them to stand fixed. You will instantly change the energy of the room and have a favorable start to your event.

Welcomes should be brief because due to a full day and in most cases an early start, your message—if meant to be meaningful and something that you want carried away with them—may not sink in. This is not the best time or place to schedule the imparting of important information.

- *dinner*

Welcome dinners are meant to be light. It is not necessary to invest major dollars making a show; instead, make your splashy display on the second night. If you still want your guests mingling and mixing, set up dinner service as a buffet. If you want to let them relax but still move around a bit, have dinner served to the table and set up dessert stations around the room.

Think about seating and how it will serve meeting your company objectives. You can either have open seating and let your guests choose where they want to sit, or have more formal seating arrangements set up. More formal arrangements can be executed in any number of ways to ensure that whomever you want seated next to another does end up there, and this can help you ensure that your top company executives are seated with key members of your participants. For example, you can have an invitation to join "x" at their table for dinner this evening sent to their guestroom with a small token gift that ties into the event's theme, and have a floor plan posted in the reception area, and dinner tables clearly marked.

Entertainment can be low key because many guests will want to head to their rooms early. If your event is not one where your guests have been invited to bring their spouses, partners or companions, dancing should not be on the agenda any night. Dancing can create uncomfortable situations for all involved, especially when combined with open bars and being far from home. What goes on in Vegas does not stay in Vegas on company functions, and rumors can run rampant in the industry and home office in a matter of minutes after an indiscretion occurs. Don't provide the fuel for marital discord and divorce—it has and does happen—and the means for personal and professional reputations to be placed in question and sometimes in shreds. Protect the reputations of your company and your guests as much as possible to help you meet company objectives—and not make industry and national headlines.

Food and Beverage Cost Considerations

Here are some food and beverage cost-saving tips that are applicable to all meal functions, both on and off property, that will help you to be able to afford the event elements that will make the most difference to the return on your event:

✔ During receptions, people tend to take less food if passed by waitstaff than if placed on a buffet table, but weigh the cost

---

Continued

of doing this and having your guests remain stationary against having them mixing and mingling, and decide which best fits your objectives.

✔ For some receptions, such as the farewell, where your guests know one another, having passed canapés is a nice, formal touch as well as a cost savings. For such service, a flat unlimited fee—not per piece charge—often can be negotiated.

✔ Putting out smaller dessert-sized plates rather than luncheon or dinner plates results in people taking less food on a buffet, but you still have to be careful to have sufficient food on hand to feed your guests.

✔ For the feeling of serving a high-end meal even though you need to save dollars, order half portions of two main entrée items. For example, combining a half portion of beef tenderloin with a half portion of chicken breast helps bring down the dollar cost per plate, while still enabling you to offer guests a selection with depth.

✔ Keep alcohol costs and behavior in check by serving one-ounce drinks instead of one-and-a-half ounce drinks.

✔ Refrain from serving salty, dry snacks, which encourage guests to drink more.

✔ Cut your champagne costs by having glasses of bubbly passed instead of poured or topped up. One company that did so did not want their guests to be able to put a dollar value on the quality of champagne that was being served, so glasses were replenished out of sight of the guests. Only select staff had access to top-of-the-line champagne and they refilled the VIP glasses from a very identifiable bottle. Guests attending the event left with the perception that they, too, were enjoying champagne far superior to the reality.

✔ Bar costs can be kept from escalating by limiting the alcohol available. Wine and beer are two options to offer guests at the reception, as well as having your venue create a customized cocktail.

✔ Have the wine stewards notify the lead event director as to when you are approaching the halfway mark of your estimated liquor consumption. You can then make an informed decision on whether or not to slow wine/beverage service or close the bar earlier than scheduled.

✔ The cost for a professionally staffed bar is less than setting up a self-serve bar where liquor can flow too freely and costs can skyrocket.

✔ Know your guests' profile. One company holding a cocktail reception spent unnecessary dollars to set up a mashed potato bar that sat untouched and left their high-fashion guests searching for low-carb options.

✔ Announcing last call only serves to drive up alcohol costs. Many guests tend to view last call as their last opportunity to stockpile drinks by ordering multiple rounds to take to their rooms or drink while the party is winding down.

Morning (Meeting Days)

Take time to carefully look at all the event elements that go into a meeting and work them to meet your objectives. Meeting event elements include:

- *breakfast*

Your goal for breakfast on meeting days is to make sure that your guests are well looked after and fed before attending your scheduled meeting. Ensure that sufficient time is allocated so that all guests can be served. As a backup, you may want to have coffee, tea and muffins set up outside the meeting room so that any guests who missed breakfast will have the opportunity to get something to eat. This will help guests focus on what is being said on stage, not on wondering how they can slip out and go get something to eat. Having them fully present is imperative, and it is especially important that they have something to eat if they have been drinking the night before.

One company scored major points with its participants at a company function by taking into consideration that many would be waking up early the first couple of days as they adjusted to time differences. The company had hot coffee and local juices, along with the morning paper, delivered to each guestroom, anticipating the attendees' needs. Another company, taking its group to the Caribbean where the pace can be more leisurely than guests who have not yet begun to unwind would like, made arrangements at the restaurant for carafes of coffee, tea and juices to be placed on each table immediately as the guests arrived and were seated. It was a little touch but noticed and appreciated, and started the day off on a peak—not valley—energy note.

Breakfast can be set up many ways at a business function, each staged to produce different results and meet a variety of company objectives. It can be held in a private room and set up buffet style (double-sided so your guests are not kept in line longer than they need be). In a private room, having breakfast served to the table limits choices and is usually not recommended. If you want your guests to be served, you could exclusively take over a restaurant on the property. Or, you could reserve a section of the restaurant, station a staff member at the front door to make sure that none of your guests are waiting in line with regular hotel guests, and allow your guests to order off the menu and sign it to their guestroom. Unless you are able to negotiate a flat rate with the hotel, costs are not as controlled this way, but you could also save money should some guests just opt for coffee and a muffin. With a private room and a set buffet menu, you are locked into paying for the number of guests that you have guaranteed the breakfast service for—not how many show up.

Breakfast Considerations

Here are some ways to save money on the breakfasts you hold:

✔ Ordering breakfast a-la-carte is less expensive than a packaged continental meal. For example, ordering sliced bagels on a per person basis offers people a choice of easily taking half the bagel rather than the whole, and allows you to separate the amount of food versus beverage ordered per person. This cuts down on the amount of food that is needed to be purchased and thus creates potentially less wastage. Packaged breakfasts often offer sliced fruit, which is more expensive than whole fruit. Ordering a-la-carte allows you to include fruit at a lower cost.

✔ If you are looking to do something different to get guests up and about during breakfast, you could consider staging a breakfast reception—if you did not hold a reception the night before. You want to avoid duplicating serving styles two meals in a row. Mini eggs Benedict, bite size muffins, and little Danish pastries can be served at various food stations. These can be accompanied with a selection of freshly squeezed juices, smoothies, teas and specialty coffees.

✔ Don't forget the little touches that show your guests that you are tuned into their needs as well as your own. One company that hosts stockbrokers always makes sure that it has top financial newspapers available in quantity in the breakfast room. It knows how important staying on top of the news is to its attendees and does what it can to make sure that they have what they require.

• *meetings*

You have designed your meeting content around your company objective, and now it is important to convey it in a manner that will be riveting and capture your attendees' attention. The first priority was ensuring your attendees have had all their needs looked after so that they can give you their full attention. Now that they have been looked after and fed, it is time to focus on matters at hand.

A simple touch of adding a dress code to your meeting—and listing it in your delegates' daily agenda—can instantly change the tone of your meeting. Business dress can project a very different image and show a different intent than casual dress.

It is equally important to look at what is taking place in the room and orchestrate what will be taking place on stage, otherwise your message and your objective can be easily lost.

You also need to ensure that your attendees' valid expectations are met.

- If you are going to require your participants to take copious notes, have everything they need at their disposal. For example, have the meeting room laid out with tables for them to write on, as opposed to making them juggle notepads on their laps. Have additional paper and pencils readily available to them.

- Make sure that the room is comfortable, not too hot or too cold, or you will lose guests' attention. Have water and glasses ready. Ensure that the chairs provided are comfortable to sit on for extended periods of time. Provide good lighting if guests will need it.

- Structure the seating arrangement if it will help you to meet a specific objective. If seating serves no purpose, leave it as open seating so that your guests can choose whom they would like to sit next to.

One concern that some attendees have is getting time to check for messages. If guests head back to their guestrooms to return calls and attend to anything urgent back in the office, you can lose people. It is important to understand their needs and devise a plan that will help them not feel torn about business priorities and allow them to relax, knowing that they can tend to anything important that does crop up and still be fully in the moment listening to what your company has to say. For example, schedule your meetings to end at 3:00 p.m., allowing your guests time to check for messages at the end of the day, still have time to handle what they need to, and reach key people within business hours before meeting for dinner activities.

Meeting Cost Considerations

Here are some cost-saving measures for meetings:

✔ If you are looking for ways to save money on audiovisual and stage productions, involve your technical director in venue choice before contracting. Room height, location of pillars and chandeliers, loading dock access, size of elevator and so forth can all affect costs. Suppliers can offer budget-saving solutions and creative options if they obtain staging knowledge of the room well in advance.

✔ Find out in advance what each speaker's AV requirements are. There is nothing worse than finding out that in an hour, one of your speakers will expect a microphone that no one was aware of. In-house AV is much more expensive when the need Is immediate.

✔ Always book your meeting room one day prior to your meeting to ensure the staging company will have time to load in, erect the audiovisual equipment and troubleshoot any glitches that may occur. This should also allow time for rehearsals. Of course, the amount of time required will vary with the amount of staging and rehearsals required. If your meeting commences at 9:00 a.m., the room should be clear from 6:00 p.m. the night before. What you spend on room rental costs can be less than incurring overtime and double-time charges for union labor or bringing in extra crew to do a fast room turnaround.

✔ Use technology to cut back on printing and postage costs. E-mail conference promotional materials and reminders, have the program and speaker materials available in electronic format, and encourage attendees to bring their PDAs and provide on-site update capabilities for people who do.

✔ If appropriate, search out suppliers that could act as sponsors and either partially or totally cover the costs. Identify their contribution and offer sponsorship benefits based on their contribution. This is usually a win-win situation and a number of the suppliers will entertain this idea in exchange for exposure and having their name attached to the event.

Continued

✔ Hire one host professional—a master of ceremonies. This "interactive symbol of energy" would emcee all proceedings, introduce the speakers, provide energy breaks, entertain, reinforce educational material and maintain the conference theme throughout. The planner/client saves both budget and time in hiring one "go to" person instead of booking different hosts, entertainers and energy break leaders for each segment of the conference.

✔ Shipping is another area of savings for meetings and other business functions. One company announces two shipping dates to all of its departments taking part. The first one is for ground shipping many weeks out, and it encourages everyone to have their heavy materials ready for this date. The company piggybacks its materials with the shipping of the display material and booths, offering the incentive of low or zero shipping costs to other departments. The second date is for air shipping a week out. Departments that have to ship on this date are billed back and have to include this expense in their budgets.

✔ Dollars can be saved creatively in the area of printing. One business introduced generic printed materials that are easily customized in-house each year to suit its new conference. This means it can pre-order printed material in bulk. The business also eliminated special envelopes for each conference and used its photocopier overprint feature (for smaller runs) to add a message to the outside of the envelope. Another company had its printer produce the meeting material at a branch location near the conference city. The shipping costs were halved. For one other company, eliminating the use of three-ring binders for the conference materials and having them spiral bound instead saved hours of labor time and materials cost. Other printing cost savings include piggybacking the main bulk of program mailings with other mailings; one company found that it reduced its postage costs by over half. Using e-mail blasts instead of postcards can also be a cost savings. It all adds up to allow you to have more funds for event elements that will impact your delegates in the way you are looking to. Better to put the printing dollars saved toward a memorable guest speaker that will have your invitees and industry buzzing.

- *coffee breaks*

Avoid choosing the wrong type of food for coffee breaks. You want your participants' attention to stay steady, not spike then crash. There are many coffee break menus that are carefully designed with health and well-being in mind, and may serve you better in keeping your guests' attention on your meeting intentions. Some companies are now including fitness coffee breaks and giving their attendees an opportunity to move around and stretch, returning to the meeting room feeling refreshed and ready to begin again.

Afternoon (Meeting Days)

- *lunch*

It is important to decide your objectives for lunch on meeting days. Do you want lunch to take on a social aspect, or do you want attendees to have a short lunchtime and return to the meeting room so that you can break early and allow them the time they need to pick up messages and return calls?

If having lunch as a social affair serves meeting your objectives better, you may want to consider ending the meeting in the early afternoon and having a later lunch, with guests free to be at their leisure after they finish. It is hard to get guests' minds back to business when lunch becomes too social—perhaps including alcoholic beverages—and it may be best to have an intense meeting with carefully timed coffee breaks in the morning and, if desired, end the day on a high social note.

You may want to have guests fed and in and out as fast as possible, and if so, a plated lunch with the appetizer or salad already in place as they enter the room is the ideal service style. A buffet could take conceivably longer, as your participants are up and about chatting and getting food.

If you are having your delegates go back to the meeting, it is recommended that you not serve alcoholic beverages. Choose foods that will keep them alert and avoid heavy menu selections that will leave them longing for a nap. If you don't, you will defeat the purpose of your afternoon session.

If you want to serve alcohol and have your guests relaxing over drinks, schedule it as part of your close of meeting events, but remember to exercise caution, as too much drinking during the day can limit attendance at evening functions and can be problematic. Always select high protein snacks if you are serving drinks after your meeting. And if any of your guests are drinking and then driving immediately after your meeting, remember the social host legal liabilities that your company needs to protect itself from.

Group Activity Days

Group activities can be both day and evening functions. They are a scheduled part of your program and attendance is mandatory. During the day, group activities can include sightseeing tours, road rally's, team building challenges, shopping excursions, sports activities, such as a golf tournament, and so on. At night, a group activity could be a dine-around program, off property dinner, nightclub tour and so on.

- *group activity*

Stage your group activities carefully. They can be a tremendous resource in producing results, but it is important to keep timing and the objectives you are trying to meet top of mind when designing them. For example, create a challenging team-building experience at the beginning of their stay so that they can grow closer and have the opportunity to share more ideas throughout the week.

For team-building events, choose your teams with care; don't leave it to chance. Decide strategically where it would benefit you to have people develop stronger relationships and assign teams accordingly.

Group activities can be custom designed with your company objectives in mind to encompass sports, sightseeing, shopping, local events and attractions. One company looking to spark their employees' innovative thinking designed a road rally event that would serve to showcase their new product. As part of the event, each team was required to produce a creative mini commercial around this new product to stimulate ideas for their upcoming product launch. The final results were shown at their farewell reception and dinner, with fun awards given out. Many of the ideas expressed in the commercials—which were very creative and fresh—were expanded on and used in the actual campaign. Their road rally, designed around their product, created the imaginative energy spark that the company was looking for. The same results would not necessarily have been delivered during a golf tournament where everyone would be focused on their individual games instead of being taken out of their element and comfort zone.

Choose your group activities and the time they take place wisely, as they can be gold mines of possibilities and opportunities toward helping you deliver company event goals.

Group Activity Cost Considerations

Here are some budget-saving group activity suggestions:

- Instead of playing 18 holes of golf and including boxed lunches, refreshment carts and dinner with an open bar, look at reducing the tournament to a half-day event, playing 9 holes and ending with a barbecue lunch, leaving the afternoon/evening at leisure. This way, you lower golf expenses and eliminate a meal and extra beverages. Those who want to play another round of golf can do so at their own expense.

- Look for less expensive group activity options that have appeal. As an alternative to their company's traditional convertible road rally, one executive suggested a flyfishing tournament with expert instruction at an exclusive club, followed by a fish fry. The event was enjoyed equally by the males and females in the group and was substantially less expensive.

- *refreshments*

If you are serving refreshments during team-building activities, make sure that what you choose is a match for what you are trying to achieve. Don't serve something mundane if you are looking to show your ingenuity to your participants. You have to set the standard in every event element that is included in their group activity—including refreshments—if you are looking to receive the same back from your attendees.

Dinners

Business function dinners over the course of a meeting, conference and incentive can be fun, festive, formal or somewhere in between. They can become group activities, for example, dine-arounds or a group experience. It's key that you keep your finger on the pulse of the event's energy as a whole and choose the right style at the right time. For example, if your guests have endured a long day of sitting still in meetings, a fun, festive dinner that gets their energy flowing and has them up and moving about (buffet dinner style) could be the perfect ending to their day, and leave them feeling energized, refreshed and ready to go back into the meeting the next day. A serious formal dinner on the end of a full day of meetings, however, can be energy draining and would be better served coming at the end of a day where the afternoon had been left at leisure, not spent in meetings, so that your guests will have had time to recharge their energies and bring their best to your event. On group activity days, where spirits are high, it is nice to have them end in a celebratory dinner.

Remember to mix up serving styles. Your guests do not want to face every meal as a buffet. Look at your day and your stay as a whole and make sure to balance out both serving styles and selections.

It is also appropriate during events that cross the span of several days to give your participants "dinner at leisure." This lets them have breathing space from the group if they choose to have dinner with some of the delegates they have gotten to know. Dinners at leisure can be at the individual's own expense or an expense that they will be permitted to expense back to the company, but either way, make sure that how it is being handled is noted in their itinerary book. They can then be financially prepared if it is at their own expense.

To guide your guests as to where to go for their night out, have menus from recommended restaurants available at your hospitality desk. If possible, secure reservations at popular restaurants and have local staff on hand at the desk to assist them with making their plans and calling in names for block reservations.

A cash allowance, which helps to control costs, can also be distributed to your attendees. You can work with your hotel to have packets made up in the denominations that you require. When distributing cash allowances, always make sure that your guests sign off on receiving them. The allowances can be handed out in envelopes or creatively tied into your theme.

- *on property*

If your attendees are going to be in meeting rooms most of the day and for their breakfasts and lunches, and your dinners will be held on the property, try to find alternate space to hold your dinners, such as a poolside barbecue, exclusively taking over one of the hotel's top restaurants, on the golf course at the end of your golf tournament or in an outdoor function space that is out of the ordinary. It is important to bring different energy into your event. It will help to breathe fresh life into your guests' days.

One company held a group dinner outside on the hotel grounds perched above the ocean. A classical guitarist played softly in the background during cocktails while the sun was setting into the ocean. It was moving and memorable. A gourmet dinner was served and a pianist was set up to provide added ambiance. They capped off the evening with a private movie screening in a function room that had been set up with reclining chairs and over-the-top movie refreshments. After the movie, guests were invited back out to enjoy a decadent dessert buffet, after-dinner drinks and cigars under the stars. The next day was a full day of leisure, so guests were able to relax, unwind and enjoy the evening, which ended with the sun coming up. The event was timed perfectly and the deals that were cemented that night under the stars underwrote the cost of the entire event and more. The long-term results and the company objectives that were met were outstanding—just like the evening.

For outdoor events, always make sure that your hotel has weather backup space in place. Outdoor heaters are advisable if temperatures tend to get nippy at the time you are holding your meeting.

- *off property*

An off-property dinner is staged to give guests a change of scenery, a life experience and a boost of energy. It may or may not cost more than holding your dinner at your resort, as you have to factor in transportation costs. An off-property dinner can be a group activity or done as a group dine-around if your purpose is to have your company executives spend quality time with carefully selected guests. Invitations can be sent to each guestroom the night before as to which restaurant they will be hosted at for dinner that evening, and what time and where to meet for transfer to dinner.

Special note: Participants' feathers and business egos can be ruffled by finding out about private in-room parties—pre-dinner cocktail parties or post-dinner nightcaps—that others have been invited to by company executives but from which they have been excluded. Be careful how such events are carried out and make sure that no one feels they did not rate an invitation back to a key executive's room—word will get around. Whatever is done must be done with finesse and without undoing all the good that your event has put into place. You simply cannot afford to have disgruntled guests.

The same applies to leisure evenings when company executives may want to invite a select guest or two to join them for dinner. If you decide to do this, select a restaurant that is not one of the restaurants that you are recommending to the rest of your guests, or else you will leave them wondering why their name wasn't on your select list. Be careful to not make any business etiquette faux pas or you can easily cancel out all that you have worked hard to produce.

Decor

Spend your decor dollars wisely. Always keep in mind that decor is one of your more fluid items. It can be molded to meet your budget requirements and depends on your choice of venue. For example, a ballroom may require more decor brought in to create a specific mood than a venue that requires very little in the way of added ambiance, such as a classy theater.

Weigh the top options when you are setting out and looking at a location in which to hold your event. Remember that simplicity can be stunning. The company that held their group dinner outside on the hotel grounds perched above the ocean chose a venue where they did not have to do a great deal to enhance the mood of the location for a very special dinner event. The terrace overlooked the ocean and was the perfect, picturesque setting for sunset cocktails, timed so that guests would be able to watch the sun set into the sea. The company planners upgraded the service to white glove for added finesse. The company chose to use the venue's crisp floor-length linen, bring in chair covers with a romantic floral arrangement tied to the back of each chair, added candelabras in place of centerpieces, and used fine china and sparking crystal. With the candles softly glowing, the location was striking and was made complete by a white baby grand and pianist in white tails that complemented the artistically designed gourmet dinner they were being served. They did not need to add more and knew to stop when they had pulled together a look of simple elegance with a touch of romance, which was what was most important to them. The movie was followed by dancing in the moonlight on the terrace and fine brandy and cigars under the trees overlooking the ocean. The cost for decor was minimal but the effect magical, meaningful and memorable. What the company chose to do in this example is to enhance and extend the natural setting as opposed to heavily theming a ballroom or outdoor location to create the same effect. The same event planning principle of extending the setting could apply to a casual party set by a resort's swimming pool, where over-the-top lounge cabanas can be created for guests to relax in over cocktails. A custom water and light show that takes part in the swimming pool can also be set up.

Decor is about creating magic. If you can't afford to drape an entire room with fiber optics, enhanced with theatrical lighting for dramatic effect, you may be able to include swags of fabric with twinkle lights, which in the right decor company's hands can create a similar illusion.

If you are handling your decor requirements in-house and not using the services of a professional event planning company, there are a few key points to remember when choosing your decor company. A full-service decor company can handle all or part of your decor: floral; rental items such as props, coat racks, table settings, cutlery, glassware, tables, chairs, linens, overlays and chair covers; and lighting requirements.

Some decor companies own their own props and have specialty divisions, such as their own in-house florist, while others subcontract what they need to bring in. Both have their pros and cons. With a decor company that owns their own props, you may be limited to using only what they can provide, unless they are willing to look outside to find what's needed to complement what they have in stock. On the other hand, they may offer a custom product that no one else can obtain. For example, one decor company handles custom linens, overlays and chair covers for a high-society clientele. Those same items are available for other clients to use after the event they were created for has taken place. Its clients have access to top-of-the-line materials and designs that cannot be found elsewhere. A decor company that subcontracts has the flexibility to work with a variety of suppliers and designers to create a look that is right for you.

Your decor needs—how extensive and elaborate they are—will determine the best fit for you. If your design needs are not complex and you have the time and inclination to do so, you may prefer one-stop shopping by going through a full-service decor company or just use them for specific event elements and work directly with florists, rental companies and so forth for the rest. The cost difference may not be great between the two ways of handling your decor requirements, but you may end up with a more pulled-together look when working through one designer as opposed to pulling the pieces together yourself from different suppliers.

Decor Cost Considerations

Here are some inexpensive decor suggestions that provide visual impact:

✔ Specialty lighting can add a feel of extravagance without the cost and be changed throughout the night to transform the room dynamics. Gobos are an inexpensive, interesting and dramatic specialty lighting effect. A gobo is a silhouette pattern (e.g., your logo) cut from metal or glass and used to project images from a spotlight onto any surface, such as the wall, floor, ceiling or drape. They deliver a lot of the WOW factor. You can keep gobos stationary, which will be very inexpensive, or use them in intelligent lighting fixtures that move around the room, which of course will cost more money. Creative special effects can add more than atmosphere to your event. Moving custom gobos were used at one event to light up the path to the main event. The cost was minimal but the effect was showstopping.

✔ Look for a location that requires little in terms of decor enhancements and is a fit for the occasion. Some settings are perfect just as they are—they don't require heavy decor to pull the look together, as is often the case when using a hotel ballroom or convention center. For example, for very exclusive society events, top fashion designers allow their store to be used as a private venue. They have a fully operational kitchen located beneath the store for caterers. Eighty people can enjoy cocktails, a sit-down dinner and a private truck "fashion show" in their facility. Each dinner table of 10 is set with flair and features one of their 8 different linen designs, matching tableware and glassware.

✔ Create a statement with one large piece rather than using 15 decor elements around the room.

✔ Concentrate on a WOW entrance treatment and look at table decor. Beautiful linens and centerpieces go a long way in creating a look or supporting a theme, and may not be as costly as standard decor vignettes.

Continued

✔ Find out what the facility has on hand that you can use to further your decor look. Some hotels have colorful overlays, chair covers and interesting centerpieces in-house and are able to throw in the incidentals at no cost.

- *entertainment*

Take care to ensure that entertainment is not offensive. It is imperative that you meet with hired entertainers to clearly outline what is and isn't acceptable behavior and content in a business setting. Your company's reputation and professionalism is at stake, and you don't want to lose credibility by hiring a performer that makes off-color jokes or is provocative in ways that are not reflective of your company standing and image.

Entertainment Cost Considerations

Here are some ways to lower entertainment costs:

✔ Use the services of an entertainment supplier in order to be able to negotiate good rates for entertainment. As well, have them go through the contract from the performer and ascertain if what they have listed is what is actually needed. Most contracts from performers are standard contracts meant for public performances, which do not pertain to the corporate event world. And some of the hospitality riders can be over the top.

✔ If the attendees are unlikely to dance, do not hire a dance band— it will be more costly if you do. Instead, look at a good background trio to create an ambience. If they bring their own sound system and lights, you can also save on technical costs.

✔ If you're planning a meeting and want to provide entertainment and a social team-building activity but don't have the budget for both, one option is to have your guests become the stars of their own event. Building on the popularity of *Canadian Idol*, *American Idol* and *World Idol*, a "Battle of the Airband" would be a budget-conscious entertainment option. Participants are formed into bands with each group learning to lip-sync to and perform a popular song. Instruction is by professional choreographers and musicians who teach the hottest pop star dance steps. The finale is a live show where costumes and props make everyone feel like a star, has the office buzzing and is an inexpensive entertainment option.

Farewell Reception and Dinner

Traditionally, the farewell reception and dinner is held on the final night. But, depending on travel times the next day, some companies opt to hold special evenings—like awards presentations—the night prior to the farewell and have the farewell designed to be a high-energy celebration. Farewell reception and dinner event elements include:

- *farewell reception*

Your farewell reception is the time to pull out all the stops. It's what is going to send your guests home on an energy high. Be sure to structure your evening so that the energy builds to a grand finale. Having drinks and appetizers passed at this stage of your event is appropriate because it is no longer necessary for your guests to be moving about. Your target tonight is your guests' enjoyment.

- *dinner*

A farewell dinner is best held on property. This gives your guests flexibility to retire early if they have to depart for the airport first thing in the morning or finish packing. Keep departure times in mind when you are scheduling entertainment and your farewell speeches. Make sure that you convey all that you want and that your grand finale takes place before guests start slipping away, but also remember to keep the momentum and energy going until the evening officially ends, in case you have participants who want to enjoy every last minute.

- *WOW factor*

Companies want to have their guests returning home talking about how inspiring their hosts' event was from a creative and cutting-edge standpoint. It is what sets the company apart from its competition and positions it as an innovative industry leader in its field.

The bar is always being raised and now it has extended to space. Richard Branson, owner of Virgin Group, has sold tickets on Virgin Galactic. His newest venture? The world's first tourist space flights, scheduled for 2008. And he used a news conference event at an air show to launch it.

Element 21 Golf Co., a golf club manufacturer, is poised to turn the International Space Station into a driving range during a spacewalk. Taking advantage of zero gravity, company representatives hope to have their company and the drive become the talk of long-distance hitters and those who aspire to be. Their new gold-plated six-iron is to be used to launch the golf shot into space, commemorating the anniversary of Alan Shepard's shots on the moon 35 years ago on the Apollo 14 mission. The company is benefiting from its space promotion idea and has received international press coverage for the product. The telephone is ringing off the hook and it has received over three million hits on its website in three months—well before the event was even scheduled to take place. Should the company representatives move forward with this event promotion, which has the perfect theme to build a business function around, it will surely help them grow their company's brand awareness even further.

Another company, a magazine celebrating their 100th issue, had a 75' x 110' vinyl mesh replica of its cover image constructed in the desert outside Las Vegas. The magazine cover replica was so big that satellites were able to photograph the image from space. The magazine arranged to have the image as seen from space displayed on the Internet, and the media gave it worldwide exposure. The company built a weekend of celebration around its out-of-the-world publicity promotion, which showcased not only the magazine's name and product but its creativity in breaking new frontiers.

Room Gifts

Room gifts do not have to be expensive but they should effectively convey creativity and caring and create meaningful memories. One company, holding their company event at Disney World, had cookies and milk on ice waiting for their participants back in their room after a long day and night of company events. Over breakfast the next morning, the "bring back the kid in all of us" treat was the hot topic of discussion and very well received. The simple, inexpensive but thoughtful gesture had lightened a long day, lifted spirits and refreshed guests' energies.

Traditionally, welcome gifts are tied into the destination, the nightly offering sets the scene for the next day's activities, and the farewell gift is one that is designed to provide a reminder of the overall event experience. It is always a good idea to have staff members accompany bell staff on room drop deliveries to ensure that no one is missed, that deliveries do not end up in the wrong rooms and that if specific items are to go to specific individuals, for example, team-designated shirts the right color and size, they are delivered to the right person. Photographs, packaged to meet more objectives, can be sent as a follow-up once your participants leave to remind them of your event and the messages you delivered, and hopefully be displayed in their offices or homes as constant reminders of what they took away.

Departure

Do not drop the ball on departure elements. Until your guests are back in their own homes with their luggage intact, you cannot rest on delivering care and concern. The attention you pay your guests' departures should be equal to the attention you paid at their arrival.

- *departure notices*

Make sure that a departure notice that lets your participants know baggage pull details, checkout procedures and transfer information is delivered to each guestroom before dinner on the final evening so that they have time to prepare. And always schedule staff to remain behind at the hotel or resort, flying home separately from the group the next day, to handle any problems such as an attendee missing their transfer or the flight, monitor the connecting flights, stay in touch with airport staff at the arrival gateway cities and do as much as they can before their return to the office.

- *hotel checkout and return airport transfers*

Work with the hotel to make checkout as effortless and efficient as possible. Let them know your departure schedule so that they can staff the front desk accordingly. Have a staff member review guests' accounts the night before to make sure that there are no charges appearing that should be on your company's master account. If you find any, have them transferred before your guest receives a copy of their bill. And take the same care with your guests' comfort on their departure as you did when they first set out. Don't drop the ball at the end. Remember to provide the same touches so that your participants' journey ends on a high note.

- hospitality rooms or late room checkouts for those with evening departures
- staff on hand to oversee express group checkout
- return airport transfers that are coordinated, comfortable and supervised
- return airport check-in, with staff on hand in major group arrival airports to assist with lost luggage and transfers to overnight hotel accommodations and so on

Set clear guidelines for your company employees as to what can be expensed back and what cannot. Let them know you will require them to provide receipts. Know going in that your guests will be expecting your key executives to pick up rounds of drinks should they be gathered together. Make sure that your executives know how to handle these situations with flair[1] and how to sidestep continually being placed in that position—unless you want them to be.

---

1   *Event Planning Ethics and Etiquette* (Wiley, 2003) offers tips and techniques.

- *master accounts*

Establish who has signing authority for the master account and how you want additional expenditures to be handled. Make sure that you have reconciled your budget going into your business function so that you know whether or not you have any leeway to add in an unexpected pleasure for your guests.

- *tipping*

On-site tipping will be an expense that needs to be estimated and included in your budget. This slush fund should be used to tip bellmen for special services, to thank specific staff overseeing your food and beverage functions and so forth. This is over and above the mandatory service charges and gratuities that are included in your function's cost. Assign a company person to be in charge of tipping so there is no duplication. Your hotel liaison will be able to guide you on how much and when tipping is appropriate. Use this information to develop a guideline for your representatives as to what is an acceptable amount and what is not.

- *communications*

Communication costs need to be estimated and a part of your budget. Pre-event communication costs can include couriers and long distance expenses, and on-site communication costs can include rented cell phones, walkie-talkies, on-site business office expenses, delivery of faxes, and registration and hospitality desk costs.

Communications Cost Considerations

Here are some suggestions for keeping communication expenses in check:

✔ Negotiate complimentary on-site use of communication devices, for example, walkie-talkies, cell phones and so forth, with destination management companies and hotels.

Continued

✔ Work with hotels to reduce or eliminate hook-up charges for hospitality desk telephones, rental fees for flip charts and markers, delivery charges for room gifts, departure notices, photocopy charges and the like.

INDEX